Systems
Software
Tools

Ted J. Biggerstaff

Microelectronics and Computer Technology Corporation
Austin, Texas

Prentice-Hall, Englewood Cliffs, New Jersey 07632

Library of Congress Cataloging-in-Publication Data

Biggerstaff, Ted J.   (date)
   Systems software tools.

   Includes index.
    1. Computer software.   2. IBM Personal Computer—
Programming.   3. C (Computer program language)
I. Title.
QA76.754.B52 1986   005.4   85-25724
ISBN 0-13-881772-3
ISBN 0-13-881764-2 (pbk.)

Editorial/production supervision
  and interior design: **Lisa Schulz**
Manufacturing buyer: **Gordon Osbourne**

Prentice-Hall Software Series, Brian W. Kernighan, Advisor

If your diskette is defective or damaged in transit, return it directly to Prentice-Hall at the address below for a no-charge replacement within 90 days of the date of purchase. Mail the defective diskette together with your name and address.

> Prentice-Hall, Inc.
> Attention: Ryan Colby
> College Operations
> Englewood Cliffs, NJ 07632

The author and publisher of this book have used their best efforts in preparing this book and software. These efforts include the development, research, and testing of the theories and programs to determine their effectiveness. The author and publisher make no warranty of any kind, expressed or implied, with regard to these programs or the documentation contained in this book. The author and publisher shall not be liable in any event for incidental or consequential damages in connection with, or arising out of, the furnishing, performance, or use of these programs.

Printed in the United States of America

10 9 8 7 6 5 4 3

ISBN   0-13-881772-3
ISBN   0-13-881764-2 {PBK.} 025

PRENTICE-HALL INTERNATIONAL (UK) LIMITED, *London*
PRENTICE-HALL OF AUSTRALIA PTY. LIMITED, *Sydney*
EDITORA PRENTICE-HALL DO BRASIL, LTDA., *Rio de Janeiro*
PRENTICE-HALL CANADA INC., *Toronto*
PRENTICE-HALL HISPANOAMERICANA, S.A., *Mexico*
PRENTICE-HALL OF INDIA PRIVATE LIMITED, *New Delhi*
PRENTICE-HALL OF JAPAN, INC., *Tokyo*
PRENTICE-HALL OF SOUTHEAST ASIA PTE. LTD., *Singapore*
WHITEHALL BOOKS LIMITED, *Wellington, New Zealand*

To my parents, *Harold and Dorothy,*
and my wife, *Christina.*

Contents

Illustrations

Tables

Preface

The structure of this book is predicated upon several ideas. First, it is easier for people to learn concepts when simultaneously presented with a basic principle and one or more specific examples of that principle. Consider the English student trying to decide whether to use "which" or "that" to introduce a clause modifying a noun. Referring to his dictionary, he finds that "which" is used for nonrestrictive clauses and that "that" is largely confined to restrictive clauses. Now, exactly what does that mean? The dictionary provides examples that clarify the contrast. "A computer language that does not allow pointers is a clumsy language." "The FORTRAN language, which is considered by many to be the first high-level language, was developed at IBM." Ah, yes, now I see. The clause introduced by "that" is necessary to identify the specific computer languages referred to by the subject of the first example sentence. In contrast, the clause introduced by "which" in the second example sentence could be eliminated and the reader would still know exactly what the subject noun phrase is referring to.

Examples provide the student with a structure he can use to derive, test, and adjust his understanding of basic principles. Examples also provide a rich set of implications—albeit quite specific—that are either not derivable from the general principle or are derivable only with great labor. In this book, I will present both the basic principles, and working examples that illustrate the basic principles.

The second idea behind this book is that people learn best by doing. There is a popular aphorism that recognizes the value of doing:

> I hear, I forget; I see, I remember; I do, I understand.

But one must perform a fair amount of preparatory work in order to start experimenting (i.e., "doing") with systems software. If a person is studying simple, standalone algorithms it is easy enough to start from scratch and develop working variations on the algorithms. If, on the other hand, the person is studying systems, there are few small, standalone parts of systems that can be extracted for experimentation. To experiment with systems software, one usually has to implement a fairly large piece of the system before much of anything starts to work in an interesting way. Thus, it is useful to have a starting framework that relieves the experimenter of the rather large task of setting up a structure in which to perform an implementation experiment. Providing such a framework is the second objective of this book. The system software described herein is intended to serve as a starting framework for:

1. Student lab assignments in an operating systems course
2. Ambitious student projects, such as quarter, senior and masters projects
3. Hobby computing projects
4. Serious software engineering developments

It is not a complete system with all of the facilities that one would find in a production system. It is a minimal, working system intended as a base to be modified and extended.

The third idea behind this book is that most current operating systems texts do a good job of presenting the general principles but are less successful at presenting the student with examples that are rich enough to have interesting internal interactions among their parts; that actually run on some real machine and, therefore, can be experimented with; that, in addition to dealing with those systems issues for which simple, elegant theories exist, deal with those scruffy, homely systems issues for which there are no simple, elegant theories; and that, because of the richness of the examples, raise a plethora of design issues and problems that most students do not encounter until they get their first job assignment to develop a complex systems design. This book is targeted to fill this gap and serve as a teaching supplement or lab book for systems courses that require hands-on development of system software, or that would benefit from the study of reasonably rich working examples with documentation.

It also is intended as a case book for the working software practitioner. In that role, it can serve as a source for ideas and software algorithms that are the starting point for real developments, or it can serve as a self-study guide for the software practitioner delving into new systems areas.

The fourth idea behind this book is that it should be complete and stand alone in the knowledge that it presents. That is, it is intended to provide at least the rudiments of the various kinds of knowledge required to develop and understand the examples. This goal requires that it present a broad array of information areas, including the C programming language, operating systems concepts, windowing concepts, communications concepts, the 8086/88 and associated hardware, and the PC-DOS operating system. It presents these various information areas not with the intent of providing a thorough, in-depth treatment, but with the intent of providing sufficient information for the student to be able to understand, modify, and extend the examples presented.

I would like to thank several people who have helped to bring this book about. First, Brian Kernighan caught several bugs and many instances of ugly constructions. Not all ugly constructions managed to get removed, but most of those you don't see are due to Brian! In addition, a number of organizational improvements were due to Brian's suggestions. Second, Jim Fegen provided enthusiasm, encouragement, and suggestions that helped to shape the book. Third, Lisa Schulz and other anonymous copyeditors put some spit and polish on my prose. Finally, my wife tolerated my absence for the long time that these programs and this book required.

Ted J. Biggerstaff

Chapter 1

Introduction

1.1 THE SYSTEMS SOFTWARE TOOL

A systems software tool is a software tool that is intimately associated with the operating system software. A window manager is a good example. It does not work well unless it has direct and complete control of the video display hardware. To make matters worse, it must also be able to affect very rapid changes to the video display. Such features are only possible if the software tools have a very strong systems component or make use of low level operating system services.

Powerful systems software tools are a relatively new phenomena, most closely associated with personal computers. The emergence of the personal computer has made powerful systems software tools possible, because personal computers have allowed a more intimate relationship between software tools and the operating system functions. With large- and medium-scale systems such intimate involvement can introduce opportunities for operating system bugs, significantly increase the complexity of the operating system or de-optimize the use of the shared resources. Thus, the powerful systems software tool is phenomena of the personal computer revolution.

From the user's point of view, systems software tools behave differently from software tools on large or medium scale systems. Like the personal computers that they typically run on, systems software tools emphasize a more direct and immediate user involvement in the computational process. They tend to be more interactive on the average than tools on large- or medium-scale computers and, thereby, to amplify the user's capabilities and operation. Spreadsheets are a good example. The course of computing with spreadsheets is seldom cut and dried. It usually consists of a series of experiments, each of which results in a slight reformulation or generalization of the spreadsheet model. With spreadsheets, even the computational formulas and their relationships are interactively provided by the user and continually adjusted and tuned as the model evolves. The user is intimately involved with every step of the computation. Personal computer software tools are designed to take advantage of the person and his or her capabilities. Raw computing is deemphasized. By contrast, software tools on large-scale systems are typically designed to take advantage of the raw compute power or massive storage available. The role of the individual in the computing process is deemphasized.

One of the reasons that systems software tools are possible is economic. The size and cost of computing hardware has changed drastically in the last twenty or so years. What used to cost hundreds of thousands or even millions of dollars can be purchased today for a few thousand. What used to fill a warehouse-size room and require expensive environmental control equipment now sits on top of a desk and operates in a normal office or home environment. The costs and sizes have dropped two to three orders of magnitude and, consequently, there is no longer as strong an economic need to share this computing hardware. Each user can have a reasonably powerful computer of his or her very own, and in addition, the user can have built-in hardware that enhances computing ability by allowing him or her to communicate with remote computers, develop sophisticated graphics, or synthesize music on a personal computer. Such software tools are available to a wide audience because of the advent of the personal computer. The changing economics of computing systems have, over a period of years, brought about the subtle shift in the character of the software tools available on personal computing equipment. This shift is clearly shown by a comparison of the characteristics of large- and medium-scale software tools against those of personal computer software. (See Table 1-1.)

The subtle difference between large-scale software tools and personal computer systems software tools results in differing emphases of the elemental structures, or building blocks, that are used in the construction of the two kinds of tools. Consider, for example, the interrupt facility support on these two kinds of systems. On large-scale systems, one typically would find interrupt facilities buried deeply in the operating system, largely unavailable to the applications programmer and,

TABLE 1-1   COMPARISON OF SOFTWARE TOOL CHARACTERISTICS

Large-/Medium-Scale Computer Software Tools	Personal Computer Software Tools
* Resource-oriented—i.e., optimizes the use of computer resources such as CPU, memory and rotating media	* User-oriented—i.e., opitmizes the user's operation
* Batch or limited interaction	* Highly interactive
* Shared resources	* Private resources

consequently, not easily available for the development of application programs. Personal computers, in contrast, provide interrupt facilities that are readily available and easily incorporated into application programs, thereby encouraging programs that are highly interactive.

In this book, we will analyze some of the elements of systems software tools by delving into their functions and structures. The kinds of elements that we will consider are:

1. Interrupt and real-time facilities
2. Communications facilities
3. Multitasking facilities
4. Window management facilities

1.2 THE ELEMENTS OF SYSTEMS SOFTWARE TOOLS

In order to understand fully the elements of systems software tools, one must master two kinds of knowledge:

1. The concepts and principles that form the basis of the software
2. The programming structures and techniques required to apply those concepts and principles

This book is largely example-driven, and even though examples are prejudiced toward the presentation of programming structures and techniques, we will always labor to supplement the examples with the concepts and principles behind them. To the degree that the student understands both aspects of the material, he or she possesses elemental system building blocks of systems software tools.

Let us consider the elements of systems software tools and consider the knowledge required to understand and work with them.

Interrupt-Driven Software

In order to develop interrupt-driven software, the student needs to understand how the hardware processes interrupts and the relationship of that processing to the software that will support it. There is a broad streak of commonality in interrupt processing on various microcomputers, even though the details may differ somewhat from microcomputer to microcomputer. Developing a general mental model of interrupt processing is the first, important task of developing interrupt-driven software. However, beyond that, the developer must know a number of specific details before the programming can begin. He or she needs to know where specific interrupt vectors are located on specific systems or, at least, where in the documentation to find that information. He or she needs to know the format of those interrupt vectors and what conventions must be obeyed by the software that supports those interrupts. Finally, he or she must understand the hidden assumptions and constraints that the interrupt software is based upon.

Asynchronous Communications

Asynchronous communications software transmits and receives data on a character-by-character basis, over communications lines, and does not depend upon common timing signals to synchronize the transmitting and receiving of those characters. The knowledge required to understand asynchronous communications software includes knowledge of the hardware mechanisms for dealing with the communications gear, the protocol for receiving a character, the protocol for transmitting a character, and the higher-level protocol for interacting with an ASCII standard terminal.

Multitasking

Multitasking software allows the user to run several programs simultaneously. For example, he or she may want to compile a program in the background while editing in the foreground. The knowledge required to understand multitasking software includes that of mechanisms for switching the CPU between processes, scheduling processes to achieve the appearance of simultaneity, loading programs, initiating programs, and terminating programs.

Window Management

Window management systems represent an extension of the notion of multitasking systems to provide a better, more simultaneous, and more intuitive presentation of the information displayed by the multiple programs running on the system. Knowledge required for window management includes the methods of representing windows, mechanisms for mapping from virtual video displays to real video displays, mechanisms for interfacing the window manager to the basic system functions provided by the PC firmware and resident operating system, and mechanisms for managing the keyboard within a multiple-window context.

1.3 THE TARGET COMPUTER

Running examples require that we be concrete and, therefore, we must focus on a specific target computer. We have chosen the ubiquitous IBM Personal Computer. The examples apply to only this machine but the associated principles apply to many similar personal computers. For example, on other machines that use the

8250 asynchronous communications chip, the protocol of application program interaction with the 8250 will be the same. The differences are likely to arise in the
details of sending and receiving information to and from the 8250. If the reader
uses the examples shown in Chapter 5 as a guide, the development of analogous
asynchronous communications software should be direct and simple.

1.4 OVERVIEW OF THE BOOK

This book is intended to be a standalone book. The book presents a variety of
information that is necessary to understand the principles and the examples given
herein, even though that information is broad in its scope. The remainder of the
book is organized as follows:

1. Chapter 2 presents a synopsis of the C programming language. This chapter
   is intended for reference purposes and does not aim to be a training source
   for the C language.
2. Chapter 3 describes the firmware and operating system services on the IBM
   PC. It presents methods for invoking these services, which will be used later
   in the examples.
3. Chapter 4 presents the principles and concepts of the hardware interrupt
   system for the PC and of the asynchronous communications equipment. The
   hardware interrupt knowledge will be critical to both of the extended examples
   that follow—the terminal emulator and the multitasking window manager.
4. Chapter 5 describes the first extended example, an interrupt-driven terminal
   emulator.
5. Chapter 6 introduces the concepts and principles of multitasking and window
   management in preparation for the second extended example.
6. Chapter 7 presents a specification and overview of the second extended example and describes some of the conventions on which the later discussion
   depends.
7. Chapter 8 presents and explains the multitasking mechanisms of the the second
   extended example.
8. Chapter 9 presents the user interface aspects of the second extended example—window and keyboard management.

Chapter 2

A Review of the C Programming Language

2.1 INTRODUCTION

The C programming language is the language of choice for recording the algorithms to be developed in this book. There are several reasons:

1. It is particularly good for writing systems programs because of its facilities for controlling the hardware at a fairly low level.
2. It is highly standardized because it has a single, recognized source for its definition. Further, by the time it was released, it was already sufficiently mature so that language designers largely resisted the urge to tinker with its definition.
3. It possesses a significant amount of machine independence, even though it allows the systems programmer fairly low-level control of the hardware.
4. It is not a toy language. It is sufficiently rich and robust to be a serious tool in the development of real-world software.

All of the examples developed in this book will be written in the C language except where we must, for one reason or another, use assembly language. As it turns out, we will be able to use C for 90+ percent of the code developed.

The C programming language was designed and developed by Dennis Ritchie at Bell Laboratories as the systems programming language of the UNIX[1] operating system. Most of the UNIX system is written in C, which may suggest something

---

[1]UNIX is a trademark of Bell Laboratories.

6

about the nature of the language. C is a language that is particularly good for writing systems programs and has been variously described as a low-level language and a high-level language. On the one hand, it is claimed that C is a low-level language because it provides mechanisms that can be used to access the lowest levels of the hardware. On the other hand, it is claimed that C is a high-level language because it provides facilities such as high-level data and control structures typical of most modern high-level languages. These two aspects of the language are complementary. The low-level facilities increase its utility on each specific machine, and the high-level facilities make it highly hardware independent and therefore applicable on a broad range of hardware. C's pointer support mechanisms provide a good example of its hardware independence. They allow the programmer to increment an array pointer without explicitly coding in information about the exact physical width of each array element. Given information about the data type of the array elements, the C compiler compiles code appropriate to that data type. Features such as this make C far more transportable than many other high-level languages and certainly more transportable than one would expect for a language that allows such intimate contact with the hardware.

This chapter is intended as a synopsis of the C language and not as a standalone training guide or as a thorough-going reference for the C language. There are readily available, good books that provide training-oriented descriptions of C or that provide thorough-going reference material on C. We will provide pointers to these books.

2.2 THE C PROGRAMMING LANGUAGE

We will describe the syntax of C constructs, provide some examples of their use, and provide some limited information about their operation. For greater detail, the reader should consult *The C Programming Language* by Kernighan and Ritchie[2]. Programmers with a knowledge of C may skip this chapter. Programmers with a knowledge of other high-level languages, may want to start with Chapter 3 and refer back to this chapter when they encounter constructs that are not clear from context.

Basic Data Types and Their Constant Forms

C provides only four basic data types, with sizes that depend on the characteristics of the host machine. These types are:

1. **char**—a character packaged as a single byte,
2. **int**—an integer the size of the machine's word,
3. **float**—a single precision floating point number, and
4. **double**—a double precision floating point number.

---

[2] Brian W. Kernighan, and Dennis M. Ritchie, *The C Programming Language*, (Englewood Cliffs, N.J.: Prentice-Hall, Inc., 1978).

Declarations of basic data types have the following forms:

```
char vbl;
int vbl;
float vbl;
double vbl;
```

where *vbl* represents any legal C variable name.

The exact machine representation of these basic data types can be varied by using the following qualifiers in variable declarations:

Qualifier	Function	Can qualify
short	Compact integer	int
long	Extended precision	int, float
unsigned	Sign bit used as data	char, short int, int, long int

Several shorthand forms are allowed:

Shorthand form	Equivalent long form
short	short int
long	long int
double	long float
unsigned	unsigned int

Notice that there is no "string" data type mentioned. Strings are not a basic data type of the C language but are formed as arrays of type **char**. Thus, there are

TABLE 2-1   TYPICAL C DATA TYPE SIZES FOR THE PC

Type	Size in bits
char	8
unsigned char	8
short	16
unsigned short	16
int	16
unsigned int	16
long	32
unsigned long	32
float	32
double	64

no string operators in the language. The C language provides operators for individual characters and the C run-time library provides C functions for string operations.

Typical sizes on the IBM PC for the various data types are shown in Table 2-1.

The examples in Table 2-2 illustrate how to form legal C constants for the basic data types and their variations.

Variable Declarations

Formats of Declarations

In the following discussion, we will use the convention that italicized identifiers are meta-variables representing some class of C expressions. For example, *iconst* represents the class of all integer constants. The meta-variables that we will use in the following discussion are defined in Table 2-3.

Using the meta-variables from Table 2-3, Table 2-4 summarizes the basic declarations available in C.

TABLE 2-2   EXAMPLES OF C DATA CONSTANTS

Example constant	Representation
10	Decimal
10L	Long decimal
0x00ff	Hexadecimal
0x000000ffL	Long hexadecimal
012	Octal
012L	Long Octal
3.75	Floating point
3.75e-3	Scientific notation
'c'	Character
'\012'	Character input by its octal value
'\n'	Newline character (decimal value 10)
'\r'	Carriage return character (decimal value 13)
'\t'	Tab character (decimal value 9)
'\b'	Backspace character (decimal value 8)
'\f'	Formfeed character (decimal value 12)
'\\'	Backslash character (decimal value 92)
'\' '	Single quote character (decimal value 39)
'\0'	Null (decimal value 0)
"string"	String (technically an array of characters)

TABLE 2-3   DESCRIPTIVE META-VARIABLES

vbl	Variable name
decl	Declaration
fixed	Any one of the identifiers char, int, long, or short
sfixed	Any one of the identifiers char, int or short
type	Any legal type identifier, e.g., char or int
utype	User defined type
iconst	Integer constant
const	Constant
func	Function name
tag	Structure or union identifier

Basic Types

The C character data type is somewhat particular to C. C character values behave like small integers with a range of 0 to 255 if unsigned, and a range of -128 to $+128$ if signed. Character variables can be assigned to using the conventional assignment operator. Character variables and constants can be used in arithmetic or logical expressions and can be mixed with integers. It is legal to do arithmetic on characters, or compare them logically with other characters or integers.

The **int**, **float** and **double** data types behave much as their counterparts in other high level languages.

Arrays

C allows arrays to be formed out of any C data type or user defined structure. For example,

```
int x[30],y[30];
```

declares two integer arrays, each with 30 entries. Multi-dimensional arrays are formed by adding a bracketed integer dimension specification for each additional dimension. For example,

```
int matrix[30] [30];
```

declares a 30 by 30, two dimensional integer array named "**matrix**." If the array is being declared as a parameter to a C function, the first dimension need not be given. That is,

```
int x[], y[], matrix[] [30];
```

would be legal if **x**, **y** and **matrix** were being declared as function parameters.

Functions

C functions may return values. The type of the value returned must be declared, unless the type is the default, i.e., **int**. For example, if "**f**" is a function that returns

TABLE 2-4   BASIC DECLARATIONS OF C

Data Object	Declaration
Character	char *vbl*;
Integer of two bytes	short *vbl*;
	short int *vbl*;
Integer of one word	int *vbl*;
Integer of four bytes	long *vbl*;
	long int *vbl*;
Unsigned char or int	unsigned *fixed vbl*;
Floating point number	float *vbl*;
Extended floating point	double *vbl*;
	long float *vbl*;
Variable initialization	*type vbl* = *const*;
Array	*type vbl* [*iconst*];
Two dimensional array	*type vbl* [*iconst*] [*iconst*];
Array parameter	*type vbl* [];
Two dimensional array parm	*type vbl* [] [*iconst*];
Array initialization	*type vbl* [] = { *const*, *const*, . . };
Pointer	*type* * *vbl*;
Function	*type func*();
Register variables	register *sfixed vbl*;
Vbls in separate compile units	extern *decl*;
Permanent storage vbls	static *decl*;
Automatic storage vbls	auto *decl*;
Structure	struct *tag* { *decl*; *decl*; . . . } *vbl*;
Array of structures	struct *tag* {*decl*; *decl*; . . .} *vbl* [*iconst*];
Creating new type	typedef *type utype*;
Union	union *tag* {*decl*; *decl* ; . . .} *vbl*;

a character, then **f** would be declared as

```
char f();
```

in any block where **f**'s result is to be used.

Pointers

C allows the programmer to deal with pointers, but in order for the compiler to be able to automatically check types and compute the details of pointer operations, it must know the data type of the item that the pointer points to. An example declaration of a pointer that points to a character is:

```
char *ptr;
```

This expression is declaring ***ptr** as a **char**, and by implication **ptr** as a pointer. That is, the compiler deals with the variable **ptr** as a machine address, and it deals with the expression ***ptr**, i.e., the de-referenced pointer, as a **char**.

One of the hallmarks of C declarations is the parallelism of structure between the declaration forms and the usage forms. In the example above, both the item being declared as a **char** and the item being operated upon as a **char** in the code body are referred to by the expression ***ptr**. This expression explicitly describes the path to the data being declared. That is, if one mentally "executes" any de-referencing operators within a declaration, i.e., * operators, one will "arrive at" the data item being declared. Similarly, if one mentally "executes" the same sequence of de-referencing operators within the code body, one will "arrive at" the data item to be operated upon by the code. We will extend this notion of mental execution of declarations when we discuss how to interpret complex declarations.

Storage Allocation Control

C provides a variety of declaration mechanisms that allow some control of the machine storage allocation. The qualifier **register** suggests to the compiler that the data should be kept in a machine register, if at all possible. The qualifier **extern** allows variables declared in one compile unit, i.e., one separately compiled file, to be used in a separate compile unit. The qualifier **static** provides for variable storage that is not dynamically allocated. Allocation of static storage occurs at the start of the program and the storage area exists "statically" during the whole execution of the program. The qualifier **auto** provides for automatic storage allocation. With automatic allocation, storage is allocated upon entry to the block in which it is declared and de-allocated upon exit. If variable storage within a block is not qualified by any of these qualifiers, the default is automatic.

Structures

C provides for structures built from any set of legal C data types. The storage for a structure is allocated as a block and can be static, automatic or dynamic. Dynamic storage is allocated and de-allocated under application program control. An example of a structure name **perrecord** is:

```
struct pair
       {
       int *ssn;
       char person [30];
       } perrecord;
```

This structure contains two fields: a pointer to an integer (probably containing some code for a social security number) and a thirty character record (probably containing the person's name).

C provides two additional important facilities. **typedef** allows the user to form his or her own types, and **union** allows the user to view a single storage area in more than one way. For example,

```
union {long i; float x;} shared;
```

allows the variable "**shared**" to store two kinds of data at different times.

Complex Declarations

Interpretation of complex declarations is sometimes difficult, but it can be accomplished in an algorithmic way. The notion behind this method of interpretation is that a complex declaration can be "transformed" in a step-by-step manner to produce a pidgin English description of the structure being declared. The order of application of the transformation rules is determined by the precedence of the operators. (See the following section on operators and in particular, see Table 2-12.) The operators of higher precedence are applied first, unless parentheses redefine the order of application.

Table 2-5 contains the transformation rules

TABLE 2-5 TRANSFORMATION RULES FOR INTERPRETING C DECLARATIONS

Form	Is transformed to
vbl	*<vbl>*
func	*<func>*
type *rxpr*	*<rxpr* type *type>*
* *rxpr*	*<rxpr* pointer to>
rxpr []	*<rxpr* an array containing>
rxpr [*iconst*]	*<rxpr* an array (with length *iconst*) containing>
rxpr ()	*<rxpr* a function that returns>
struct *tag rxpr1 rxpr2*	*<rxpr2* structure defined by tag *tag*, with fields *rxpr1>*
struct *tag rxpr*	*<rxpr* structure defined by tag *tag>*
struct *rxpr1 rxpr2*	*<rxpr2* structure with fields *rxpr>*
union *tag rxpr1 rxpr2*	*<rxpr2* union defined by tag *tag*, with members *rxpr1>*
union *tag rxpr*	*<rxpr* union defined by tag *tag>*
union *rxpr1 rxpr2*	*<rxpr2* union with members *rxpr>*
storeclass rxpr	*<rxpr* storage class *storeclass>*
{*rxpr*;}	*<rxpr>*
{*rxpr1*; *rxpr2*;	{*<rxpr1* and *rxpr2>*;
(*rxpr*)	*rxpr*

In this table, *rxpr* represents a transformed string enclosed in angle brackets, and *storeclass* is defined as **extern** or **register** or **auto** or **static**.

In the foregoing rules, the fully translated part of the declaration is represented by the meta-symbol *rxpr*. In an actual translation, *rxpr* would be a string of pidgin English surrounded by angle brackets (i.e., "< >"). The angle brackets are just a syntactic device to distinguish the portion of the declaration that has been translated from the portion that has not. Only the outer angle brackets of a fully translated portion need to be retained if the meaning of the phrase within is clear. For example,

```
<func> ()
```

might be transformed to the phrase

```
<<func> a function that returns>
```

but, for ease of reading, it is more properly translated to

```
<func a function that returns>
```

At the discretion of the translator, inner brackets may be retained where they help to avoid ambiguity.

The secret of this method is to start with the inner-most identifier and apply transformation rules from Table 2-5 such that the fully transformed region of the declaration expands outward until the whole declaration is transformed. As will be clear from the following example, there may be more than one expanding translated region at times during the translation process.

If at some point during the translation two alternative operators can be chosen for translation, as in

```
"....   * <transformed_phrase> ()      ....."
```

then choose the one with the higher precedence to transform first. In the foregoing case, the "()" operator has higher precedence than "*", so the declaration becomes

```
"...   * <transformed_phase a function that returns>  ..."
```

Let's follow the complete translation of a complex declaration:

```
struct pair  { int *ssn; char person[30];}
        *(*findary()) [];
```

Transforming this example produces the following series of steps:

```
struct pair  { int *ssn; char person[30];}
        *(*<findary a function that returns>) [];

struct pair  { int *ssn; char person[30];}
        *(<findary a function that returns pointer to>) [];

struct pair  { int *ssn; char person[30];}
        *<findary a function that returns pointer to> [];
```

```
struct pair  { int *ssn; char person[30];}
       *<findary a function that returns pointer to
             an array containing>;

struct pair  { int *ssn; char person[30];}
       <findary a function that returns pointer to
             an array containing pointer to>;

struct pair  { <ssn pointer to type int>;
                <person an array (with length 30)
                       containing type char>;}
         <findary a function that returns pointer to
             an array containing pointer to>;

struct pair  <ssn pointer to type int and
             person an array (with length 30)
                       containing type char>
         <findary a function that returns pointer to
             an array containing pointer to>;

<findary a function that returns pointer to
    an array containing pointer to
       structure defined by tag pair
             with fields
                  ssn pointer to type int and
                  person an array (with length 30)
                        containing type char>;
```

This pidgin English is directly translatable into a picture that makes the declaration even clearer (see Figure 2-1).

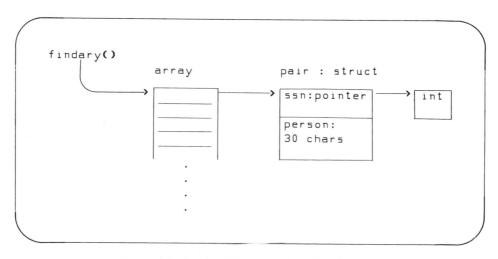

Figure 2-1 Graphical Representation of Declaration

Operators

Arithmetic Operators

C provides the conventional binary arithmetic operators for multiplication, division, addition, and subtraction (see Table 2-6). They are prioritized in the conventional way (see Table 2-12). C also provides the conventional unary operators plus and minus. In addition, the modulo function, often provided as a callable function within other languages, is provided in C as an operator.

In addition to the conventional operators, C provides a shorthand notation, the $++$ and $--$ operators, for the frequently occurring operations of increment and decrement. These operators can be used within an expression whose main purpose is the computation of some value that is a function of the variables to be incremented or decremented. The secondary purpose of the expression is incrementing or decrementing the variables used in the expression. The $++$ and $--$ operators must provide both a value for use in the computation of the expression and a side effect to accomplish the incrementing or decrementing computation. For example,

```
x = (++y) + 10;
```

will increment y and then use the new value of y in the computation of x. In the case that $++$ (or $--$) precedes the variable, the incrementing (or decrementing) takes place before the value is fetched for use in the main line computation. If $++$ (or $--$) appears after the variable, the value used in the main line computation is the value of the variable before the increment or decrement operator is applied. That is, the increment or decrement occurs after the variable is used.

TABLE 2-6 ARITHMETIC OPERATORS

Oper	Name	Example	Explanation
*	Multiply	x*10	x times 10
/	Divide	x/10	x divided by 10
%	Modulo	x%10	x modulo 10
+	Add	x+y	x plus y
−	Subtract	x−y	x minus y
++	Increment	++x	Increment x before use
−−	Decrement	x−−	Decrement x after use
−	Unary minus	−x	Negate value of x

Relational and Logical Operators

Table 2-7 summarizes the relational and logical operators. See Table 2-12 for information on the precedence of these operators.

TABLE 2-7   RELATIONAL AND LOGICAL

Oper	Name	Example	Explanation
>	Greater	x > y	Nonzero if x greater than y
> =	Greater or equal	x > = y	Nonzero if x greater than or equal y
<	Less	x < y	Nonzero if x less than y
< =	Less or equal	x < = y	Nonzero if x less than or equal y
= =	Equal	x = = y	Nonzero if x equal y
!=	Not equal	x != y	Nonzero if x not equal y
!	Unary negation	!flag	Nonzero if flag is 0
&&	Logical and	x && y	Nonzero if x and y nonzero
| |	Logical or	x | | y	Nonzero if x or y nonzero

Assignment Operators

In addition to the conventional assignment operator, C allows a short form for the frequently occurring form

$$x = x \ \langle op \rangle \ y;$$

where $\langle op \rangle$ represents operators such as **+** or **−**. C allows this form to be shortened to

$$x \ \langle op \rangle = y;$$

Table 2-8 defines the set of operators that can be used in this short form.

TABLE 2-8   ASSIGNMENT OPERATORS

Oper	Name	Example	Explanation
=	Assignment	x = 10;	x gets the value of 10
op =	op Assignment	x op = y;	Equivalent to x = (x) op (y) for op one of + − * / % << >> & ^ |

Storage Related Operators

C provides a powerful implementation of pointers that allows them

1. To be used like arrays, and
2. To used and manipulated in machine independent ways.

The array like usage of pointers provides a notationally convenient way to manipulate data types referenced by pointers. For example, any pointer **p** can be operated upon as if it were an array using the notation

```
p[i]
```

to access the (i + 1)-th data item in the referenced block. Indeed, the name of a declared array is implemented as a pointer, and can be treated either as an array by using the [] operator, or as a pointer by using the * operator. So de-referencing **p** with the * operator produces the zeroth element of the array, i.e., **p[0]**.

Pointers are updated in a machine storage independent way. Suppose that **p** is a pointer to some known storage type, such as a two byte wide integer. Incrementing **p** produces a new pointer pointing to the succeeding integer element in the array. That is, if **p** contains 0x0440 before adding 1 to **p**, it will contain 0x0442 after adding 1. Thus, by adding 1 to a pointer **p**, we are not adding the integer 1 to the address represented by **p**. We are adding the integer number of bytes contained in one instance of the integer storage type, i.e., the integer 2, to the address referenced by **p**. It follows that **p[i]** and *(**p**+**i**) access the same data item.

Access to structure members is provided by the **.** operator, as in

```
employee.lastname
```

which accesses the **lastname** member of the **employee** structure. For the case where we have a pointer to the structure, C provides the − > operator for accessing members of the structure. Continuing with the preceding example, we could use the expression,

```
p->lastname
```

given that **p** is a pointer to a structure named **employee**.

C also provides an operator, **&**, to take the address of the location referenced by its operand. Hence, **&p[0]** produces the same address as **p**, and the same address as **&*p**. More generally,

```
&p[i] == (p + i) == &*(p + i).
```

To maintain this independence between storage allocation details and the use of such information in the application code, C provides the **sizeof** operator to symbolically refer to the size in bytes of the storage allocated for a type or object.

```
sizeof(double)
```

produces the number of bytes in a double precision type, and

```
sizeof p
```

TABLE 2-9   STORAGE RELATED OPERATORS

Oper	Name	Example	Explanation
[]	Array element	a[47]	Access 48th element of a
−>	Structure pointer	ptr−>son	Gets son member of structure at ptr
.	Structure member	sreg.ax	Gets ax member of sreg
*	Dereference pointer	*ptr	Value at ptr
&	Address	&ptr	Address of ptr
sizeof	Storage size	sizeof(x)	Number of bytes reqd by x

produces the number of bytes allocated for the object **p**. If **p** is an array, for example, this would be the number of bytes allocated for the array.

The **sizeof** operator allows the user to write storage implementation independent code. For example, the function **alloc** requires the size in bytes of the storage block to be allocated. Thus, to allocate an array that will hold 100 integers, the programmer can write

```
alloc(100 * sizeof(int))
```

and this will get the right amount of storage independent of the particular compiler or machine integer size conventions.

Bitwise Operators

C provides operators to operate upon packed fields of bits. These are summarized in Table 2-10.

TABLE 2-10   BITWISE LOGICAL AND SHIFT OPERATORS

Oper	Name	Example	Explanation
~	One's complement	~0xff	Word constant 0xff00
&	And	x & y	x ANDed with y bitwise
|	Or	x | y	x ORed with y bitwise
^	Exclusive Or	x ^ y	x Exclusive ORed with y
<<	Left shift	x << 2	x shifted left 2 pos
>>	Right shift	x >> 2	x shifted right 2 pos

Miscellaneous Operators

The remaining operators, summarized in Table 2-11, include the function invocation operator and three somewhat unconventional, but highly useful operators. The first of these somewhat unconventional operators is the "type cast" operator, which allows for explicit type conversions. For example,

```
fraction = x - (float) ((int) x);
```

produces the fractional part of the real variable **x** by subtracting the integer part of **x** expressed as a real number. The integer part is produced by casting **x** to an **int**, and then, immediately back to a **float**.

The conditional expression operator provides a value returning conditional structure that can be embedded within an expression. For example,

```
return(errorflag < 0 ? errorflag : posresult);
```

could be the return statement of a function that returns the value of some error flag, if the flag is negative, or otherwise returns some positive result computed elsewhere in the function.

Finally, the comma operator allows one to string together a set of computations where otherwise only one would be allowed. The value returned is the value of the last expression. This operator is frequently used in **for** loops that must initialize two or more variables, such as in

```
for(i=1, sum=0; i<max; ++i) { . . . . . . . . }
```

Operator Precedence

Table 2-12 defines the precedence and associativity of C's operators. When a variable or expression might be the operand of more than one operator, by virtue of the fact that it appears between two operators in some expression, the

TABLE 2-11 MISCELLANEOUS OPERATORS

Oper	Name	Example	Explanation
( )	Function	fact(n)	Call fact function with n
(*type*)	Type cast	(int) x	Convert x to int
? :	Conditional expression	x<y?5:10	If x < y, value is 5 else 10
,	Comma	++i,++j	Discard value of i and use j

TABLE 2-12   OPERATORS ORDERED BY PRECEDENCE LEVEL

Level	Type	Operators					Assoc.
15	Primary	()	[]	.	->		L to R
14	Unary	!	~	++	--	-	R to L
		(type) *	&	sizeof			
13	Arithmetic	*	/	%			L to R
12		+	-				L to R
11	Shift	<<	>>				L to R
10	Relational	<	<=	>	>=		L to R
9		==	!=				L to R
8	Bit logical	&					L to R
7		^					L to R
6		|					L to R
5	Logical	&&					L to R
4		||					L to R
3	Conditional	?:					L to R
2	Assignment	=	+=	-=	*=	/=	R to L
		^=	&=	>>=	<<=	%=	
		|=					
1	Comma	,					L to R

operator with the highest precedence will be the one with which it is associated by the compiler. Consider, the expression

$$*p[5]$$

Since the precedence of the [] operator is greater than that of the * operator, **p[5]** will be computed first and then the de-referencing operator, *, will be applied to the result.

If competing operators are at the same precedence level, then the Assoc. column in Table 2-12 reveals the order in which the operators are executed, either left to right or right to left.

Statement and Blocks

The Simple Statement

A simple statement is a syntactically valid string terminated by a semicolon (see Figure 2-2).

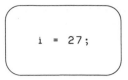

Figure 2-2 Example of a Simple Statement

A simple statement may be a declaration, an assignment, or a function call. It may be placed anywhere on a line or may be spread over several lines. Of course, variables, strings, and constants should not be broken over lines.

Blocks

A block, sometimes called a compound statement, is a series of legal C statements surrounded by braces. The general form is found in Figure 2-3.

```
{statement1 statement2 . . .statementn}
```

Figure 2-3 Block or Compound Statement Form

An example is given in Figure 2-4.

```
{
xtrows = col / maxcolp1;
col %= maxcolp1;
row += xtrows;
row %= maxrowp1;
}
```

Figure 2-4 Example of a Block

A block may be placed anywhere a simple statement may be placed.

The if Statement

The **if** control structure has two basic variations: 1) the simple **if** form, without an

else clause, and 2) the general **if**, with the **else** clause. The general forms are shown in Figure 2-5.

```
if (expr)                    /*Simple if*/
        statement



if (expr)                    /*General if*/

        statement1
else
        statement2
```

Figure 2-5 if Statement Forms

In the simple **if** statement, *statement* is executed if the value of the expression *expr* evaluates to nonzero. Control falls out of the **if** if *expr* evaluates to zero. The general form of the **if** statement is similar except that *statement2* is executed when *expr* evaluates to zero. Either *statement1* or *statement2* may be another **if** statement. Brackets may be used to assure that each **else** is associated with the proper **if**. Without brackets, the rule is that an **else** associates with the nearest **if**.

The conditional expression after the **if** must be enclosed in parentheses. The first statement of the **if** follows immediately after the conditional expression of the **if** with no intervening identifiers, i.e., C has no "then" clause identifier. The statements may be any legal C statement or block of statements.

Three examples are shown in Figure 2-6.

The switch Statement

The **switch** statement has the form shown in Figure 2-7.

The **switch** statement compares the value of its expression *expr* against a number of constant values (i.e., *const1* through *constn-1*) and executes the associated statement set. If no constant value is equal to *expr* and a **default** case is present, the default statement set is executed. If none of the constants are equal and no **default** branch is present, the whole **switch** construct is a null statement.

```
if (col == incol)        /*Simple if*/
        {
        putchar(c);
        return;
        }


if (c == CTRLZ)          /*General if*/
        return(EOF);
else
        return(c);


if (isalpha(c))              /*Else-if Idiom*/
        return(LETTER);
else if (isdigit(c))
        return(DIGIT);
else
        return(c);
```

Figure 2-6 Example of **if** Statements

break statements typically are used to exit from a **switch** statement. If the last statement in a statement set is not a transfer of control (e.g., **break** or **return**) control will fall through to the succeeding statement set. This allows a single case to have multiple labels. Be careful, however. Omission of an intended transfer of control statement at the end of a case is a common C error.

An example of a **switch** is shown in Figure 2-8. This **switch** example is a variation on the interrupt service routine in Chapter 5. When an asynchronous interrupt occurs, a machine character register called the "interrupt identification register" (**iir**) is set to an even integer value indicating what kind of event caused the interrupt. This **switch** statement dispatches control based on the kind of interrupt event. These event classes include transmission error ('\006'), the arrival of a byte of data from the modem ('\004'), the freeing of the transmission register ('\002'), or a change in modem status ('\000') such as a change in the "Clear To Send" signal. This application of the **switch** statement is quite typical.

The while Loop

The **while** loop has the form shown in Figure 2-9.

```
switch (expr)
        {
        case const1:
                statement set 1

        case const2:
                statement set 2

        case const3:
                statement set 4
                .
                .
                .
                .
                .
        default:
                statement set n
        }
```

Figure 2-7 Form of a **switch** Statement

```
switch(iir)
        {
        case '\006':
                note_error(iir);
                break;
        case '\004':
                buffer_data();
                break;
        case '\002':
                thrfree = 1;
                break;
        case '\000':
                msr_change();
                break;
        default:
                return;
        }
```

Figure 2-8 Example of a **switch** Statement

```
while(expr)
          statement
```

Figure 2-9 Form of a **while** Loop

The **while** loop executes *statement* as long as the value of the conditional expression *expr* is nonzero. If *expr* is zero on entry, the **while** construct produces no action. An example of a **while** loop is given in Figure 2-10.

```
int argc ;
char *argv[];

while (--argc>0 && (*++argv)[0] == '-')
        {                /* Process program options */
        .
        .
        .
        }
```

Figure 2-10 Example of a **while** Loop

The example is a C idiom for processing a C program's options. The **while** loop will continue to execute as long as the count of arguments remaining to be processed (i.e., **− −argc**) is positive and the first character of the current argument string (i.e., **(* + +argv)[0]**) is a minus sign. The **for** loop example (see page 27) completes this C idiom by supplying a typical body for this **while**.

The do-while Loops

The **do-while** loop has the form shown in Figure 2-11. The **do-while** loop executes *statement* at least once. The loop test is done at the bottom of the loop. The loop continues to execute *statement* as long as the value of the conditional expression *expr* is nonzero. This construct is convenient in those cases where the loop must always execute at least once, regardless of the value of the expression *expr*.

```
    do
              statement
    while (expr);
```

Figure 2-11 Form of a **do-while** Loop

```
    do
                   putchar('\n');
    while (i-- > 0);
```

Figure 2-12 Example of a **do-while** Loop

The example in Figure 2-12 terminates a string being written to **stdout** and follows it with **i** blank lines for **i** greater than or equal to 0.

The for Loop

The **for** loop has the form shown in Figure 2-13.

```
    for(initial expr ; while expr ; update expr)
            statement
```

Figure 2-13 Form of a **for** Loop

Here, the the *initial expr* expression is executed before the loop, the *while expr* expression is executed at the top of each loop, and *update expr* is executed at the bottom of each loop. The loop continues to execute as long as the value of *while expr* is nonzero. The **for** loop is equivalent to the loop shown in Figure 2-14.

```
    initial expr;
    while (while expr)
            {
            statement
            update expr;
            }
```

Figure 2-14 **for** Loop Equivalent Construct

An example of a **for** loop is shown in Figure 2-15.

```
char *s;

for(s=argv[0]+1; *s!='\0'; s++)
        switch (*s)
                {
                case 'd':
                        debug = TRUE;
                        break;
                case 'f':
                        frugal = TRUE;
                        break;
                default:
                        printf(''Illegal option\n'');
                        break;
                }
```

Figure 2-15 Example of a **for** Loop

This example is a candidate for the body of the **while** example given earlier. This **for** loop is an instance of a C idiom for processing C program options. It allows two options indicated by the letters "d" and "f," and diagnoses any other letter as an "Illegal option."

The **for** initializes the string **s** to point to the second character of the option string (i.e., **argv[0] + 1**). The body of the loop executes as long as the first character of *s* (i.e., ***s**) is not the string terminator (i.e., '**\0**'). At the bottom of the loop body, **s** is updated to point to the next character of the string (i.e., **s++**).

The break Statement

The **break** statement exits from the closest (i.e., innermost) **for**, **while**, **do-while**, or **switch**. It causes control to transfer to just after the affected construct. The **break** statement often simplifies the construction of error processing code. See the **switch** example (Figure 2-8) and the **continue** example (Figure 2-16) for examples of the use of **break**.

The continue Statement

The **continue** statement causes the closest (i.e., innermost) **for**, **while**, or **do-while** to begin its next iteration immediately. An example is given in Figure 2-16.

```
#define TRUE 1
#define ENDOP  '\117'    /*Second char sent for END function key*/
#define CURUP  '\110'    /*Second char sent for UP CURSOR function key*/
#define CURLFT '\113'    /*Second char sent for LEFT CURSOR function key*/
#define CURRGT '\115'    /*Second char sent for RIGHT CURSOR function key*/
#define CURDWN '\120'    /*Second char sent for DOWN CURSOR function key*/
char c,getc_noecho();
int x,y;                 /*Column, row position of cursor*/
        .
        .
        .

printxy("Move cursor to desired position, Hit End key to complete",24,0);
while (TRUE)            /*User moves cursor to select screen position*/
        {
        if((c=getc_noecho()) != '\0')  /*First char not function key signal*/
                {send_bell(); continue;}

        if((c=getc_noecho()) == ENDOP)  /*Second char is exit loop char*/
                break;

        switch(c)
                {
                case CURUP:
                        if(y > 1) move_cursor(--y,x);
                        break;
                case CURDWN:
                        if(y < maxrow) move_cursor(++y,x);
                        break;
                case CURRGT:
                        if(x < maxcol) move_cursor(y,++x);
                        break;
                case CURLFT:
                        if(x > 1) move_cursor(y,--x);
                        break;
                default:
                        send_bell();
                }
        }
```

Figure 2-16   Example of **continue** and **break** Statements

   The foregoing loop illustrates the use of both the **continue** and the **break** statements. This loop is designed to let the user move the cursor (via calls to **move_cursor**) to a place on the screen where he or she wants the application program to place data. The program keeps track of the current cursor position in **x** and **y** while providing the user immediate feedback by moving the cursor each time the user presses a cursor function key. Since the number of key strokes is indefinite, the **while** loop must be a "do forever"-style loop. The **break** statement associated with **ENDOP** test is the **while** loop exit mechanism. The **break** statements inside the **switch** are the **switch** exit mechanisms. The **continue** statement at the top of the loop forces the next iteration of the **while** loop whenever the user types a nonfunction key.[3] The loop body is organized into two distinct parts to handle two characters on each iteration, that is, the function key signal character and the function key designation character. If a nonfunction key is pressed, only one character is available to be processed, and the **continue** statement causes the second part of the loop body to be bypassed.

The goto Statement and Labels

The **goto** construct is included in C for completeness, but it should be used very sparingly. **goto**s are not inherently evil. It is just that with a few minutes of thought one can almost always think of a clearer, more elegant way to express the code.

One place in which **goto**s are most justified is in error processing where, because of the nature of the error, one wants to jump out of several nested loops, **switch**es, and so on. In such a case, the **goto** will allow you to organize a block of error reporting and fixup code that is similar to an interrupt service routine. It gets control on some exception condition. In Figure 2-17, the code is probably clearer than if the error exit were through the same path as the success exit. In the latter case, we probably would have to introduce error filter code at each exit level to guide control to the proper place at the level that is to handle the error. This is one of the few cases in which the **goto** may actually simplify the structure of code.

```
while (expr)
        {
        for(init; cond; update)
                {
                if (error check) goto bailout;
                . . .
                }
        }


bailout:
        report error and fix up
```

Figure 2-17 Example of the **goto** Statement

---

[3]Function keys on the PC generate two characters. The first character is a NUL (\000) that serves as the function key signal character, and the second is an ASCII character assigned to the function key. For example, the cursor down key generates the character pair (\000,\120) where these values are expressed in octal. The same character pair expressed in hexadecimal is (0x00,0x50).

Functions and Programs

A C function has the general form shown in Figure 2-18.

```
type func ( arglist )
        arglist declarations
        {
        local variable declarations
        statements
        }
```

Figure 2-18 Form of a C Function

This form declares a function whose name is *func*. If *func* is preceded by *type* (which is optional), *func* returns a value of type *type*. Returning a value is accomplished with the **return** statement, as in

```
return(x);
```

which returns the value of the variable **x**. **x**'s type must be consistent with the type of the function. The type of a function that has no explicit type declaration is **int**. A statement of the form

```
return;
```

returns no value. A program or function may be written without an explicit **return** statement. In this case, the **return** is implied by the fact that control can reach the end of the function's top level block without encountering a **return** statement. Such a function behaves as if there were a **return** statement just at the end of the block.

An example function is given in Figure 2-19.

```
fil(buf, s, c)
        char *buf;
        int s;
        char c;
        {
        while (s--)
                *buf++ = c;
        }
```

Figure 2-19 Example of a C Function

This function fills a buffer, pointed to by **buf**, with s copies of the character **c**. It returns without a value by falling off of the end of the top-level block. The output of the function is the contents of the buffer pointed to by **buf**.

Function parameters are always passed by value, but because of the flexibility of C, at the programmer's discretion, some of those values may be addresses of variables, as in the case of **buf**. Such a case is equivalent to passing a variable "by reference." Arrays are passed by reference when the programmer uses only the name of the array without any subscripting information. With subscripting information, as in **a[5]**, the array reference represents a single element and as such is passed by value. If this is not the intention of the programmer, he or she may use the **&** operator to turn the array element into a pointer to the element. For example, **&a[5]** is a pointer to an array whose zeroth element is the fifth element of the array **a**.

Functions are called with the form

```
func (arg1,arg2,......);
```

Functions can recursively call themselves.

A main program is just a C function whose function name is **main** and there is only one of them per program. An example of a main program is given in Figure 2-20. This program counts the number of characters in **stdin** and writes out the results on **stdout**. It operates in two modes, wordy and frugal, depending upon the variable **frugal**, which is set from the program parameter list. Notice that a main program has two parameters. In Figure 2-20, these are called **argc** and **argv**. **argc** is an integer indicating how many parameters the program was called with and **argv** is an array of pointers to the strings that are the program's parameters. If the foregoing program was compiled and loaded onto a file **count.exe**, the command

```
count -f <longfile
```

would count the characters on the file **longfile** and print the frugal answer on **stdout**. Without the "-f" parameter, it would print the wordy answer.

Formatted Input/Output

C provides routines for reading and writing data under control of a format. The arguments *arg1*, *arg2*, and so on, can be written to standard output, to any arbitrary

```
#include <stdio>

main(argc,argv)
int argc;          /*Number of program arguments*/
char *argv[];      /*An array of pointers to strings, one per argument*/
        {
        long nc;
        char *s;
        int frugal = 0;
        while (--argc>0 && (*++argv)[0] == '-')
                {          /*Process program options */
                for(s=argv[0]+1; *s!='\0'; s++)
                        switch (*s)
                        {
                        case 'f':
                                frugal = 1;
                                break;
                        default:
                                printf("Illegal option\n");
                                break;
                        }
                }
        nc = 0;
        while (getchar() != EOF) ++nc;
        if (frugal)
                printf("%ld\n",nc);
        else
                printf("Number of characters = %ld\n",nc);

}
```

Figure 2-20 Example of a C **main** Program

stream, or to an in-memory string, respectively, by the set of functions shown in Figure 2-21.

```
printf(format, arg1, arg2, ...);
fprintf(stream,format, arg1, arg2, ...);
sprintf(string,format, arg1, arg2, ...);
```

Figure 2-21 Formatted Output Functions

Similarly, data may be read into arguments *arg1*, *arg2*, and so on, from standard input, from any arbitrary stream, or from an in-memory string, respectively, by the set of functions shown in Figure 2-22.

```
scanf (format, arg1, arg2, ...);
fscanf (stream,format, arg1, arg2, ...);
sscanf (string,format, arg1, arg2, ...);
```

Figure 2-22 Formatted Input Functions

In the case of input, the arguments *arg1*, *arg2*, etc., must be pointers to the locations where the data is to be stored.

format is a string that consists of field specifiers interspersed with constant strings. The constant strings are printed as is on output and must be matched exactly by the incoming data stream on input. A field specifier has the form described in Figure 2-23.

Figure 2-24 defines the meanings of the various conversion characters. The character % is included as a literal in a format (rather than the syntactic marker for a field specification) by doubling it. Thus, %% in a **printf** format will print as a single %.

Examples of formatted input and output statements are found in Figures 2-25 and 2-26.

```
% [-] [*] [w] [.p] [l] c

where

MetaSymbol          Meaning
_____          _____


    []              An optional portion of the specifier.

    -               Causes left justification, for print
                    functions only.

    *               Suppresses assignment of the field to a
                    variable, for scan functions only.

    w               Width, an integer defining the width of
                    the field for both the scan and print
                    functions, if w has leading zeros the
                    field will be zero padded on output.

    p               Precision, an integer defining the maximum
                    number of characters to be printed if the
                    field is a string, or the number of digits
                    to be printed to the right of the decimal
                    point if the field is floating point.

    l               The letter l indicates a long integer or a
                    double floating point, for both input and
                    output.

    c               The conversion character as defined in
                    Figure 2-24.
```

Figure 2-23 Field Specifier

The variables within a **scanf** call must be "*address pointers*," not simple variables. Array names are by their nature address pointers, but simple variables such as an **int** require use of the **&** operator to form the target address, which is to receive the data.

Conversion Character	Meaning
d	Decimal conversion.
o	Octal conversion.
b	Binary conversion. (Extension to K&R standard.)
x	Hexadecimal conversion (0x prefix acceptable on input but not required).
h	Short integer, input only.
u	Unsigned decimal conversion, output only.
c	Character conversion.
s	String conversion. On output, the length of the string is the minimum of the precision (if present) and the length of the string up to the null byte that marks the end of the string. On input, the length of the resulting string is the minimum of the precision and the number of non-white space characters available from the current position, where white space is defined to be blanks, tabs and newlines.
e	Output of a float or double is presented in engineering notation, that is, in the format [-] d.ddddddE[+ or -]xx where the number of digits to the right of the decimal is given by the precision with a default of 6. On input, this is a synonym for the f specification.
f	Float or double conversion. On output, this is formatted as [-]dddd.ddddd where the number of digits to the right of the decimal point is given by the precision with a default of 6. On input, either the f or e format is acceptable.
g	On output, use the shorter of %e or %f.

Figure 2-24 Format Conversion Characters

```
char funame[9],drive,filename[9],ext[3],title[5],lastname[20],salut[32];
int in_value;
FILE *tracefl;

printf("%s: Error on input [%d]\n", funame, in_value);
fprintf(tracefl,"Writing out file %c:%s.%s\n", drive, filename, ext);
sprintf(salut,"Dear %s %s;\n", title, lastname);
```

Figure 2-25 Examples of Formatted Output

```
char arraynam[9],title[5],lastname[20],salut[32];
int number,dim1,dim2;
FILE *datadefs;

scanf("%d",&number);
fscanf(datadefs,"%s[%d,%d]",arraynam,&dim1,&dim2);
sscanf(salut,"Dear %s %s;",title,lastname);
```

Figure 2-26 Examples of Formatted Input

Preprocessor Statements

The preprocessor statements are summarized in Figure 2-27.

2.3 THE C COMPILER

The compiler we will use for examples in the remainder of the book is the C86 compiler from Computer Innovations, Inc. This compiler implements the C language and C library as specified in Kernighan and Ritchie (1978).[4] With the addition of certain library functions that will be explained in detail in the forthcoming chapters, all examples should port with a minimum of effort to any C compiler that meets the Kernighan and Ritchie standard.

[4]Kernighan and Ritchie, *The C Programming Language*.

Form	Meaning
#define *ident token*	Replace each *ident* with *token*.
#define *ident*(*id1*,*id2*,...) *token-strg*	*token-strg* is macro definition. Each occurrence of *ident*(*arg1*,*arg2*,...) is replaced by *token-strg*, where each *idn* within *token-strg* is replaced by the corresponding *argn* in *ident*(*arg1*,*arg2*,...)
#undef *ident*	Undefine preprocessor definition of *ident*.
#include "*filename*"	Replace line with the contents of *filename*.
#include <*filename*>	Replace line with the contents of system file in standard location.
#if *const_expression*	Check *const_expression* for non-zero.
#ifdef *ident*	Check for preprocessor definition of *ident*.
#ifndef *ident*	Check for undefined preprocessor symbol.
#else	Compile lines between previous preprocessor #if test and this statement, if the test was true, else skip those lines.

Figure 2-27 Preprocessor Statements

```
#endif                              If there is a
                                    preceding #else and
                                    the
                                    preceding #if test was
                                    false, then
                                    compile the lines
                                    between the #else and
                                    this statement, else
                                    skip those lines. If
                                    there is no preceding
                                    #else between this
                                    line and the previous
                                    #if test, and the #if
                                    test was true, compile
                                    the lines between the
                                    #if test and this
                                    statement, else skip
                                    them.
#line constant ident                Use constant as the
                                    line number of the
                                    next line and ident as
                                    the file name in
                                    diagnostics.
```

Figure 2-27   (Continued)

EXERCISES

2.1. Develop a C program to parse C declarations and produce pidgin English descriptions according to the rules given in this chapter. See Table 2-12 for the precedence and associativity constraints. This exercise will take one to three weeks of effort depending on generality and flexibility required, and depending upon whether or not parser generating tools are used.

Chapter 3 ━━━━━

Access to System Services

━━━━━━━━━━━━━━━━━━━━━━━━━━━━

3.1 BASIC FUNCTIONS

The extended examples developed in later chapters will require knowledge about how to deal with the keyboard and the video display, as well as how to gain access to other operating system services. Many of the required primitive support functions are accessible via interrupts. This section will overview the interrupt functions provided in ROM or provided by MS-DOS and will describe how to invoke these interrupt functions. In addition, it will provide pointers to IBM documentation that will allow the reader to further expand his or her knowledge of the primitive support functions. The reader is well advised to read this section with a copy of the *IBM Technical Reference Manual*[1] and the *IBM Disk Operating System Manual*[2] close at hand, as they will richly supplement this discussion.

BIOS Functions

The IBM PC ROM contains the Basic I/O System (BIOS), which interfaces to the I/O gear attached to the PC. The objective of BIOS is to provide an interface that insulates the programmer from the details of the specific hardware attached to the PC. Most programs, including DOS, use BIOS to perform I/O and to provide other system services. Among the services provided by BIOS are:

---

[1]*IBM Technical Reference Manual*, rev. ed. 2.02 (Boca Raton, Fla.: IBM: April 1983), sec. 2.

[2]*Disk Operating System by Microsoft, Inc.*, 1st ed. Version 2.00 (Boca Raton, Fla.: IBM and Microsoft: January 1983), App. D.

1. Keyboard management
2. Disk management
3. Printer management
4. Screen management
5. Communications management
6. Equipment checks
7. Time of day

Figure 3-1[3] provides a map of PC memory showing areas that are germane to BIOS. BIOS programs are resident starting at memory address FE000. Listings of these programs are given in the *IBM Technical Reference Manual*.[4] Even though they are written in assembly language, these listings are highly informative because they are extensively commented. Even nonassembly language programmers will learn a great deal from reading the comments, especially those comments that preface the main routines.

To invoke one of the software callable BIOS routines, the programmer must put the arguments of the routine into the specified registers and then generate a "software interrupt." An assembly language instruction "**int**" is provided for this

Starting Address in Hex

00000	BIOS Interrupt Vectors
00080	Available Interrupt Vectors
00400	BIOS Data Area
00500	User Read/Write Memory
C8000	Disk Adapter
F0000	Read Only Memory
FE000	Bios Program Area

Figure 3-1 PC Memory Map

[3]*IBM Technical Reference Manual*, p. 2-10.
[4]*IBM Technical Reference Manual*, App. A.

purpose on the Intel 8088 and 8086. All this sounds like BIOS routines have to be called from assembly language. Typically, they do, but later we will describe a C callable assembly language routine, **sysint**, that will do all of the work for us. For now, we will describe the BIOS hardware/software mechanisms involved in invoking BIOS routines.

Each software callable BIOS entry point is associated with an interrupt number, and when the software generates an interrupt with that specific interrupt number as the operand of the **int** instruction, the hardware causes control to be transferred to the associated BIOS entry point. The address of the target BIOS routine (called an "interrupt vector") can be found at the absolute address, that is four times the interrupt number. For example, interrupt 0x10[5] is associated with the BIOS routine that manages the video display. The interrupt vector for interrupt 0x10 is stored at 0x40—i.e., 0x4 times 0x10. If you look at location 0x40 with the debugger and you are not using any application programs that alter that interrupt vector, you will find

$$65 \ F0 \quad 00 \ F0$$

at this location. This represents the 8086/8088 address F000:F065[6]—that is, paragraph number F000 (or absolute address F0000) and offset F065. The absolute address is generated by shifting the paragraph number left four bits and adding the offset. Thus, the absolute address of the video interrupt routine is F0000 + F065, or FF065. To verify that this is really the video interrupt routine, the reader should use the debugger to look at F000:F065, unassemble the code there, and compare this to the code listing in the *IBM Technical Reference Manual*.[7]

Table 3-1[8] provides a list of the interrupt vectors to be found in low memory. The BIOS interrupts are numbered from 0x0 at absolute address 0x00 to 0x1F at absolute address 0x7C. These interrupts are organized into several groups based on their general characteristics. The first eight interrupts (0 to 7) are basic system services:

1. Interrupts to handle catastrophes—e.g., divide by zero, power interruption, and arithmetic overflow
2. Interrupts that are required by the debugger—e.g., single step and breakpoint
3. The interrupt that prints the screen

---

[5] When it is not clear from context, we will use the C convention for representing hexadecimal numbers.

[6] The 8086/8088 family stores a word in memory with the bytes reversed. Thus, F065 is stored in memory as 65F0.

[7] *IBM Technical Reference Manual*, App. A.

[8] *IBM Technical Reference Manual*, p. 2-5.

TABLE 3-1   BIOS INTERRUPT VECTORS

Address (Hex)	Interrupt Number	Name	BIOS Entry
0-3	0	Divide by Zero	D_EOI
4-7	1	Single Step	D_EOI
8-B	2	Nonmaskable	NMI_INT
C-F	3	Breakpoint	D_EOI
10-13	4	Overflow	D_EOI
14-17	5	Print Screen	PRINT_SCREEN
18-1B	6	Reserved	D_EOI
1D-1F	7	Reserved	D_EOI
20-23	8	Time of Day	TIMER_INT
24-27	9	Keyboard	KB_INT
28-2B	A	Reserved	D_EOI
2C-2F	B	Communications	D_EOI
30-33	C	Communications	D_EOI
34-37	D	Disk	D_EOI
38-3B	E	Diskette	DISK_INT
3C-3F	F	Printer	D_EOI
40-43	10	Video	VIDEO_IO
44-47	11	Equipment Check	EQUIPMENT
48-4B	12	Memory	MEMORY_SIZE_DETERMINE
4C-4F	13	Diskette/Disk	DISKETTE_IO
50-53	14	Communications	RS232_IO
54-57	15	Cassette	CASSETTE_IO
58-5B	16	Keyboard	KEYBOARD_IO
5C-5F	17	Printer	PRINTER_IO
60-63	18	Resident BASIC	F600:0000
64-67	19	Bootstrap	BOOT_STRAP
68-6B	1A	Time of Day	TIME_OF_DAY
6C-6F	1B	Keyboard Break	DUMMY_RETURN
70-73	1C	Timer Tick	DUMMY_RETURN
74-77	1D	Video Initialization	VIDEO_PARMS
78-7B	1E	Diskette Parameters	DISK_BASE
7C-7F	1F	Video Graphics Chars	0

The next group of eight interrupts (8 to F) are associated with external devices and they are generated by the hardware, not the software. All of the signal lines associated with these interrupts are connected to the 8259A interrupt processor, which acts as arbiter, deciding which interrupt signal will get the attention of the 8088 CPU when there is more than one interrupt pending. These signal lines come from the timer circuits, the keyboard hardware, the communications hardware, the diskette hardware, and the printer hardware. Signals on these lines will cause the currently active application or operating system program to be interrupted in order to service those signals. We will delve deeply into this type of interrupt in Chapter 5 when we consider asynchronous communications.

The next group of eleven interrupts (10 through 1A) are the main body of the software callable BIOS routines. These interrupts provide the basic I/O services for floppy disk drives, cassette drives, the keyboard, the video display, the asynchronous communications hardware, the clock, and the printer. In contrast to the previous group of interrupts that occur asynchronously with respect to the executing application program, these interrupts are synchronized with the executing application program by virtue of the fact that they are invoked by it, much like a subroutine. In this chapter, we will develop C interfaces to several useful and important interrupts in this group.

The next two interrupts allow the application program to have greater control over its execution than might otherwise be possible. These are reserved for the application program. If the application program wants to capture and process Ctrl-Break keys, it can store a vector in interrupt 1B (location 6C-6F) that points to its own code. That code will be called whenever the Ctrl-Break key is struck by the user. Similarly, interrupt vector 1C (location 70-73) is reserved for programs that have real-time processing requirements, such as a program that must track the position of the mouse and update the mouse's cursor position on the monitor. This code is called 18.2 times per second by the interrupt that updates the PC's clock.

The last group does not contain interrupt vectors but rather pointers to BIOS data.

DOS Functions

DOS provides operating system services via interrupts 0x20 through 0x3F, and they are documented in Appendix D of the *IBM Disk Operating System Manual*. These interrupts are intended to be the mechanism by which application programs interact with DOS. It is probably wise always to try to use DOS calls rather than direct calls to BIOS routines when you have a choice, because we can reasonably expect each new version of DOS to be compatible with the previous version. New machines may have different ROM functions, but the DOS interrupts probably will remain compatible over many successive versions and over a range of hardware versions.

Among the DOS interrupts, one interrupt (0x21) is special in that it is organized into a large number of subfunctions. A subfunction is invoked by placing the function number in the high order byte of the accumulator (**ah**) and executing interrupt 0x21. In a later section, we will develop a C callable function, **bdos**, which invokes the functions of interrupt 0x21. Table 3-2[9] summarizes the groupings of functions within interrupt 0x21:

[9]*IBM Disk Operating System*, pp. D-12 and D-13.

TABLE 3-2 FUNCTIONS OF DOS INTERRUPT 0x21

Function no. (hex)	Function
0-12	Traditional character device I/O
12-24	Traditional file management
25-26	Traditional non-device functions
27-29	Traditional file management
2A-2E	Traditional non-device functions
2F-38	Extended function group
39-3B	Directory group
3C-46	Extended file management group
47	Directory group
48-4B	Extended memory management group
4C-4F	Extended function group
54-57	Extended function group

In the following sections, we will develop several C functions that access basic functions not normally available from high-level languages. Furthermore, we will use these C functions later to develop several application programs.

C Interface to BIOS Functions

We will examine a C callable function, **sysint**, that allows the execution of the 8086/88 **int** instruction from a C program. **sysint** is written in assembly language and allows the user to specify values that the 8088 registers are to have just before the **int** instruction is executed. In addition, it returns a C structure containing the values of the registers just after the **int** instruction is executed.

The specification of **sysint** is

```
int sysint(vec,sreg,rreg)
unsigned char vec;      /*interrupt number to be executed*/
struct regval *sreg;    /*registers before int execution*/
struct regval *rreg;    /*registers after int execution*/
```

where **regval** is a C structure defined as

```
struct regval { int ax,bx,cx,dx,si,di,ds,es;}
```

With permission from Computer Innovations, Inc., we have included the assembly code implementation of **sysint** in Figure 3-2. (See Appendix A for the ".h" files.)

This function is worth some analysis in that it includes some highly clever assembly coding. The basic problem requiring the clever coding is that the 8086/88 **int** instruction requires that the interrupt type be coded into the instruction as immediate data. Calling from C, we have to pass in the interrupt number as a

```
            include model.h

;           execute an interrupt with registers set up

            include prologue.h

;           entry  1, the interrupt vector ( *4 for absolute address )
;                  2, pointer to register values for call
;                  3, pointer to area to save returned register values
;           exit   machine status register value returned as func value
;           structure for register values is
;                    struct regval {unsigned ax,bx,cx,dx,si,di,ds,es;}

if      @BIGMODEL
a1      equ     @ab+4
a2      equ     @ab+6
a3      equ     @ab+10
ELSE
a1      equ     @ab+4
a2      equ     @ab+6
a3      equ     @ab+8
ENDIF


        public sysint

if      @bigmodel
sysint  proc    far
else
sysint  proc    near
endif

        cld                     ;for dos 2.0

        push    ds              ;save important registers
        push    es
        push    bp
        mov     bp,sp           ;set our arg pointer

        mov     bl,a1[bp]       ;get interrrupt number
        cmp     bl,025h
        jz      sysinta
        cmp     bl,026h
        jz      sysinta
        push    ax              ;dummy on stack for return
```

Figure 3-2 Assembly Code for **sysint**

```
sysinta:

        pushf                           ;push the flags for return
        pop       dx                    ;make a copy of flags
        push      dx
        push      cs                    ;and the code segment
        call      dummy                 ;push the ip
dummy:
        pop       ax                    ;get ip value
        sub       ax,offset dummy
        add       ax,offset sysint1
        push      ax                    ;return address
        and       dh,0ch                ;clear I and T flag bits
        push      dx
        xor       bx,bx                 ;clear bx
        mov       es,bx                 ;and es
        mov       bl,a1[bp]             ;get int trap number
        shl       bx,1                  ;*2
        shl       bx,1                  ;*2 again (thats 4)
        push      es:word ptr 2[bx]
        push      es:word ptr [bx]                      ;thats the entry data

IF      @BIGMODEL
        LES       BX,dword ptr A2[BP]
ELSE
        mov       bx,a2[bp]             ;get source registers
ENDIF

        mov       cx,8                  ;move values to registers
mtor01:
IF      @BIGMODEL
        PUSH      WORD PTR ES:[BX]
ELSE
        push      word ptr [bx]
ENDIF
        inc       bx
        inc       bx
        loop      mtor01                ;push all 8 words
        pop       es
        pop       ds
        pop       di
        pop       si
        pop       dx
        pop       cx
        pop       bx
        pop       ax

        iret                            ;simulate an interrupt
```

Figure 3-2 (Continued)

```
sysint1:
        mov     bp,sp               ;restore bp
        pushf                       ;save result flags for return

        push    es                  ;get returned register values
        push    ds
        push    di
        push    si
        push    dx
        push    cx
        push    bx
        push    ax
IF      @BIGMODEL
        LES     BX,dword ptr A3+2[BP]
ELSE
        mov     bx,a3+2[bp]     ;get destination address
ENDIF
        mov     cx,8
rtom01:
IF      @BIGMODEL
        POP     ES:WORD PTR [BX]
ELSE
        pop     ss:word ptr [bx]
ENDIF
        inc     bx
        inc     bx
        loop    rtom01

        pop     ax                  ;result flags for user
        pop     bp                  ;dump rubbish from stack
        pop     bp
        pop     es
        pop     ds                  ;restore segment registers
        ret                         ;all done
sysint  endp

        include epilogue.h

        end
```

Figure 3-2 (Continued)

parameter, and just to complicate matters a bit, BIOS routine parameters are passed through registers. The final complication is that the BIOS routines must return using an **iret** (interrupt return) instruction, which undoes the effects of the interrupt. That is, the interrupt that calls a BIOS routine (or any interrupt for that matter) saves the **ip**, **cs**, and **flags** registers on the stack and loads the **ip**, **cs**, and **flags** registers with the values for the target BIOS routine. Therefore, the last instruction an interrupt routine must execute is an **iret** instruction, which restores the **ip**, **cs**, and **flags** registers from the stack, thereby resuming execution at the address just after the location at which the interrupt occurred.

Thus, **sysint** must accomplish three basic goals:

1. Set up the stack to simulate the occurrence of an interrupt (i.e., put the proper **ip**, **cs**, and **flags** registers values on the stack so that the final **iret** instruction in the interrupt service routine will work properly)
2. Load the registers (from the C structure) with the proper pre-interrupt data
3. Simulate an **int** instruction

The stack is set up with the proper **ip**, **cs**, and **flags** registers by the code from **sysint** shown in Figure 3-3.

```
1       sysinta:

2               pushf                   ;push the flags for return
3               pop     dx              ;make a copy of flags
4               push    dx
5               push    cs              ;and the code segment
6               call    dummy           ;push the ip
7       dummy:
8               pop     ax              ;get ip value
9               sub     ax,offset dummy
10              add     ax,offset sysint1
11              push    ax              ;return address
12              and     dh,0ch          ;clear I and T flag bits
13              push    dx
14              xor     bx,bx           ;clear bx
15              mov     es,bx           ;and es
16              mov     bl,a1[bp]       ;get int trap number
17              shl     bx,1            ;*2
18              shl     bx,1            ;*2 again (thats 4)
19              push    es:word ptr 2[bx]
20              push    es:word ptr [bx]               ;thats the entry data
```

Figure 3-3 Setting Up a Simulated Interrupt

Lines 1 through 11 produce a stack that contains (among other things) the information that will be used by the BIOS **iret** instruction to return to the label **sysint1** in **sysint**. It contains

```
ip (offset of sysint1)

cs (current segment)

flags (unaltered)
```

Lines 12 through 20 set up the stack with the **ip**, **cs**, and **flags** values used to simulate the **int** call of the BIOS routine. Lines 2 through 4 copy the **flags** register into **dx** so that the interrupt and trap flags can be cleared later in line 12. Since **sysint** will use an **iret** instruction to simulate the **int** instruction, the **flags** register must be put onto the stack so that the **iret** instruction will pick it up. However, a true **int** instruction clears the interrupt and trap flags to inhibit interrupts and traps while the interrupt service routine is executing. To simulate the clearing of the interrupt and trap flags, **sysint** puts the **flags** register on the stack with the flags already cleared (line 12). When the **iret** instruction causes the **flags** register to be loaded from the stack, it will appear just as if a true **int** instruction was executed. In addition, the **iret** instruction will pick up the **ip** and **cs** of the target BIOS routine. To set up the proper **ip** and **cs** on the stack, **sysint** zeroes the **bx** and **es** registers (lines 14 and 15), gets the interrupt number (line 16), and multiplies it times 4 to get the address of the interrupt vector (lines 17 and 18). Lines 19 and 20 push the **cs** and **ip** of the interrupt vector onto the stack. The stack now looks like:

```
ip (offset of BIOS routine)

cs (segment of BIOS routine)

flags (T and I flags clear)

ip (offset of sysint1)
```

```
cs (current segment)

flags (unaltered)
```

The remaining code in **sysint** loads the registers by first pushing them on the stack and then popping them into the appropriate registers. An **iret** instruction is used to simulate the interrupt, after which the results are loaded into the appropriate C structure.

C Interface to DOS Functions

BIOS routines have few frills over and above their basic functions. You often want a bit more functionality, and many DOS functions provide this. For example, the BIOS keyboard management function will read a character from the keyboard. In contrast, DOS function 1 will perform the read, echo the character to the screen, and check for and process the Ctrl-Break key if one is present. The more recently added DOS functions provide even more service. For example, function 0x3f allows you to read from a file or device providing support for I/O redirection. When possible, the user should use the DOS functions. Appendix D of the IBM DOS manual describes the DOS functions that are available.

Notice that we have referred to these as "functions" rather than interrupts. Recall that these functions are all available through one DOS interrupt, number 0x21. The specific DOS function desired is indicated by putting the function number in **ah**. Of course, we could access these functions by setting up **ah** appropriately and then calling **sysint**, but there is an easier and more direct way to call simple DOS functions. Use the C support function **bdos**. The specification of **bdos** is

```
int bdos(fcode,dx)
int fcode, dx;
```

where **fcode** contains the DOS function code and **dx** contains an integer parameter to be loaded into the **dx** register. **bdos** returns the value of the accumulator, **ax**, as its result. For more complex DOS functions that have more extensive register requirements, **sysint** may be used.

The assembly code that implements **bdos** is shown in Figure 3-4.

```
          include model.h

;         call bdos for simple services

          INCLUDE PROLOGUE.H
          public bdos
IF        @BIGMODEL
BDOS      PROC      FAR
ELSE
BDOS      PROC      NEAR
ENDIF


          push      bp
          mov       bp,sp
          mov       ah,@AB[bp]
IF        @BIGMODEL
          PUSH      DS
          lds       DX,dword ptr @AB+2[BP]  ;**
else
          mov       dx,@AB+2[bp]
ENDIF
          int       21h
IF        @BIGMODEL
          POP       DS
ENDIF
          pop       bp
          ret

BDOS      ENDP
          INCLUDE EPILOGUE.H
          end
```

Figure 3-4 bdos Implementation (Courtesy of Computer Innovations, Inc.)

Now it is time to put **sysint** and **bdos** to use. We will develop a few basic functions that are not readily available in C, but that we will need for the applications to be developed later in the book. In the course of this development, the reader will learn where to find the information describing all BIOS and DOS functions and will learn the basics of developing interfaces to BIOS and DOS functions.

3.2 APPLICATION OF THE BASIC FUNCTIONS

Keyboard Management

Reading without Echo

For the most part, the existing C language I/O functions are satisfactory for reading data from the keyboard. There is at least one notable exception, however. In a number of applications, input from the keyboard may need to be processed by the application program before it is echoed to the screen, and under some conditions the application program may not want to echo it to the screen at all. Further, such applications will want to read characters from the keyboard unbuffered. That is, they require that each character be sent to the application program one at a time when they are typed, not buffered into a group that is only sent to the application program when terminated with a **newline** character. For example, a full-screen editor may respond to some input characters as data and to others as commands. Therefore, the editor must process each incoming character from the keyboard individually and decide how to handle it. The standard C I/O functions create a problem in that they insist on both buffering and echoing the characters read from the keyboard. Hence, we need a **get character** function that reads data unbuffered from the keyboard and does not echo it to the screen. This function is named **getc_noecho**.

The specification for this function is:

```
char getc_noecho()
```

and it is implemented by the code shown in Figure 3-5.

getc_noecho makes use of DOS function 7 which is described in Appendix D of the IBM DOS manual. It reads the keyboard without echo and waits if no

```
char getc_noecho()
/*       this function behaves like getc except that the
         character is not echoed to the display.
         It uses dos 0x21 interrupt with function 0x7.
*/
         {

/*       Declare structures which contain the register
         values before and after a system interrupt
         executed by the C function sysint.
```

Figure 3-5 getc_noecho Implementation

```
 */
                struct regval { int ax,bx,cx,dx,si,di,ds,es; };
                struct regval sreg ;
                struct regval rreg;

                sreg.ax = 0x700;              /*function is 0x7 */
                sysint(0x21,&sreg,&rreg);
                return(rreg.ax & 0xff);
                }
```

Figure 3-5 (Continued)

character is available. The resulting character is returned in **al**. Thus, the last statement of **getc_noecho** masks out that character and returns it.

Function 7 does not check for Ctrl-Break, so nothing will happen until the user types a character. Alternatively, we could use DOS function 0x8, which would perform the same DOS function except that a Ctrl-Break character would cause a 0x23 interrupt. Generally, DOS handles a 0x23 interrupt but there are occasions in which the application program may want to handle its own Ctrl-Break interrupts. On those occasions, the application program will want to supply a Ctrl-Break handling routine and re-vector interrupt 0x23 to that routine. Chapter 5 will supply the reader with enough knowledge about the interrupt system to handle this kind of option. For now, we will be satisfied to let DOS handle Ctrl-Break.

The foregoing version of **getc_noecho** is a bit clumsy. We have the alternative of using **bdos** instead of **sysint** and this results in the simpler version shown in Figure 3-6.

```
char getc_noecho()
/*      this function behaves like getc except that the
        character is not echoed to the display.
        It uses dos 0x21 interrupt with function 0x7.
 */
        {

        int bdos();
        return(bdos(0x7,0) & 0x00ff);
        }
```

Figure 3-6 Simpler **getc_noecho** Implementation

Each call to **getc_noecho** returns a single character for each key struck. The exception to this is in the case of the extended character codes for keys such as Alt shifted keys, the cursor movement keys, and so forth. For these keys, BIOS returns two character codes: 0x00 (NUL), indicating an extended character code is to follow, and a second ASCII code defining the specific extended character. For example, the Home key generates the ASCII code 0x00 followed by 0x47 (decimal 71). The extended character codes are defined in the *IBM Technical Reference Manual*.[10]

Under the assumption that extended character codes are possible, the typical usage of **getc_noecho** is a call to **getc_noecho** followed by a check for a NUL byte, and if one is found, a second call to retrieve the extended character code.

DOS Functions Preferred

DOS functions are preferred over direct BIOS interrupts in those circumstances where you have an option. **getc_noecho** is a case in point. We could have opted to make direct calls to the BIOS interrupt routine for **getc_noecho**, but we chose not to for a very good reason. We would have limited the generality of **getc_noecho**. There is a nontrivial difference between the DOS and BIOS-based implementations of **getc_noecho** that would become obvious if we tried to use the BIOS-based **getc_noecho** in a C filter program. I/O redirection works only if we do the input by using a DOS read function because DOS, not BIOS, handles the redirection. The BIOS implementation would read from the keyboard regardless of whether or not **stdin** was redirected. The DOS-based version, on the other hand, will read from the appropriate source—the keyboard, a file, or another program—depending upon whether or not redirection has been specified.

Filter programs are powerful programming tools that are typically used with I/O redirection. That is, while they are designed to read from **stdin** and to write to **stdout**, they typically take their input from a file or another program. To take input from a file, the user places the symbol "<" in front of the file name on the command line, as in

```
filterprog <infile
```

Alternatively, input may be taken from the output of another program if the user places the pipe symbol, " | ", between the programs, as in

```
program1 | program2
```

In this example, the output of **program1** becomes the input of **program2**.

Similarly, the output of a filter program is often redirected to a file, or another program, as in the foregoing example. To direct the output to a file, the user places

[10]*IBM Technical Reference Manual*, sec. 3.

the symbol ">" in front of the file name, as in

```
filter <infile >outfile
```

The concept of I/O redirection is a valuable feature that can benefit the programmer by making his or her programs more widely applicable. We certainly do not want to eliminate that capability. Therefore, the second version of **getc_noecho** is the preferred version.

Testing for Characters

getc_noecho waits on characters at the keyboard and returns control to the calling routine only when a character is typed. In many cases, an application program may want to read a character if one is present, but may want to go on to other tasks if one is not present. For example, if the application program is also responding to other input media such as game paddles or joysticks, it may not be feasible to wait for character input. Indeed, in a game situation, the character input may be optional and highly infrequent. Therefore, the application wants to respond to the keyboard only if there is a character or characters waiting.[11] This is the rationale for a function, **check_keyboard**, which checks the keyboard for waiting characters. It is implemented with the code shown in Figure 3-7.

```
int check_keyboard()      /*Returns 0xff if character waiting, else 0x0*/
          {
          int bdos();
          return(bdos(0xB,0) & 0x00ff);
          }
```

Figure 3-7 check_keyboard implementation

The structure of this function parallels that of **getc_noecho** and requires little explanation. Suffice it to say that we are using DOS function 0xB and it returns 0xff in **al** if a character is available and 0x00 in **al** if not. Since it is not good practice to depend on DOS clearing **ah** for you, we mask out **ah** leaving only the bit pattern

---

[11]The BIOS keyboard management function buffers up to 15 characters allowing the application program to read the characters at its convenience. When the 15-character buffer overflows, the system beeps at the user to slow his typing down. Any overflow characters are lost.

in **al**. It is also worth mentioning that DOS function 0xB will cause a Ctrl-Break interrupt to occur if a Ctrl-Break keystroke is pending.[12]

Screen Management

To provide a context for functions that we are about to develop, we present four different models of screen management. These models will clarify the requirements for the primitive functions needed to support each screen management model. In the following section, we will develop some of these primitive functions in detail and thereby establish the "nuts and bolts" connection between the notions of the screen management model and the facilities provided by DOS and BIOS. In later chapters, we will develop typical examples of user interfaces based on the various screen management models.

For the purposes of this discussion, we will divide screen management models into four basic classes:

1. The "linear or line-oriented model" treats the screen as a scroll of paper in which new information is added at the bottom and old information scrolls off the top.

2. The "full-screen or form-based model" treats the screen like a blackboard allowing information to be organized spatially, and written and removed from arbitrary areas of the screen.

3. The "multi-window model" organizes the screen into separate areas—that is, windows—and associates each window with a separate program. This class is recursive in that the screen architecture model local to any specific window may be any one of these four basic classes.

4. The "desktop model" extends the multi-window model with the notion that the screen is a desktop containing in addition to the windows, graphical icons representing objects—for example, in-boxes, out-boxes, and folders—that are sitting on the desk. Associated with the icons are menus that "pop-up" on command and describe the kind of processing that can be performed on that object.

[12]The keyboard management routines check for Ctrl-Break and generally execute a software interrupt (0×23) when one occurs. The only opportunity for a Ctrl-Break interrupt to be executed is when certain DOS function calls are made by the application program. For example, Ctrl-Break is checked for when the application program is either reading a character or checking to see if a character is waiting. This explains why some applications get into an infinite loop that is unbreakable. If an infinite loop does not contain the appropriate DOS function calls, it can lock up the machine, and ultimately, require a reboot to break the loop. On the other hand, infinite loops that invoke the keyboard management functions will allow Ctrl-Break interrupts, as long as the DOS invocation is not one of those that inhibit Ctrl-Break processing. Therefore, use of functions that inhibit Ctrl-Break processing should only be done with great care.

Each of these successive models is a superset of the previous model. That is, the full-screen model provides all of the capabilities of the line-oriented model plus a number of additional capabilities of its own.

Application programs that use a linear screen management model are among the easiest to write in that they require only very simple screen management code. They use straightforward writes to the screen and show the complete record of user interaction as a linear sequence of the data and commands typed by the user, interleaved with the application program responses. In addition to being the easiest to write, such programs tend to be the least satisfactory from a human factors viewpoint. That is, they are not "user-friendly." They tend to be difficult to use and allow the user only a very few options during the processing. Since all of the primitive functions required to develop applications based on the linear model are already built into the source language, we will not consider them further at this point. We will, however, develop some full-screen functions for use by extended examples to be presented in later chapters. The desktop model is mentioned for completeness, but is beyond the scope of this book and we will not consider it further.

In contrast to the linear model, the full-screen model is not currently well supported in most application languages, even though some languages such as BASIC provide a few of the functions required. In fact, an industry market segment has been created by the need of users for libraries of such functions. While we will not develop a complete package at this point, we will develop a few of the primitive building blocks required to support two-dimensional screen management, and provide the reader with sufficient knowledge to build his or her own library of support functions.

In order to support a two-dimensional model of screen management, a package must be able to perform certain basic services:

1. Clear the screen.
2. Move the cursor to an arbitrary point on the screen—e.g., move the cursor to a data field.
3. Write a string of characters to the screen without disturbing other information on the screen—e.g., update a field.
4. Change the attributes of characters on the screen—e.g., change a field from normal display to highlighted display to indicate the application program's locus of attention.
5. Determine the current position of the cursor—e.g., in order to move the cursor a number of lines or columns relative to its current position.
6. Read the data character at a given cursor position.
7. Vertically scroll blank lines up or down into some area of the screen.
8. Horizontally scroll blank columns left or right in some area of the screen.

We will not develop C functions for all of these functions, but we will develop

TABLE 3-3   video_io INTERRUPT FUNCTIONS

Function no.	Function	Returns
0	Set Display Mode	
1	Set Cursor Type	
2	Set Cursor Position	
3	Read Cursor Position	Row, column and mode
4	Read Light	Position plus trigger status
5	Select Active Display Page	
6	Scroll Active Page Up	
7	Scroll Active Page Down	
8	Read Character/Attribute	Character/attrib at curr pos
9	Write Character/Attribute	
10	Write Character Only	
11	Set Color Palette	
12	Write Dot	
13	Read Dot	Dot at row,col
14	Write Teletype	
15	Current Video State	Mode, Num Columns, and Page

enough functions that the interested reader can extend and modify them to his or her own purposes.

The reader should get out a copy of the *IBM Technical Reference Manual* and turn to the BIOS listing in Appendix A. Read the prologue to the **video_io** interrupt (0x10) routine. It will make the following routines quite obvious. Table 3-3 summarizes the functions available within the **video_io** interrupt routine.

Clearing the Screen

We will start by developing a routine to clear the screen called **cls**. The way to make **cls** work really fast is to use the **video_io** scroll function which is invoked by putting 0x6 in **ah** and executing a **video_io** (0x10) software interrupt. The implementation of **cls** is shown in Figure 3-8.

```
cls()
/*      This function clears the screen leaving the cursor
        positioned at its current position.
*/
        {

/*      Declare structures which contain the register
        values before and after a system interrupt
        executed by the C function sysint.
```

Figure 3-8   cls Implementation

```
*/
          struct regval { int ax,bx,cx,dx,si,di,ds,es; };
          struct regval sreg ;
          struct regval rreg;

          sreg.cx = 0;           /*upper left corner of screen (0,0)*/
          sreg.dx = 0x184f;      /*lower right corner (24,79)*/
          sreg.bx = 0x700;       /*normal attribute for scrolled lines*/
          sreg.ax = 0x600;       /*bios function for scrolling*/

          /*now call bios*/

          sysint(0x10,&sreg,&rreg);
          }
```

Figure 3-8 (Continued)

The **video_io** routine provides two kinds of scrolling, up when **ah** = 6 and down when **ah** = 7. It does not matter since we are clearing the whole screen, so we will choose up. This is set up by the statement

```
          sreg.ax = 0x600;       /*bios function for scrolling*/
```

The area of the screen to be scrolled is defined by the registers **cx** and **dx** such that (**ch**,**cl**) = (row, column) of the upper left-hand corner and (**dh**,**dl**) = (row,column) of the lower right-hand corner. This is accomplished by the statements

```
          sreg.cx = 0;           /*upper left corner of screen (0,0)*/
          sreg.dx = 0x184f;      /*lower right corner (24,79)*/
```

Finally, we have to chose the attribute of the scrolled lines by putting the display attribute bit pattern into **bh**.

```
          sreg.bx = 0x700;       /*normal attribute for scrolled lines*/
```

This statement requires a bit of background information. The IBM PC display buffer is set up with a pair of bytes defining each character on the screen. One byte contains the ASCII code of the character and the second byte contains the display attributes of that character—for example, inverse video, normal, highlighted, blinking, and so on. (See the *IBM Technical Reference Manual*[13] for definitions of the bit patterns.) Table 3-4 provides C **#define** statements that will be

---

[13]*IBM Technical Reference Manual*, p. 1–138.

used later in the book. For **cls**, we will use constants for the attributes so that our intention is clear. Later in the book, we will use C **#defines** for such constants, which is the preferred practice.

TABLE 3-4   C **#defines** FOR DISPLAY ATTRIBUTES

```
#define NORM_ATTR 0x07           /*normal or blank attribute*/

#define INV_ATTR 0x70           /*inverse video attribute*/

#define NORMBLNK_ATTR 0x87      /*normal blinking attribute*/

#define INVBLNK_ATTR 0xf0       /*inverse video blinking*/

#define NORMHLIT_ATTR 0x0f      /*normal with highlighting*/

#define INVHLIT_ATTR 0x78       /*inverse video with highlighting*/

#define NORMBLNKHLIT_ATTR 0x8f  /*normal,blinking,highlighting*/

#define INVBLNKHLIT_ATTR 0xf8   /*inverse, blinking,highlighting*/

#define UNDERLINE_ATTR 0x01     /*underline attribute*/
```

These combinations are constructed from the atomic values given in Table 3-5.

TABLE 3-5   ATOMIC DISPLAY ATTRIBUTES

Value	Attribute
0x00	Nothing is displayed
0x01	Character is underlined
0x07	Normal character (white character on black)
0x0f	Normal character with highlighting
0x70	Inverse video (black character on white)
0x80	Blinking character

Scrolling Windows

cls uses a special case of a more powerful BIOS routine for scrolling window areas on a screen. The next logical step is to write a C function called **scroll_window** that can take full advantage of this capability. We will make good use of **scroll_window** in later chapters.

scroll_window is a modest generalization of **cls**. We will simply turn the BIOS parameters into C parameters, thus making the full power of the **video_io** function available from C. The implementation of **scroll_window** is shown in Figure 3-9.

```
scroll_window(row1,col1,row2,col2,n,attrib,fnc)

/*    This function scrolls a window whose upper
      left corner is (row1,col1) and whose lower
      right corner is (row2,col2). The window is
      scrolled n lines and the new lines have
      attribute attrib (e.g., attrib = 0x07 is a blank line)
      fnc specifies the bios function (6-scroll up,7-scroll dwn)
      If n = 0, the whole window is blanked.
*/

      unsigned int row1,col1,row2,col2,n,attrib,fnc;
      {

/*    Declare structures which contain the register
      values before and after a system interrupt
      executed by the C function sysint.
*/
      struct regval { int ax,bx,cx,dx,si,di,ds,es;};
      struct regval sreg ;
      struct regval rreg;

      sreg.ax = (n & 0xff) _ ((fnc << 8) & 0xff00);
      sreg.cx = (col1 & 0xff) _ ((row1 << 8) & 0xff00);
      sreg.dx = (col2 & 0xff) _ ((row2 << 8) & 0xff00);
      sreg.bx = (attrib << 8) & 0xff00;

      /*now call bios with function fnc*/
      sysint(0x10,&sreg,&rreg);
      }
```

Figure 3-9 scroll_window Implementation

It should be clear that

```
                scroll_window(0,0,24,79,0,0x07,6);
```

is equivalent to

```
                                cls();
```

for a 25 line by 80 column display.

Moving the Cursor

Another basic capability that we will require is positioning the cursor at an arbitrary position on the screen. Again, this function, which we will name **move_cursor**, is provided directly by the **video_io** routine function 2. The implementation of **move_cursor** is shown in Figure 3-10.

```
move_cursor(row,col)
/*      this function moves the cursor to position (row,col)
        It uses bios 0x10 interrupt with function 2.
*/
        unsigned int row,col;
        {
        unsigned int xtrows;

/*      Declare structures which contain the register
        values before and after a system interrupt
        executed by the C function sysint.
*/
        struct regval { int ax,bx,cx,dx,si,di,ds,es; };
        struct regval sreg ;
        struct regval rreg;
/*      Screen wrap logic --
        This logic wraps to top of screen if necessary.
*/
        if(row > maxrow || col > maxcol)
                {
                xtrows = col / maxcolp1;
                col %= maxcolp1;
                row += xtrows;
                row %= maxrowp1;
                }

        sreg.dx = col;
        sreg.dx |= (row << 8) & 0xff00;
        sreg.bx = 0;

/*      col to dl and row to dh      */
/*      screen number to bh          */

        sreg.ax = 0x200;            /*bios function 2*/
        sysint(0x10,&sreg,&rreg);
        }
```

Figure 3-10 move_cursor Implementation

move_cursor uses several global variables that describe parameters of the display. For the monochrome display, these global variables are defined as

```
int maxcol = 79;       /*max col number of screen*/
int maxrow = 24;       /*max row of screen*/
int maxcolp1 = 80;     /*max col of screen + 1*/
int maxrowp1 = 25;     /*maxrow + 1*/
```

These global variables are used for the cursor wraparound logic. The objective of this logic is to make the screen look like a circular buffer of characters, 2,000 characters in length—that is, 25 lines of 80 characters each. If a column position exceeds 79, it is wrapped into its proper position on a lower row. If the row position, or the column and row positions taken together, exceeds the lower right-hand corner of the screen, the cursor is wrapped around to the proper position at the top of the screen. This logic generalizes the wraparound logic of BIOS which, because it is working with single byte definitions of row and column, can only handle positions less than or equal to 255. If we depended on the BIOS logic, we would not get full-screen wraparound for values of the column position greater than 255 (i.e., for values over 3 + lines).

Notice that the **move_cursor** code sets **bh** to the display page number by setting **bx** to 0. For the monochrome display, we just set this to zero since there is only one page.

Writing to the Display

Now that we can move the cursor, the next logical capability is that of writing a string to the display. Of course, C provides several functions that will write characters to the screen (e.g., **printf**), but they give us no control over the attribute values. So if we want to write a field in inverse video, we are out of luck. **writln** remedies this omission. Consider the implementation shown in Figure 3-11.

```
writln(str,attrib)
        char *str;
        unsigned int attrib;
        {
        unsigned int row, col, mode;


/*      Declare structures which contain the register
        values before and after a system interrupt
        executed by the C function sysint.
```

Figure 3-11   writln Implementation

```
*/

        struct regval { int ax,bx,cx,dx,si,di,ds,es; };
        struct regval sreg ;
        struct regval rreg;

        read_cursor(&row,&col,&mode);
        for (; *str != 0x00;)
                {
                sreg.ax =*str & 0xff;           /* char to be output*/
                sreg.ax |= 0x0900;              /* bios function */
                sreg.bx = attrib & 0x00ff;      /* attribute to bl*/
                sreg.cx = 1;                    /* #of times to write char*/

                /* bh contains display page (0 for monochrome display)*/

                /* write character to screen */
                sysint(0x10,&sreg,&rreg);
                col++;
                move_cursor(row,col);
                ++str;
                }
        }
```

Figure 3-11 (Continued)

writln writes the string in **str**, starting at the current position of the cursor, and continues until the string is exhausted. **writln** uses the function **read_cursor** (defined on p. 66) to retrieve the current position of the cursor. Since the display buffer is one long string and since the cursor position is bumped by one position each time, writing a string that extends over the end of a line will cause the string to wrap around to the following screen line at the end of each screen line. Similarly, a string that extends over the lower right-hand boundary wraps around to the top left-hand boundary of the screen.

The parameter **attrib** is the display attribute to be associated with each character to be written. Refer to Tables 3-4 and 3-5 for legal values of **attrib**.

Finding Cursor Position

Many programs need to be able to determine the position of the cursor at any given time. We will present a function, **read_cursor**, that reads the current row, column, and mode of the cursor. (See Figure 3-12.)

```
read_cursor(row,col,mode)
/*
        This function reads the current cursor position
        and returns its row, column and mode.
        Note that row, col and mode are pointers.
*/
        unsigned int *row,*col,*mode;
        {

/*      Declare structures which contain the register
        values before and after a system interrupt
        executed by the C function sysint.
*/
        struct regval { int ax,bx,cx,dx,si,di,ds,es; };
        struct regval sreg ;
        struct regval rreg;

        sreg.bx = 0;        /*display page no*/
        sreg.ax = 0x0300;   /*bios function to read cursor*/

        sysint(0x10,&sreg,&rreg);
        *row = (rreg.dx >> 8) & 0xff ;
        *col = rreg.dx & 0xff;
        *mode = rreg.cx;
        }
```

Figure 3-12 read_cursor Implementation

read_cursor uses **video_io** function 3 to read the (row, column) position of the cursor into registers (**dh**, **dl**) and the mode into register **cx**. These results are returned in the C variables **row**, **col**, and **mode**.

Reading the Display Buffer

Another capability we need is a routine that can read characters from the video display buffer. The display buffer appears as part of the PC's address space and can be read and written just as any other part of memory. For the monochrome display, the display buffer begins at paragraph address 0xb000 (i.e., absolute address 0xb0000), and for the color monitor the display buffer begins at paragraph address 0xb800 (i.e., absolute address 0xb8000). Rather than code these constant addresses into our routine, we will let the BIOS **video_io** routine figure out which kind of monitor we have and where the display buffer is located.

The implementation of **fetch_dchar** shown in Figure 3-13 uses the BIOS

```
char fetch_dchar(row,col)
/* fetch display character at (row,col).
   cursor is moved to (row,col) and left there*/

        unsigned int row,col;


        {

/*      Declare structures which contain the register
        values before and after a system interrupt
        executed by the C function sysint.
*/
        struct regval { int ax,bx,cx,dx,si,di,ds,es; };
        struct regval sreg ;
        struct regval rreg;

        move_cursor(row,col);

/* bh must be current display page*/

        sreg.bx = 0;
        sreg.ax = 0x0800;        /*bios video fnc 8*/
        sysint(0x10,&sreg,&rreg);
        return ((char) (rreg.ax & 0x00ff));
        }
```

Figure 3-13 fetchd_char Implementation

The implementation of **fetch_dchar** shown in Figure 3-13 uses the BIOS **video_io** routine to read the data character at a given (**row**, **col**) position of the display. **fetch_dchar** reads the character from the display buffer at (**row,col**) by moving the cursor to (**row, col**) and invoking **video_io** function 8. The character is returned to **fetch_dchar** in the low-order byte of the accumulator (**al**) and the attribute of the character is returned in the high-order byte (**ah**). As it stands, **fetch_dchar** throws the attribute byte away, but if the user desired to retrieve it as well, he or she could redeclare **fetch_dchar** as an unsigned **int** and return both values. The calling routine would then be responsible for separating the values. The cursor is left at (**row, col**).

With this basic set of routines, the reader should be able to perform most screen management functions within a form-based screen architecture. These routines are the basic set of routines from which other more complex functions can be built. Further, you now know where to look for system functions and how to access them. By reading through the various DOS and BIOS functions documented in the IBM manuals, you will find many gems that you will want to add to your library.

EXERCISES

3.1. Explain some advantages and disadvantages of the operating system interface to application programs being implemented using interrupts.

3.2. Investigate the available DOS functions and extend the set of support functions. Consider extensions for PC graphics.

3.3. Write a simple full screen program editor. (This is a one month to one quarter project, depending on the number of edit commands implemented.)

3.4. Develop a data acquisition program that treats the screen as a form that might be used by librarians. The form contains the following fields: Title, Author(s), Publication Type (i.e., book, periodical, conference, journal, thesis), Pages, Volume, Number, and Publisher. Use the up arrow key and down arrow key to move from field to field, and the back arrow and forward arrow to move within a field. Consider allowing the use of the home, ins, del, and backspace keys for local editing. The end key causes the information entered onto the form by the user to be written to a file. See the documentation for the UNIX program *refer*[14] for the definition of the format of the output file. (This exercise should be about a one- to one-and-one-half month project for a first-year graduate student.)

---

[14]M. E. Lesk, "Some Applications of Inverted Indexes on the Unix System," *Unix User's Manual Supplementary Documents (4.2 BSD)*, (Berkeley, Calif.: University of California, March 1984), See also Bill Tuthill, "Refer—A Bibliography System," *Unix User's Manual Supplementary Documents (4.2 BSD)*, (Berkeley, Calif.: University of California, March 1984).

Chapter 4

Interrupt
and Communications
Hardware

4.1 INTRODUCTION

In Chapter 3, we introduced interrupts that could be issued by the software for the purposes of invoking DOS or BIOS functions. These interrupts are caused by execution of the 8086/88 **int** instruction. In contrast, hardware interrupts are caused by signals generated by various pieces of hardware within the PC. For example, the timer chip generates a signal 18.2 times per second that causes the CPU to update the memory location containing the current time of day. The timer is typical of the kind of hardware function that requires interrupt support. It is one that:

1. Is operating asynchronously with the activities of the CPU
2. Requires intermittent servicing and interaction with the CPU
3. Requires only a relative small portion of the CPU's computing resources
4. Must be serviced without delay

In fact, there are several such pieces of hardware on the PC. They include, in addition to the timer, the keyboard processor, the asynchronous communications equipment, the disk drives, and the printer. Since the 8086/88 chip has only one input line for interrupt signals, multiple pieces of hardware needing connection presents a problem. How can we connect these several pieces of equipment to the single interrupt input line? And once we have solved the connection problem, what do we do about concurrent requests for service from the CPU? This problem is resolved by the introduction of the 8259A interrupt processor chip.[1] The job of this chip is:

1. To allow multiple interrupt lines (up to eight per 8259A) to be logically connected to the CPU
2. To arbitrate between simultaneous interrupt signals (i.e., choose highest priority) and sequence the servicing of those signals
3. To enable or disable individual interrupt lines at the behest of the currently running CPU program
4. To inform the CPU of the interrupt number associated with a currently firing interrupt

In the following sections, we will examine the structure of the hardware involved in interrupt processing and describe its behavior in a working PC.

4.2 THE INTERRUPT HARDWARE

Figure 4-1 shows the key elements involved in interrupt processing on the IBM PC: the 8086/8088 CPU, the 8259A interrupt processor, and the 8288 bus controller. The roles of each piece of hardware will become clear as we view the overall behavior of the group. Let us follow through the actions associated with an interrupt signal on line IRQ4—that is, a signal originating in the asynchronous communications element.

Given that no higher priority interrupts are pending (i.e., interrupts 0 through 3) and interrupt 4 has not been masked off, the 8259A signals the 8086/88 by making its **INT** pin go high. The interrupt will be honored by the 8086/88, if the **if** flag in the **flags** register is set.[2] The 8086/8088 signals the bus controller (i.e., the 8288) via the status lines S0-S2 to put the first of two interrupt acknowledge signals to the 8259A onto the $\overline{\text{INTA}}$ line. At the same time, the CPU reserves the bus for future communication with the 8259A. The 8086/8088 once again signals the bus controller on lines S0-S2, asking it to send a second interrupt acknowledge signal to the 8259A. Upon receipt of the second interrupt acknowledge signal, the 8259A puts onto the bus a byte whose value is the interrupt number associated with the specific interrupt line signaling—that is, 0xC for line IRQ4. (See Table 4-1.) The CPU reads the byte off of the bus and multiplies it times four to get the absolute address of the interrupt vector—that is, 0x30 for line IRQ4.

---

[1]See Application Note AP-59 in *iAPX 86,88 User's Manual* (Santa Clara, Calif.: Intel Corporation, 1981).

[2]The **if** flag is set with an **sti** instruction and cleared with a **cli** instruction by the software running on the 8086/8088.

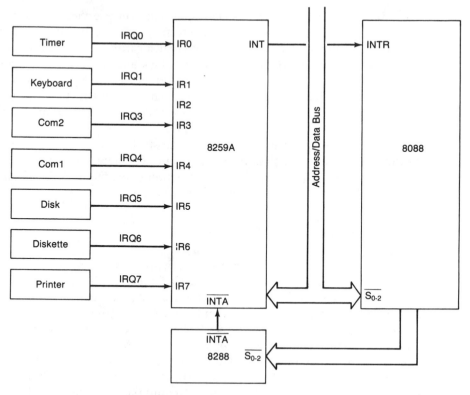

Figure 4-1 IBM PC Interrupt Hardware

TABLE 4-1 INTERRUPT LINE ASSIGNMENTS FOR THE PC

Line	Intr No (Hex)	Vector Address	Function
IRQ0	8	20-23	Timer Interrupt
IRQ1	9	24-27	Keyboard Interrupt
IRQ2	A	28-2B	Reserved
IRQ3	B	2C-2F	Asynch Com2 Interrupt
IRQ4	C	30-33	Asynch Com1 Interrupt
IRQ5	D	34-37	Disk Interrupt
IRQ6	E	38-3B	Diskette Interrupt
IRQ7	F	3C-3F	Printer Interrupt

The 8086/8088 saves the state of the machine. First, it pushes the **flags** register onto the stack. It then clears the interrupt enable flag (**if**) and the trap flag (**tf**), thus preventing intervening interrupts and traps. This will allow the interrupt service routine to run with interrupts disabled until it gets to a point in its execution where it can safely re-enable interrupts. For some interrupt service routines, interrupts are never re-enabled until the routine returns with the **iret** instruction, which will re-enable interrupts by reloading the **flags** register from the stack. Finally, the 8086/8088 pushes the **cs** and **ip** registers onto the stack and reloads them with the **cs** and **ip** values stored at the interrupt vector address—that is, the vector stored at absolute address 0x30 for line IRQ4. Thus, the next instruction executed will be the first instruction of the interrupt service routine. After the interrupt servicing is complete, the **iret** instruction at the end of the interrupt service routine reloads the original **ip**, **cs** and **flags** register from the stack, thus returning the machine to the state it was in at the time of the interrupt. The next instruction that the 8086/8088 will execute after the **iret** is the instruction immediately following the instruction it was executing when the interrupt occurred.

Internal Structure of the 8259A

Figure 4-2 is a diagram of the 8259A interrupt processor.[3] The status of the interrupt processor is kept in three registers: the IRR (Interrupt Request Register), the ISR (In-Service Register), and the IMR (Interrupt Mask Register). The IRR is used to keep track of which interrupt input lines are requesting service. A signal on line IRn causes bit n in the IRR to be set to 1. The ISR contains a record of interrupts that are currently being processed. Finally, the IMR contains a record of which interrupts are turned on (i.e., a 0 in the corresponding bit of the IMR) or off (i.e., a 1 in the corresponding bit). The priority resolver decides which lines requesting service will receive service. It takes into account the IMR and the relative priorities of other interrupts either requesting service or being serviced. The highest priority interrupt is chosen, the CPU is informed via the control logic section, and when an INTA is received, the corresponding bit is set in the ISR.

The read/write logic analyzes input to the 8259A recognizing various commands for initializing or changing the state of the processor. The cascade buffer/comparator is used when a number of 8259As are cascaded in order to allow more than eight interrupts. This is not germane to the PC, which has only one 8259A.

Features of the 8259A

Fully Nested Mode

By the nature of the device, the 8259A imposes a priority structure on the interrupts it is handling. That is, for any two interrupt requests that occur simultaneously, one will be given service over the other based on their respective priorities. This is the normal mode of operation, and it is called *fully nested mode*. Figure 4-3 is an example of 8259A behavior when it is operating in fully nested mode. The

[3]*iAPX 86, 88 User's Manual* (Santa Clara, Calif.: Copyright Intel Corporation, 1981), p. A-142.

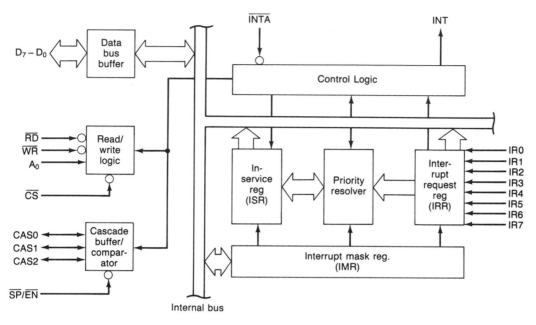

Figure 4-2 Structure of the 8259A

priorities go from the highest priority of 0 to the lowest of 7. This diagram assumes that all interrupts are turned on—that is, the IMR is all zeros. This diagram also assumes that interrupts are currently enabled in the CPU whenever we show an interrupt request event. In a real application, there would be short periods (during critical sections of interrupt service routine code or during the issuing of commands to the 8259A) when interrupts would be disabled. The dollar signs ($) show which interrupt levels can accept interrupts at each point in time based on the contents of the ISR. Time is assumed to be running down the diagram.

At first, all interrupt levels can accept interrupts because no bit is set in the ISR. The first interrupt occurs at level 5 and once it is acknowledged by the CPU, the corresponding bit in the ISR is set and the only interrupt levels that can honor interrupts are levels 4 through 0. In the second state, signals occur on input lines IR3, IR4, and IR7 simultaneously. The priority resolver eliminates IR7 because a higher priority interrupt (5) is already in service. It eliminates IR4 because IR3 is of higher priority. Thus, IR3 is the winner and that interrupt is issued to the CPU. In the following state, we can see that the interrupt was acknowledged by the CPU and bit 3 in the ISR was set. Thus, the service routine associated with interrupt 5 is suspended and the one associated with interrupt 3 gets control of the CPU. The next event is that the 8259A receives a non-specific EOI (End Of Interrupt). That is, it receives a signal that some interrupt service routine has completed its work, but the signal contains no information as to the interrupt with which it is associated (hence, the "nonspecific"). In fully nested mode, it is easy to deduce which interrupt has completed. It is the highest priority interrupt in service, so bit 3 in the ISR is

EVENT	Status Item	IS7	IS6	IS5	IS4	IS3	IS2	IS1	IS0
	ISR Status	0	0	0	0	0	0	0	0
	Priority	7	6	5	4	3	2	1	0
	Can Honor Ints	$	$	$	$	$	$	$	$
INTERRUPT REQUESTS				*					
	ISR Status	0	0	1	0	0	0	0	0
	Priority	7	6	5	4	3	2	1	0
	Can Honor Ints				$	$	$	$	$
INTERRUPT REQUESTS				*		*	*		
	ISR Status	0	0	1	0	1	0	0	0
	Priority	7	6	5	4	3	2	1	0
	Can Honor Ints						$	$	$
NON-SPECIFIC EOI									
	ISR Status	0	0	1	0	0	0	0	0
	Priority	7	6	5	4	3	2	1	0
	Can Honor Ints				$	$	$	$	$
INTERRUPT REQUESTS				*		*			
	ISR Status	0	0	1	1	0	0	0	0
	Priority	7	6	5	4	3	2	1	0
	Can Honor Ints					$	$	$	$

Figure 4-3 Fully Nested Mode Behavior

reset making every interrupt level below 5 once again eligible to receive interrupts. Since interrupt request 4 is still pending, it will be honored. Interrupt 7 loses again.

From this short example, the nature of fully nested mode should be clear. The interrupt levels have stack-like character with any higher priority interrupt level able to cause a lower priority interrupt in service to be suspended. As soon as the higher priority is complete, the lower priority level is allowed to resume if in service or fire if it has a request pending. Not all applications require this kind of fixed priority scheme, and as we shall see later, the 8259A is flexible enough to allow a number of different modes of operation. First, however, we need to understand more about the End Of Interrupt command to the 8259A.

End Of Interrupt Command

The End Of Interrupt (EOI) command is intended to inform the 8259A of the completion of an interrupt service routine so that the 8259A can update its internal data structures. The EOI command comes in three flavors: non-specific, specific, and automatic. Because the PC operates in fully nested mode, we will be using non-specific EOIs exclusively, but we will explain all three types for completeness.

The non-specific EOI is the simplest of the three types. It can be used whenever the 8259A can algorithmically determine which interrupt level has just completed service. Operating in fully nested mode makes interrupt level determination easy and is exactly the situation in which non-specific EOIs are useful. The rule is that non-specific EOIs may be used whenever the current interrupt being serviced is always the highest priority interrupt level. Therefore, do not use non-specific EOI if you use the set priority command or special mask mode.

A specific EOI command, as its name implies, includes a designation of the priority level being completed. This is required in those cases in which the priorities of the interrupt levels may have changed during the interrupt service routine processing.

The automatic EOI mode causes the automatic issuing of an EOI at the trailing edge of the last acknowledge pulse from the CPU. This simplifies the code of the interrupt service routine because it does not have to issue an EOI. Nevertheless, this is a risky way to operate and should be used only in those circumstances where the interrupt pulses occur at a predetermined rate rather than sporadically. Otherwise, an interrupt service routine on a given level can be interrupted by another interrupt at the same level, given interrupts remain enabled. This risks overrunning the stack.

Table 4-2 summarizes the various EOI modes and their characteristics.

TABLE 4-2   END OF INTERRUPT SUMMARY

EOI Type	Operation	When Used
Non-specific	Reset highest priority ISR bit.	Fully nested mode, typically.
Specific	Reset specified ISR bit.	With changing priorities.
Automatic	Reset ISR bit after associated interrupt acknowledged by CPU	Interrupts at predetermined rate, non-sporadic and with need to reduce code.

Priority Rotation

Not every application desires interrupts to be prioritized, or at least not statically prioritized. The 8259A allows the priorities to be varied in order to achieve differing effects. The priorities can be equalized so that over the long term each device gets an equal level of service. This is accomplished by "automatic rotation of priorities." The effect is equivalent to going to the end of the line after receiving service at a bank teller's window. Once serviced, you have to wait until others waiting for service get their turn before you get another opportunity for service. This avoids one customer monopolizing the teller. Similarly, automatic rotation of priorities causes a circular rotation of the priorities on receipt of each EOI, so that the interrupt level that just completed servicing (i.e., the one sending the EOI) now becomes the lowest priority interrupt. Over a period of time, each interrupt level spends roughly the same amount of time at each level, if all are firing at roughly the same rate.

There are two types of automatic rotation:

1. Rotate on non-specific EOI, and
2. Rotate in automatic EOI mode.

Rotate on non-specific EOI is accomplished by issuing a variation on the non-specific EOI. Rotate in automatic EOI mode is accomplished by the application service routine issuing commands that set and clear the mode. These commands will be described in detail later when we discuss the programming of the 8259A.

Figure 4-4 shows an example of rotate on non-specific EOI. In this example, interrupt levels 6 and 4 are in service. When the level 4 service routine completes, it issues a rotate on non-specific EOI command. This causes the ISR bit 4 to be reset and the priorities to be rotated such that interrupt level 4 becomes the lowest-level priority.

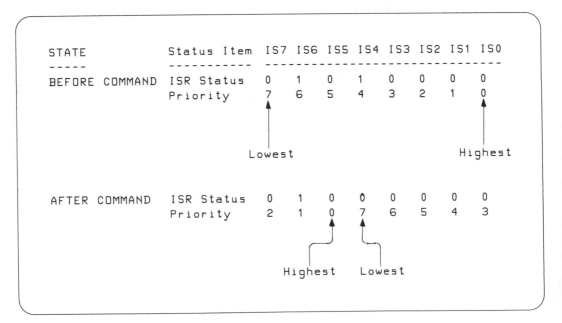

Figure 4-4 Rotate on Non-specific Command

If the using application requires some scheme other than equalization of the priorities, the 8259A allows two other commands that give greater control to the service routine. These are:

1. Rotate on specific EOI command
2. Set priority command

For the applications in this book, we will have no use for rotation of priorities. If the reader desires further details, he or she is referred to the *iAPX 86,88 User's Manual*.

Interrupt Masking

The 8259A provides a method for turning individual interrupts off and on—that is, setting and resetting bits in the IMR. The application program may read and write the IMR directly by reading and writing the PCs I/O port 0x21. This provides more selective control than that provided by the CPU instructions **cli** and **sti**, which turn all interrupts off and on, respectively.

The 8259A also provides a facility called "Special Mask Mode." When the command to enter Special Mask Mode is issued from an interrupt service routine, the in-service interrupt level is masked off and all interrupt levels, both lower and higher than the current level, are temporarily enabled. The current level is, of course, masked off. When this mode is reset, the operation reverts to its previous mode—for example, fully nested mode.

Interrupt Triggering

The 8259A provides two kinds of triggering on interrupt requests: level triggering and edge triggering. As the names suggest, each causes the recognition of an interrupt request by particular features of the electrical signals. The level-triggering mode will recognize an interrupt request whenever the level of the signal is high, whereas the edge-triggering mode will recognize an interrupt request only when the signal goes from low to high.

Level triggering is useful in only a few special cases such as when an interrupt service routine must be executed repeatedly until the signal disappears. Edge triggering is more common and well mannered. It is used in those cases where a single service computation satisfies the interrupt. The PC uses edge triggering.

Interrupt Status

The 8259A provides two mechanisms for interrogating its status.

1. Reading the interrupt registers ISR, IRR and IMR
2. Polling

The ISR and IRR registers are read by a two-step process. First, a read register command is issued to the 8259A and this command selects which register is to be read. Then, the next read command to the 8259A will return the value of the selected register. In contrast, reading the IMR is accomplished by a direct read to one of the 8259A communication ports (0x21). The details of how these registers can be read are given in the section on programming the 8259A.

Polling is an alternative to interrupts. Polling allows the CPU software to issue a poll command to the 8259A. If there are interrupt requests pending on the 8259A, the next read command from the CPU will cause the 8259A to put the interrupt number of the highest-level interrupt onto the data bus. The software running in the CPU must read this number and perform the transfer of control. The vectoring is not automatically done in hardware as it is for interrupts. The advantage of polling is that it allows more than 64 interrupt request lines, whereas the upper limit allowed under a hardware interrupt regimen is 64 lines.

Interrupt Cascading

Interrupt cascading is the name given to the use of multiple 8259As to increase the number of possible interrupts to more than eight. In cascade mode, there is one master 8259A and a number of slave 8259As reporting to the master. The output of each slave is connected to one of the inputs of the master 8259A. The inputs of the slaves are connected to the devices that can generate the interrupt signals.

The fully nested nature of the interrupt vectors that we saw with only one 8259A is not preserved in the cascade mode. Once one interrupt level is being serviced in a slave, all of the other levels in that slave are inhibited because of the behavior of the fully nested priority scheme within the master. That is, the master will not accept any more interrupts (higher priority or not) from that slave, because once the ISR bit for that level is set in the master, that master level is inhibited until the service routine is complete.

This is not the kind of behavior we want. We would like all of the interrupts to behave as if they were operating in fully nested mode on one gigantic interrupt processor. That is, we would like to have higher priority interrupts on a slave to be able to interrupt lower, in-service interrupts on the same slave. Special fully nested mode allows this kind of behavior.

Buffered mode is a feature that is required where the system data bus requires buffering. This is used in, but is not limited to, cascade mode. This feature allows the 8259A to properly control bus drivers that buffer data between the 8259A and the system bus. This feature is used in the PC because the PC has a multiplexed bus.

Reading and Writing Ports

In order to implement facilities described in the following sections, we will need to understand how the CPU communicates under software control with the various processor chips (e.g., the 8259A) within the PC. The 8259A can be programmed by the software running on the CPU. Similarly, other chips need to be enabled or disabled, sent parametric information, or have their status checked. In general, such CPU processor communication is establish through reading and writing pre-assigned I/O ports. The 8259A, for example, is assigned ports 0x20 and 0x21 on the PC for the purposes of communication with the software running on the CPU.

The C86 compiler provides four assembly language functions for reading and writing ports. These are:

```
unsigned char inportb(portno)
unsigned int portno;

unsigned int inportw(portno)
unsigned int portno;

unsigned char outportb(portno,value)
unsigned int portno;
char value;

unsigned int outportw(portno,value)
unsigned int portno;
unsigned int value;
```

inportb and **outportb**, respectively, read and write one byte from/to port **portno**. Analogously, **inportw** and **outportw**, respectively, read and write a word from/to port **portno**. We will use **inportb** and **outportb** in the extended examples developed in the following chapters.

Programming the 8259A

The programming of the 8259A is accomplished in two separate phases: initialization and operation. 8259A programming is accomplished by writing data to two I/O port addresses associated with the 8259A, ports 0x20 and 0x21.

The 8259A distinguishes between data bytes associated with initialization and operation by

1. The specific port address they are written to (the A0 bit of the address)

2. Bit patterns in the data bytes

3. What other data bytes preceded a given data byte

Initialization

The two classes of data bytes are called Initialization Command Words (ICWs) and Operational Command Words (OCWs). The specific command words are given names of the form ICW2, where the trailing integer generally indicates the byte's proper position in the programming sequence, although OCWs may be given in any order. Figure 4-5[4] provides a definition of the ICW formats that are germane to the IBM PC. ICW3 is not used on the PC.

The high order bit of the port address is considered a part of the command word in the sense that the 8259A uses this information to determine what specific command word a given data byte represents. Operationally, this translates into a specific sequence of writes to ports. For example, three command words written to ports 0x20, 0x21, and 0x21 will be interpreted as ICW1, ICW2, and ICW4 if bits D4, D1, and D0 are set in ICW1. Bit D4 set on a write to port 0x20 identifies the command as an ICW1. Bit D1 indicates that there is only one 8259A in the configuration and, therefore, there is no need for an ICW3 command word to indicate whether or not this 8259A has a slave 8259A attached to it. Finally, bit D0 indicates that an ICW4 will be sent.

Now, let's back up and go through each ICW and explain its fields and their effects, starting with ICW1. As we said, bit D0 indicates to the 8259A whether or not we intend to send an ICW4. In the case of the PC, since no ICW4 would cause an 80/85 mode of behavior, we must send the ICW4. Bit D1 tells the 8259A whether or not there are multiple interrupt processors cascaded to allow more than eight interrupts. The PC uses only eight, making this field 1. Bit D2 is used for 80/85 mode only and is ignored in 86/88 mode. Therefore, the PC uses zero for this field. Bit D3 indicates whether the interrupt processor is to trigger on signal edges or signal levels. The PC uses edge-triggered mode. Bit 4, along with bit A0 of the port address, identifies this command as an ICW1. Finally, bits D5-D7 are specific to 80/85 mode and are, consequently, zeroed for the PC.

ICW2 establishes the upper 5 bits of all interrupt types (i.e., numbers) associated with this 8259A. Consequently, this establishes exactly where in memory the interrupt vectors will reside. For the PC, ICW2 is 0x08—that is, the lowest interrupt number in the set of eight is interrupt 0x08. The 8259A ORs this number with the 3-bit integer type of the IRQ line pulsed and sends that quantity to the 8088. Clearly, this will produce exactly the sequence of interrupt types from 0x08 to 0x0F.

Notice that the only thing that identifies an ICW2 as such, other than the fact that it immediately follows an ICW1, is that it is sent to port 0x21 (i.e., A0 = 1).

---

[4]*iAPX 86, 88 User's Manual* (Santa Clara, Calif.: Copyright Intel Corporation, 1981), p. B-74.

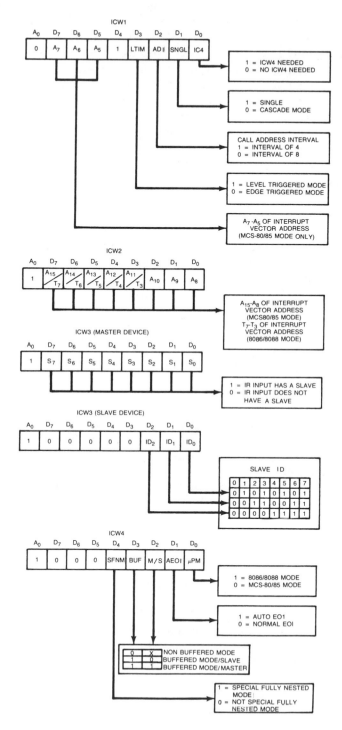

Figure 4-5 Initialization Command Words (ICWs)

81

Finally, ICW4 provides a number of critical items of information. Bit D0 designates whether the 8259A is being used in an 80/85 or an 86/88 environment. Bit D1 defines what kind of EOI regimen to expect. The PC uses normal EOI mode, meaning that the PC interrupt routines will send an EOI when they have completed their processing, rather than letting the 8259A generate one automatically. Bits D3 and D2 determine buffering mode and whether the 8259A is a slave or a master. For the PC, these select buffered and slave. The buffered designation indicates to the 8259A the role of one of its output signals (SP/EN). For buffered mode, this signal is used in gating data onto the system bus. Since there is only one 8259A on the PC, it is not a master. Bit D4 specifies the special fully nested mode, which is relevant only to cascaded configurations. Since the PC is not cascaded, this bit is zero.

Figure 4-6[5] is an excerpt from the IBM BIOS code, which initializes the 8259A during system startup. As a general rule, all interrupts should be disabled via a **cli** instruction whenever sending commands to the 8259A's ports. In fact, interrupts are disabled by the very first instruction in the BIOS startup code and are off when the code in Figure 4-6 is executed.

```
INTA00   EQU    20H        ;8259 PORT
INTA01   EQU    21H        ;8259 PORT
         .
         .
         .
         MOV    AL,13H     ;ICW1-EDGE, SNGL, ICW4
         OUT    INTA00,AL
         MOV    AL,8       ;SETUP ICW2-INT TYPE 8 (8-F)
         OUT    INTA01,AL
         MOV    AL,9       ;SETUP ICW4-BUFFRD, 8086 MODE
         .
         .
         .
```

Figure 4-6 BIOS Initialization of 8259A

The reader can verify that the Initialization commands sent (13H, 8, and 9) do indeed define the set of ICWs that we claimed were used to initialize the PC.

[5]*IBM Technical Reference Manual*, rev. ed. (April 1983), p. A-9.

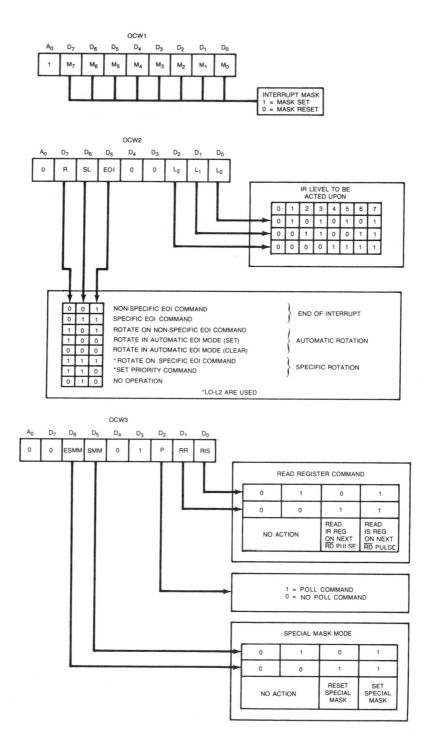

Figure 4-7 Operational Command Words (OCWs)

Operation

After the interrupt processor has been initialized, there are occasions when changes need to be made to its state. The most common such change is the masking on or off of specific interrupts. Such state changes are accomplished via OCWs, which may be sent in any order.

Figure 4-7[6] provides a definition of OCW formats for the 8259A interrupt processor. The most commonly used OCW is OCW1. It allows the executing program to turn individual interrupts off and on by changing the value of the IMR. All bits in OCW1 are data bits. None are used to identify the data byte as an OCW1 command. After the initialization sequence is complete, any data byte written to port 0x21 will be interpreted as an OCW1 and used to reset the IMR. The following example exhibits the use of an OCW1 command to mask interrupt IRQ4 on—that is, after execution of this code, interrupts on line IRQ4 will be issued on to the CPU by the 8259A.

```
disable_ints();
outportb(0x21,(inportb(0x21) & 0xef));
enable_ints();
```

Interrupts should be disabled whenever programming the 8259A. Therefore, the assembly language routines **disable_ints** and **enable_ints**, respectively, execute the 8086/8088 instructions **cli** and **sti**. The assembly language routines **inportb** and **outportb**, respectively, read a byte from and write a byte to the port number specified by their first argument. The correspondence of IRQ line numbers to bit positions is one for one—that is, bit 0 is the mask for IRQ0, and so on. Hence, the mask 0xef has a zero in bit position 4. A zero in the corresponding bit position turns the interrupt on and a one turns it off. It is common to use the phrases "masks on" and "masks off," respectively, to mean turn interrupts on and off.

OCW2 is distinguished by the fact that it is written to port 0x20 and by the bit pattern in bits D3-D4. A 00 pattern identifies an OCW2. OCW2 provides three classes of commands: end of interrupt signaling, automatic rotation commands, and specific rotation commands. The opcode for the command is specified by bits D5-D7 and the specific interrupt to be operated upon, if there is one, is specified by bits D0-D2. Figure 4-8 provides definitions of the various commands possible.

The bit patterns are determined by the roles of the individual bits. The EOI bit specifies that the command is some type of rotation. The SL bit specifies whether or not the interrupt level bits (L0-L2) are used. Finally, the R bit indicates whether or not the operation is some type of priority rotation. For our purposes, only the non-specific EOI command will be used.

[6]*iAPX 86, 88 User's Manual* (Santa Clara, Calif.: Copyright Intel Corporation, 1981), p. B-76.

```
Bits   Class                  Command
----   -----                  -------
001    End Of Interrupt       Non-specific EOI Command
011                           Specific EOI (Intrpt type required)
101    Automatic Rotation     Rotate on non-specific EOI
100                           Rotate in automatic EOI mode (set)
000                           Rotate in automatic EOI mode (clear)
111    Specific Rotation      Rotate on specific EOI (Intrpt type
                              required)
110                           Set priority (Intrpt type required)
010                           No operation
```

Figure 4-8 OCW2 Command Format

The following example is drawn from the end of an interrupt service routine that will be developed in a later chapter. It is typical of the use we will make of OCW2.

```
#define EOI     0x20       /*Non-specific EOI*/
             .
             .
             .
disable_ints();
outportb(0x20,EOI);        /*Signal completion of
                              interrupt processing*/
enable_ints();
```

OCW3 is distinguished by the fact that it is written to port 0x20 and the bit pattern in bits D3-D4. A 01 pattern identifies an OCW3. OCW3s are used to ascertain interrupt status and to alter interrupt masking.

The bits RR and RIS are used to select a read register operation, where RR enables the read and RIS identifies which register—RIS = 0 identifies IRR and RIS = 1 identifies ISR. After an OCW3 is issued, the next read to port 0x20 will return the value of the selected register. The safest way to use this facility is to turn off the interrupts while issuing the writes and reads to port 0x20. This assures that the selected register will not change between the first write and the second read. In certain situations, intervening interrupts can change the selection. In contrast to reading the status of the IRR and ISR registers, the status of the IMR register is directly accessible by a read to port 0x21. No setup operations are required.

The register status reading facility is most useful for interrupt service routines that need to know the status of other interrupts before taking some action. For example, a service routine may want to allow disk reads or writes to complete before moving data around in memory.

Another type of status checking is polling. The P bit of OCW3 indicates polling and, if specified, it will override register status reading. Polling allows an alternative to in-memory vector tables and allows the application program more of a role in dispatching control to the interrupt service routine.

The ESSM and SMM bits are used to set and clear the special mask mode. We will have no use for this facility.

In this section, we have emphasized those facilities that we will make use of in the succeeding chapters of the book and deemphasized the others. For the interested reader, the Application Note AP-59[7] provides extended detail on these facilities. It is recommended for the serious practitioner who intends to develop applications using the 8259A.

In the previous sections, we have focused exclusively on the generic interrupt services (i.e., the 8259A services) without providing much insight into the hardware that makes use of those services. In the next section, we will describe in detail one piece of application hardware, the Asynchronous Communications Element, which uses the interrupt services of the 8259A.

4.3 ASYNCHRONOUS COMMUNICATIONS

This section provides a detailed example of hardware, the Asynchronous Communications Element (ACE), that uses the interrupt services of the 8259A. The section also provides the background detail that will be required for the Interrupt Driven Terminal Emulator to be developed in the next chapter. In order to understand the ACE fully, we must present some background information on asynchronous serial communications. This will provide context for the discussion in the following sections and chapter.

Serial Asynchronous Communications

The ACE is designed to send and receive serial data and to do so asynchronously. Now, exactly what does that all mean? First, we will consider the notion of serial transmission vis à vis parallel transmission, and analyze the tradeoffs of these two alternatives.

Serial Communications

Consider two computers that need to send ASCII character data back and forth to each other. What are the options? Since digital data is sent in discrete chunks, we have two obvious options. We can let a chunk be a single character (parallel

---

[7]*iAPX 86, 88 User's Manual.*

transmission) or let a chunk be a single bit (serial transmission). If we send character chunks, we will have to have one data line per bit, or eight data lines for an extended ASCII character. Further, if we want to send both ways at the same time (i.e., full-duplex transmission), we will need sixteen lines, not to mention a few lines for control signals. This is technically feasible within a single physical installation and will allow much faster, and therefore much greater capacity transmission than with serial transmission schemes. However, stringing that much wire is an expensive proposition. Furthermore, without significant added cost, we have no switching capability. That is, we cannot easily switch the connections among various computers as our needs dictate.

An alternative that would simplify the wiring requirements would be to use the existing telephone network to transmit data from computer to computer. In contrast to custom wiring, wiring for ordinary telephones is available nearly everywhere, does not require much capital investment, and provides switching facilities that allow any phone line in the world to be connected to any other phone line in the world. Its drawbacks are that the transmission medium is largely analog, and the data transfer scheme is inherently serial. Serial transmission provides slower transmission—that is, lower data rates—than parallel transmission. Nevertheless, the positive aspects outweigh the negative aspects for many transmission systems except those with very high data traffic requirements. For microcomputers, the case is clear. We need an inexpensive but flexible system (i.e., one with switching capabilities), and we really do not need extremely high data rates. So we are led to serial transmission almost by default.

In order to transmit data over telephone lines, we have to transform the data in two ways:

1. It has to be transformed from internal, parallel format to a bit at a time serial format. This is the main job of the ACE.
2. It has to be put into analog format (i.e., tones) for transmission over voice lines. This is the job of the modem.

Of course, the inverse operations have to be accomplished at the receiving end. Figure 4-9 exhibits the structure required for communication of serial data over switched phone lines.

Asynchronous Communications

The distinction between synchronous and asynchronous transmission systems is the existence or nonexistence of a clocking control signal to synchronize the transmission of data. In synchronous transmission systems, there is a separate control wire for synchronizing the transmitter and receiver. When a signal appears on this control wire, the receiver reads the data off the data wire (or wires). There is no such synchronizing mechanism in asynchronous transmission systems so that synchronization must be achieved by different means. For the serial asynchronous trans-

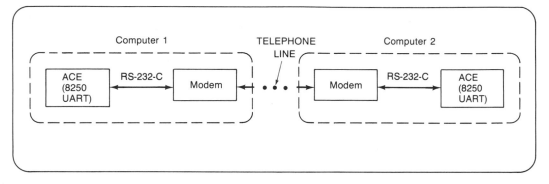

Figure 4-9 Serial Data Transmission over Telephone Lines

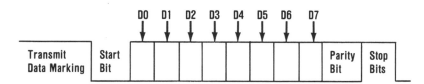

Figure 4-10 Serial Data Format

mission system provided by the ACE, the synchronizing mechanism is the start bit that precedes each stream of data bits (see Figure 4-10[8]).

The start bit allows the receiving ACE to synchronize its internal clock to the incoming character. Thereafter, it will use its internal clock to sample the incoming signal at approximately the middle of each incoming bit and shift the sampled value (one or zero) into the end of a shift register. When the stop bit arrives, signaling the end of the character, the ACE moves the assembled character into a holding buffer and signals the CPU that a character has been received. The ACE is designed to stay in step with the transmitter only through the end of a single character, so it must resynchronize for every character it receives.

The hallmark of asynchronous transmission is the fact that characters can arrive at any time. Between characters, the line is held at high (1) by convention. This is called the "marking condition," or just simply "marking." The "space" condition (or "spacing") is the term applied when the line goes low (0). A start bit is defined as the line held at 0 (spacing) for 1-bit time. Any shorter time will be interpreted as line noise. The stop bit is defined to be the line held at 1 (marking) for 1-, 1½-, or 2- bit times, depending on how the ACE is initialized. Both the

[8]*IBM Technical Reference Manual*, rev. ed. (April 1983), p. 1–226.

sender and receiver must be initialized to the same size stop bits. In general, proper communication between the transmitter and receiver requires that both are initialized to handle the same number of data bits (5, 6, 7, or 8), the same parity convention (odd, even, or none), and the same stop bit length. If one is initialized differently from the other one, transmission errors will result.

The foregoing discussion provides sufficient context for the forthcoming discussion of the ACE. The interested reader can find further detail in McNamara[9] or Jordan et al.[10]

RS-232-C Interface Standard

Figure 4-9 defines the interface between the ACE and the modem as an RS-232-C interface. Since the ACE interacts with this interface, we will require some knowledge of its structure and behavior in order to fully understand the ACE. To that end, this section will provide a short introduction to RS-232-C interfaces.

RS-232-C is a standard[11] for connecting *Data Terminal Equipment* (DTE) and *Data Communication Equipment* (DCE) for serial communications. For the application we are discussing, the PC is the DTE and the modem is the DCE. Since the standard uses the terms DTE and DCE, we will use them when describing the standard.

If the modem is external to the computer, the RS-232-C interface manifests itself as a multiwire cable between the computer and the modem with a 25-pin D-shell connector on either end. Figure 4-11[12] shows a "D" shell connector with the pins labeled with the RS-232-C signal names, and how these signals relate to the DTE and DCE. Internal modems have become popular lately and are often on the same board as the ACE, in which case the user sees only the modem input/output connector, a modular telephone jack. In this case, the data format shown in Figure 4-10 is transmitted on the ACE/modem board. Nevertheless, the signals we shall be discussing are still the same RS-232-C signals and behave the same way.

Only ten or less of these signals are required for most communications software operating on the PC. Table 4-3 describes these signals, the connector pins that they are associated with, their class, and their direction. For a more complete list and description of the signals, see the EIA standard.

---

[9]John E. McNamara, *Technical Aspects of Data Communication*, 2d ed., (Digital Press, 1982).

[10]Larry E. Jordan and Bruce Churchill, *Communications and Networking for the IBM PC*, (Bowie, Md.: Robert J. Brady Co., 1983).

[11]Electronic Industries Association, EIA Standard RS-232-C, "Interface Between Data Terminal Equipment and Data Communication Equipment Employing Serial Binary Data Interchange," (August 1969).

[12]*IBM Technical Reference Manual*, rev. ed. (April 1983), p. F-2.

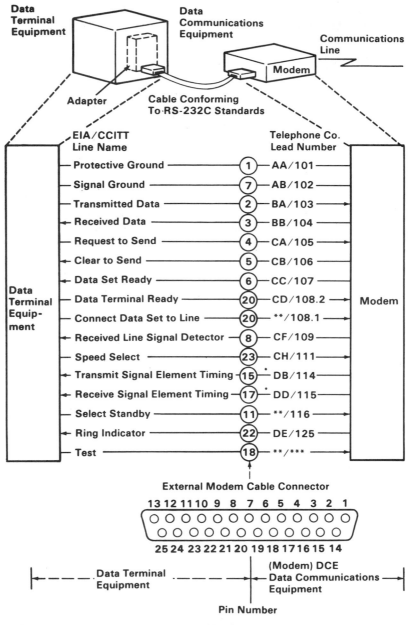

Figure 4-11 RS-232-C Connector and Signals

TABLE 4-3 RS-232-C SIGNALS RELEVANT TO PC

Signal	Pin	Gnd	Class Cntrl	Data	Direction From	To
Protective Ground	1	X				
Signal Ground/Common Return	7	X				
Transmitted Data	2			X	DTE	DCE
Received Data	3			X	DCE	DTE
Request To Send (RTS)	4		X		DTE	DCE
Clear To Send (CTS)	5		X		DCE	DTE
Data Set Ready (DSR)	6		X		DCE	DTE
Data Terminal Ready (DTR)	20		X		DTE	DCE
Ring Indicator (RI)	22		X		DCE	DTE
Received Line Signal Detector or Carrier Detect (RLSD or CD)	8		X		DCE	DTE

We will discuss the function of each signal in the context of its application for connecting the PC (through the ACE) to the modem.

1. *Protective Ground*: An optional circuit usually grounded to the equipment frame. It plays no part in the signaling system.

2. *Signal Ground*: This is a zero volt reference signal. All other signals are positive or negative with respect to this signal.

3. *Transmitted Data*: This is the wire on which the DTE (PC) passes characters to the DCE (modem) in the format given in Figure 4-10. According to the standard, data may not be passed on this circuit unless the following four signals are all ON: RTS, CTS, DSR, and DTR. When data is not being passed, this circuit is held in marking condition (high).

4. *Received Data*: This is the wire on which the DCE (modem) passes characters to the DTE (PC). This circuit is held in marking condition (high) when no data is being passed.

5. *Request To Send (RTS)*: The DTE (PC) is asking the DCE (modem) for permission to send data. The DCE (modem) will respond with a Clear To Send (CTS) if it is OK.

6. *Clear To Send (CTS)*: The DCE responds to an RTS telling the DTE (PC) that it is OK to send data over the data line.

7. *Data Set Ready (DSR)*: DSR ON signals the DTE (PC) that the DCE (modem) is connected to the communications channel and ready to transmit. For autodialing systems, it means that dialing is complete and a connection has been established. In essence, this is signaling that the DCE equipment is ready for communications.

8. *Data Terminal Ready (DTR)*: This signal is from the DTE (PC) telling the DCE (modem) that the DTE equipment is ready for communications.

9. *Ring Indicator (RI)*: This signal is used in auto-answer modems. It is a signal from the DCE (modem) to the DTE (PC), indicating that the modem is receiving ringing tone. That is, someone is calling the modem. We will not use this signal in the projects of this book.

10. *Received Line Signal Detector (RLSD)*: This signal is also sometimes called carrier detect. This is a signal from the DCE (modem) to the DTE (PC) telling the PC that it has received a suitable data carrier signal. When such a carrier signal is detected by the modem, it often lights an LED on the modem to tell the user the status. This signal is produced by the remote transmitter for the purpose of "carrying" the transmitted data from the remote modem to the receiving modem. When this signal is off, that is, the receiving modem is not detecting carrier, the Received Data circuit is held in the marking condition (i.e., 1). That is to say, no data can be received, which makes sense since there is no carrier signal to carry that data.

In the context of the PC communicating with the modem, how do these signals behave with respect to one another? That is, what does the PC have to do to transmit and receive data over a communications line? For the purposes of this book, we are interested only in the protocol for one case, full-duplex[13] communication between the ACE and a modem. In the larger context, the ACE/modem combination links the PC to a distant host computer in full-duplex mode over telephone lines. For the reader who is interested in variations such as half-duplex communication, he or she should read McNamara[14] or Nichols et al.[15]

The RS-232-C protocol is a transmission-oriented protocol. That is, transmission requires that the PC step through a multistep signaling protocol before it can actually transmit data. Receiving data, on the other hand, is quite simple, requiring little or no handshaking. Let's look at transmitting and receiving protocols.

In order to transmit data, the PC must go through the protocol summarized in Figure 4-12, where time is running from the top of the diagram down. First, the PC turns on DTR assuring the modem of equipment readiness on the part of the PC. Second, the modem signals back that it also is ready via a DSR signal. Therefore, connection to the remote computer has been established and the equipment is ready. This is a static situation that should not change once it is established. In fact, when the DTR signal is turned off or interrupted, the modem will turn the

---

[13]Full-duplex communications means that signals are traveling in both directions simultaneously. The modem accomplishes this magic by the convention that the transmission and reception occur in two distinct voice frequency ranges on the telephone lines. Therefore, the two signals do not interfere with each other.

[14]McNamara, *Technical Aspects of Data Communication*.

[15]Elizabeth A. Nichols, Joseph C. Nichols, and Keith R. Musson, *Data Communications for Microcomputers*, (New York: McGraw-Hill Inc., 1982).

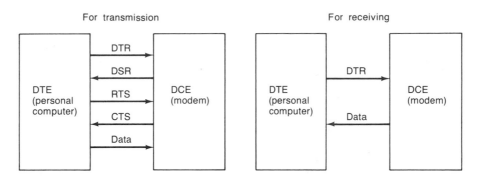

Figure 4-12 RS-232-C Full-Duplex Handshaking

DSR signal off and drop the line to the remote computer. Turning off the DTR signal is the convention for termination of a session.

After the PC has received a DSR signal from the modem, it asks for permission to send a character by sending an an RTS signal to the modem. When the modem responds with a CTS signal, the PC will send the character. The RTS and CTS signals, taken together, indicate readiness of the communication channel for transmission. These signals are more volatile than the DTR/DSR pair, which only establish equipment-readiness status. By the RS-232-C standard, when the RTS signal goes off, the modem will turn off the CTS signal shortly thereafter.

Strictly speaking, the RSLD signal is not required by the RS-232-C standard for transmission. However, from a practical standpoint, it really is required by some modems because of their design. Some modems will drop the communications line if they are not getting a carrier from the remote modem. The assumption is that if the remote modem is not sending a carrier signal, the connection must be broken, so the line is dropped. In any case, when carrier is lost, the CTS signal goes off. So at the very best (i.e., if the line is not dropped), a temporary loss of carrier from the remote modem implies another cycle of RTS/CTS handshaking. At worst, a loss of carrier means that the connection to the remote computer must be reestablished.

The conditions for receiving data are far less stringent than those for transmission. Basically, the DCE will send data to the PC any time it is receiving DTR, regardless of any other signals. That is, there is no RTS/CTS handshaking for sending data from the modem to the PC. The modem just passes through the data it receives as long as the PC is expressing equipment readiness (DTR). This is why we call RS-232-C a transmission-oriented protocol.

The ACE Hardware

The main role of the ACE is to serialize and deserialize data. That is, it accepts characters to be transmitted to the remote computer and shifts them out to the modem one bit at a time. Similarly, it accumulates a stream of incoming bits in a register until a complete character has been accumulated and then notifies the CPU that a character is available. All of this is accomplished under the direct control of the CPU. The CPU must interact with the ACE to effect the proper communication with the modem. For example, the CPU must cause the ACE to initialize its internal clock to operate at the desired baud rate; it must assure that the ACE follows the proper RS-232-C signaling conventions; it must feed characters to the ACE for transmission and fetch characters received by the ACE; and it must set up the ACE's interrupt generation system if it wants the ACE to signal it via interrupts.

Most of the ACE functionality is contained in a single chip, the INS8250 Universal Asynchronous Receiver Transmitter, or UART for short. This chip accomplishes a great deal. It serializes character data for transmission, and in the course of that serialization it adds start bits, stop bits, and parity bits. The parameters of this serialization process are under the control of the application program running in the CPU. For example, by programming the INS8250, the application program can affect serialization as well as deserialization. It can vary the number of data bits allowing 5, 6, 7, or 8; it can define the stop bit length to be 1, $1\frac{1}{2}$, or 2 bits long; and it can vary the baud rate from 50 to 9,600 baud.

The application can program the 8250 in other ways as well. It can choose to be notified of important events within the 8250 via interrupts or it can choose to poll the 8250 for status information. The BIOS system provides several software interrupts for the purpose of polling the 8250. The application program can issue and check the status of the modem control functions, and even perform hardware assisted diagnosis of the 8250's operation.

Communicating with the 8250

How does the CPU communicate with the 8250 for the purposes of programming the chip, fetching incoming data, or storing outgoing data? All CPU/8250 communications is accomplished through a set of I/O ports reserved for that purpose. These I/O ports are tied to specific 8250 registers and signals. The I/O ports for the primary 8250 ACE are at addresses 0x3f8 through 0x3fe, and the I/O ports for the secondary 8250 ACE are at 0x2f8 through 0x2fe. There is one wrinkle in this scheme. Bit 7 in the Line-Control Register (LCR) allows several of these port addresses to serve double duty. Bit 7 is called the Divisor Latch Bit (DLAB), and its value affects which registers are accessed for I/O addresses 0x3f8 and 0x3f9 (as well as I/O addresses 0x2f8 and 0x2f9). Table 4-4[16] defines the association between I/O port address and 8250 registers.

The role of each of these registers is suggested by the logical data flow diagram of Figure 4-13. This diagram shows the data flow relationships between the application program (on the left), the 8250 registers, and the modem (on the right).

---

[16]*IBM Technical Reference Manual*, rev. ed. (April 1983), p. 1–225.

TABLE 4-4   I/O PORT ADDRESSES OF 8250 ACE REGISTERS

I/O Decode (in Hex)		Register Selected	DLAB State
Primary Adapter	Alternate Adapter		
3F8	2F8	TX Buffer	DLAB=0 (Write)
3F8	2F8	RX Buffer	DLAB=0 (Read)
3F8	2F8	Divisor Latch LSB	DLAB=1
3F9	2F9	Divisor Latch MSB	DLAB=1
3F9	2F9	Interrupt Enable Register	
3FA	2FA	Interrupt Identification Registers	
3FB	2FB	Line Control Register	
3FC	2FC	Modem Control Register	
3FD	2FD	Line Status Register	
3FE	2FE	Modem Status Register	

The data flows between the application program and the 8250 can be organized into two classes:

1. Initialization of the ACE
2. Operation of the ACE

During initialization of the ACE, the application program deals with three or four registers, depending on whether or not the interrupt generation capability of the 8250 is to be used. The application program will set the baud rate by writing the Divisor Latch Registers. It will set the data character length, the number of stop bits, and parity information by writing the Line-Control Register (LCR). As an alternative to writing these registers directly, the application program may use BIOS interrupt 0x14 with a function number of 0 (i.e., **ah** = 0). It is a convenient way to initialize the baud rate, character length, number of stop bits, and parity information all in one step.

Additional initialization steps require the application program to write the Modem Control Register (MCR) in order to enable or disable the 8250's interrupt generation system. If interrupt generation is enabled, the application program must also initialize the Interrupt Enable Register (IER) in order to define exactly what types of interrupts it wants to see. The IER allows the separate enabling or disabling of four different interrupt causes:

1. Transmission errors
2. The arrival of data in the Receiver Buffer Register (RBR)
3. The Transmitter Holding Register (THR) becoming empty
4. Any change in the modem status (e.g., a change in the CTS Signal)

During regular operation, the application program reads and writes the remaining registers. Consider the process of transmitting a character to the modem. Before transmission of a character, the application program will write the MCR register to assert RTS and DTR signals. In addition, it will read the Modem Status

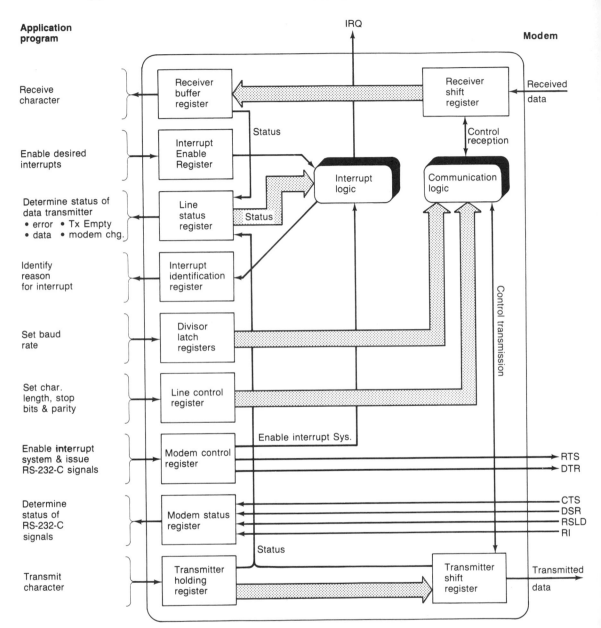

Figure 4-13 Logical Data Flow for the ACE

Register (MSR) to assure that the 8250 is receiving CTS and DSR signals from the modem. It will also read the Line Status Register (LSR) to assure that the THR is empty, and at some point in the processing it will examine other bits in the LSR to check for errors. Finally, it will write the THR with a data character to be sent.

TABLE 4-5 LINE-CONTROL REGISTER DEFINITION

Line-Control Register	Bit(s)	Name	Value	Specification Meaning
``\n 7	6	5	4	3	2	1	0 \n```				
	0-1	Word Length	00	Data character length is 5 bits.
			01	Data character length is 6 bits.
			10	Data character length is 7 bits.
			11	Data character length is 8 bits.
	2	Stop Bit Length	0	Stop bit length is 1 bit time.
			1	If word length is 5 bits, then stop bit length is 1 1/2 bit times. If word length is 6, 7 or 8, then stop bit length is 2 bit times.
	3	Parity Enable	0	Parity generation (transmission) and checking (receiving) are disabled.
			1	Parity bit is generated and checked for.
	4	Even Parity	0	If parity is enabled (i.e., bit 3 = 1), a parity bit is generated (or checked) to make the number of 1's in data + parity odd.
			1	If parity is enabled, a parity bit is generated (or checked) to make the number of 1's in data + parity even.
	5	Stick Parity	0	Stick parity is disabled.
			1	If parity is enabled (i.e., bit 3 = 1) and even parity specified (i.e., bit 4 = 1), then parity bit has a constant value of 0. If parity is enabled (i.e., bit 3 = 1) and odd parity specified (i.e., bit 4 = 0), then parity bit has a constant value of 1.
	6	Set Break	0	Set break is disabled.
			1	The Transmitted Data line is forced to spacing condition (logical 0) and remains there as long as this bit is 1, regardless of the contents of any other registers. This is an alerting signal to the remote CPU.
	7	Divisor Access Latch bit	0	Allows access to THR, RBR and IER registers.
			1	Allows access to DLLSB and DLMSB registers.

Receipt of a character requires the use of other registers. If the application program is using polling to manage incoming data, it will read the LSR to determine whether or not an unread character is waiting in the RBR. It probably will check the error bits in the LSR at the same time. It will read the RBR whenever data is available.

If the application program is using interrupts to manage incoming data and possibly to monitor the THR, the error bits, and changes in status of modem signals, it will read the Interrupt Identification Register (IIR) to determine what caused each interrupt. Once the source of the interrupt is determined, the application program will read one of several different registers to reset the specific interrupt on the 8250 chip.

1. Reading the LSR resets error or break interrupts
2. Reading the RBR resets the data available interrupt
3. Reading the IIR or writing the THR resets the THR empty interrupt
4. Reading the MSR resets the modem status change interrupt

Be aware that these actions only reset the interrupt types on the 8250 chip. The 8259A mask register may also have to be reset, and the CPU interrupt flag will have to be re-enabled before the application program can receive another interrupt.

The following sections provide specifications of the detail contents of each of the 8250 registers.

The Line-Control Register (LCR)

The Line-Control Register is at port address 0x3fb. This 8-bit register contains information that establishes the format of the data characters to be transmitted and received. The LCR is defined in Table 4-5.

The Divisor Latch Registers (DLLSB and DLMSB)

The Divisor Latch Registers, Least Significant Bit and Most Significant Bit, are at 0x3f8 and 0x3f9, respectively, for DLAB = 1. These two 8-bit registers, taken together, contain the divisor used by the baud rate generator. The baud rates generated for various values of this 16-bit baud rate divisor are defined in Table 4-6.

TABLE 4-6 BAUD RATE GENERATOR DIVISORS

Generated Baud Rate	Divisor Value (Hex)	Generated Baud Rate	Divisor Value (Hex)	Generated Baud Rate	Divisor Value (Hex)
50	0x0900	300	0x0180	2400	0x0030
75	0x0600	600	0x00c0	3600	0x0020
110	0x0417	1200	0x0060	4800	0x0018
134.5	0x0359	1800	0x0040	7200	0x0010
150	0x0300	2000	0x003a	9600	0x000c

Line Status Register (LSR)

This register is at port address 0x3fd and it contains communications status information. The LSR is defined in Table 4-7.

TABLE 4-7 LINE STATUS REGISTER DEFINITION

Line-Status Register	Bit(s)	Name	Value	Specification Meaning
7 6 5 4 3 2 1 0	0	Data Ready	0	No complete character in RBR.
			1	Complete character in RBR. (Reset by reading RBR or by rewriting LSR.)
	1	Overrun Error	0	No overrun error.
			1	New character moved into RBR before previous character read from RBR. (Reset by reading LSR.)
	2	Parity Error	0	No parity error.
			1	Inappropriate parity in character received. (Reset by reading LSR.)
	3	Framing Error	0	No framing error.
			1	Invalid stop bit in character received. (Reset by reading LSR.)
	4	Break Interrupt	0	No break interrupt.
			1	Received data line held in spacing condition for more than one full word transmission time (i.e., more time than required to transmit start bit, data bits, parity bit and stop bits). (Reset by reading LSR.)
	5	THR Empty	0	Transmitter holding register contains data.
			1	Transmitter holding register is empty and can accept a character for transmission. (Reset when a character is loaded in the THR.)
	6	TSR Empty	0	Transmitter shift register contains data.
			1	Transmitter shift register is empty. (Reset when a character is moved from THR to TSR.)
	7		0	This bit is permanently zero.

Interrupt Identification Register (IIR)

This register, at port address 0x3fa, is used when the interrupt generation capability of the 8250 is being used. It indicates whether or not an 8250-generated interrupt is pending; if one or more is pending, it identifies the one with the highest priority. The IIR is defined in Table 4-8.

TABLE 4-8   INTERRUPT IDENTIFICATION REGISTER DEFINITION

Interrupt Identification Register	Bit(s)	Name	Value	Meaning
7 6 5 4 3 2 1 0	0	Interrupt Pending	0	An 8250 generated interrupt is pending.
			1	No interrupt is pending.
	1-2	Interrupt ID	11	Receiver line status interrupt (error or break).
			10	Receiver data available.
			01	Transmitter holding register (THR) empty.
			00	Modem status change ($\overline{CTS}$, $\overline{DSR}$, $\overline{RI}$ or $\overline{RLSD}$).
	3-7		00000	These bits are always zero.

Interrupt Enable Register (IER)

The Interrupt Enable Register, at port address 0x3f9 when DLAB = 0, allows the application program to selectively enable or disable each of the four types of interrupts that the 8250 can generate. This register must be set when the application program is expecting interrupts to be generated by the 8250. The IER is defined in Table 4-9.

TABLE 4-9   INTERRUPT ENABLE REGISTER DEFINITION

Interrupt Enable Register	Bit(s)	Name	Specification Value	Meaning
7 6 5 4 3 2 1 0	0	Enable Data Available	0	No interrupt generated when data is received.
			1	An interrupt generated when data is moved into the RBR register.
	1	Enable THR Empty	0	No interrupt generated when the THR goes empty.
			1	An interrupt generated when the THR goes empty.
	2	Enable Receive Line Status	0	No interrupt generated on line status change.
			1	An interrupt generated on line status change.
	3	Enable Modem Status	0	No interrupt generated on modem status change.
			1	An interrupt generated on modem status change.
	4-7		0000	These bits are always zero.

Modem Control Register (MCR)

This register, at port address 0x3fc, controls the signaling to the modem and the interrupt signaling to the 8259A interrupt processor. It also provides a facility to test the functioning of the 8250. The MCR is defined in Table 4-10.

TABLE 4-10   MODEM CONTROL REGISTER DEFINITION

Modem Control Register	Bit(s)	Name	Specification Value	Meaning
7 6 5 4 3 2 1 0	0	DTR	0	The $\overline{\text{DTR}}$ line is forced to 1, signaling the modem that the data terminal is not ready.
			1	The $\overline{\text{DTR}}$ line is forced to 0, signaling the modem that the data terminal is ready.
	1	RTS	0	The $\overline{\text{RTS}}$ line is forced to 1, which tells the modem that the PC is not requesting to send a character.
			1	The $\overline{\text{RTS}}$ line is forced to 0, asking the modem if it is clear to send a character.
	2	OUT1		Unused.
	3	OUT2	0	The interrupt signal line from the 8250 to the 8259A is disabled.
			1	The interrupt signal line from the 8250 to the 8259A is enabled. Required if interrupts are to be used.
	4	LOOP	0	No self test of 8250.
			1	Self test of 8250 with 8250 outputs tied to 8250 inputs. Sent data immediately received.
	5-7		000	These bits are always zero.

Modem Status Register (MSR)

This register, at port address 0x3fe, contains information about the state of the RS-232-C signals. The MSR is defined in Table 4-11.

TABLE 4-11   MODEM STATUS REGISTER DEFINITION

Modem Status Register	Bit(s)	Name	Value	Specification Meaning
7 6 5 4 3 2 1 0	0	DCTS	0	No change of $\overline{CTS}$.
			1	CTS has changed since last time MSR was read.
	1	DDSR	0	No change of $\overline{DSR}$.
			1	DSR has changed since last time MSR was read.
	2	TERI	0	No change of $\overline{RI}$.
			1	RI has changed from on to off since last time MSR was read. Trailing edge of $\overline{RI}$ detected.
	3	DRLSD	0	No change of $\overline{RLSD}$.
			1	RLSD has changed since last time MSR was read.
	4	CTS	0	Not clear to send a character to the modem.
			1	A character may be sent to the modem.
	5	DSR	0	The modem is not in the ready state.
			1	The modem is ready.
	6	RI	0	No ringing signal has been detected.
			1	Ringing signal has been detected.
	7	RLSD	0	Not receiving line signal from modem.
			1	Line signal detect is being received from modem.

Receiver Buffer Register (RBR)

This register is at port address 0x3f8 when DLAB = 0, given that the CPU is reading the port. The address references a different port if written by the CPU. This register contains a character that has been received from the modem on the Received Data line. The data character bit numbers of the received character correspond one for one with the bit numbers of the RBR register. That is, the least significant bit of the character is stored in RBR bit 0.

Transmitter Holding Register (THR)

This register is at port address 0x3f8 when DLAB = 0, given that the CPU is writing the port. This address references the RBR on a read. This register contains a character that is to be transmitted to the modem on the Transmitted Data line. The data character bit numbers of the character to be transmitted correspond one for one with the bit numbers of the THR register—that is, the least significant bit of the character is stored in THR bit 0.

EXERCISES

4.1. BIOS provides a facility for reading the asychronous communications gear. Thus, a program could poll the asynchronous communications element for incoming characters. Why might this strategy fail? How might it fail—that is, what would be the symptoms?

4.2. Explain why the keyboard needs interrupt support.

4.3. Suppose you are designing a smart microwave oven with a time-of-day clock, a keypad for data input and a programmable cook control feature—that is, each minute is divided into two cycles, an "on" cycle and an "off" cycle. Various keys and keypad sequences are used to set the time of day, the number of minutes and seconds for the oven to cook, and the cook control level. What hardware would need interrupt support? What hardware could be polled? Justify your claims. Design software architecture for such an oven.

Chapter 5

A Terminal Emulator

5.1 INTRODUCTION

The objective of this chapter is to build a program that makes the PC emulate a terminal and thereby allow the user to communicate with mainframe computers over telephone lines. Of course, if that were all that we were to do, we would not have accomplished very much except make an expensive, powerful piece of hardware behave like a less expensive, less powerful piece of hardware. The real advantage is gained by appropriately mixing the power of the personal computer with the power of the mainframe computer. For example, one thing that we would like to do is to transfer files from one to the other. It is much cheaper to dial up the mainframe computer, move a file from it to the personal computer, drop the connection with the mainframe computer, and edit the file on the personal computer. Once we are satisfied with the file, perhaps after hours of editing, we can reverse the procedure and move the file back to the mainframe. The total telephone bill will cover only that time necessary to transmit the file in either direction.

What makes a terminal emulator an interesting problem, and one whose solution structures are widely applicable, is the fact that it is a real-time program. That is, it is a program that must service two pieces of gear, the keyboard and the communications gear, both of which are operating in real-time and neither of which is synchronized to the program running on the personal computer. When a character arrives at the communications gear, the terminal emulator must be ready to store that character away for future processing. Similarly, the program must always be ready to accept characters from the keyboard. In its spare time, the program must process those stored characters and manage the screen.

There are two basic architectures for such a program: polled and interrupt driven. We will compare and contrast these two approaches in order to choose one for implementation.

An emulator with a polling architecture services each separate task in order. The emulator's main loop consists of a series of repetitive tasks:

1. Service the communications gear, handling incoming characters
2. Service the keyboard, handling recently typed characters
3. Finally, write data characters to the screen, or modify the screen appropriately when terminal control sequences are received

This series of instructions is repeated until the program exits. Figure 5-1 graphically illustrates the structure of a terminal emulator that uses polling as the method of operation.

In a polled design, one has to take care that the main loop is fast enough to catch all incoming characters, so that characters do not overrun the communications gear. That is, the operational timing of a design based on polling is highly sensitive to the organization of the code. In contrast, an interrupt driven emulator performs real-time tasks on a demand basis. When a character arrives at the communications gear, the main program is interrupted, its state saved, and control transfers to a special routine called an interrupt service routine. This routine processes the interrupt (e.g., saves the character in a buffer) and then returns control to the place where the main program left off.

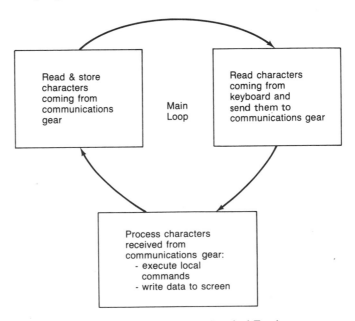

Figure 5-1 Polled Design for a Terminal Emulator

A polling based terminal emulator design for the IBM PC has a fatal flaw. The programmer cannot unconditionally control the length of time it takes to traverse the polling loop because of the possibility of BIOS or DOS interrupts issued from the C run-time routines. Suppose, for example, that we added a file transfer capability to the terminal emulator. That would require writing information to the disk. Disk writes are handled by interrupts, so that while the disk write is progressing, incoming characters from the communications gear are likely to be missed. Of course, the problem is not limited to interrupts for disk reads and writes. All interrupts (e.g., keyboard, display, timer, print spooler, etc.) provide some opportunity for slowing the polling just enough to miss one or more incoming characters. Therefore, a polling architecture is inadequate for a general-purpose terminal emulator on the IBM PC.

By contrast, an interrupt-based design is far less likely to miss incoming characters because of the demand basis of servicing interrupts. When an event occurs that needs servicing, the hardware gives immediate control to the service routine, as long as no other higher priority interrupts are active. The only way data can be lost is if the machine becomes computationally saturated, either because we are asking the machine to do more processing than it was designed for or because the interrupt service routines are too long. Therefore, care will be taken to keep interrupt service routines short and perform as much of the interrupt processing as possible outside of the interrupt service routine.

The next section will apply these general ideas by developing an interrupt based terminal emulator for the PC. Later sections will provide more of the the technical details so that the interested programmer can use and modify these programs to suit his or her own needs.

The last section of the chapter will develop the notions of special terminal control sequences. A control sequence is a special series of characters (sometimes called an "escape sequence") that the mainframe sends to the terminal in order to clear the screen, move the cursor about, scroll windows, and so forth. If the user wants to use a full-screen editor such as the UNIX editor VI[1] with the terminal emulator, he or she needs to be able to define such control sequences for the mainframe computer and to enhance the terminal emulator to respond to them appropriately.

5.2 ANATOMY OF A TERMINAL EMULATOR

Figure 5-2 graphically illustrates the data flow architecture of an interrupt-driven terminal emulator. The key data structures are two circular buffers, one named **o**, which stores characters arriving from the keyboard, and one named **a**, which stores

---

[1]William Joy and Mark Horton, "An Introduction to Display Editing with VI," *UNIX Programmer's Manual,* 7th ed., Vol. 2c, (Berkeley Calif.: University of California, November 1980).

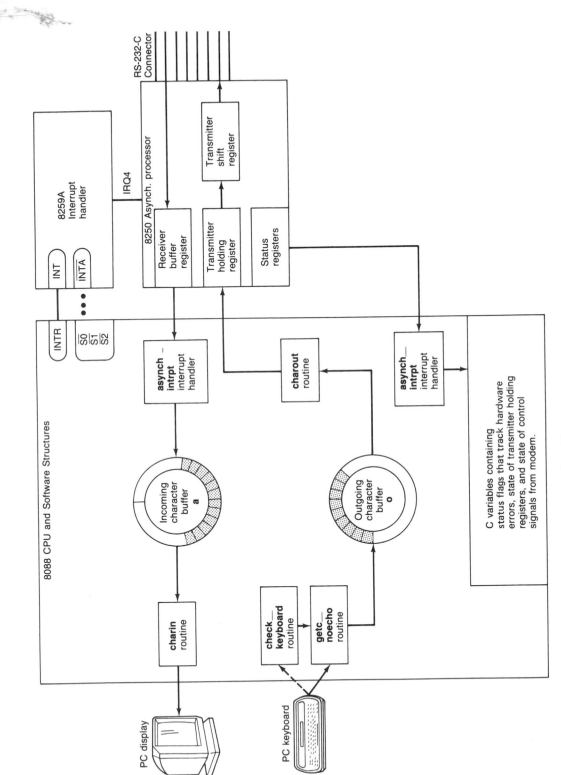

Figure 5-2 Terminal Emulator Data Flow

characters arriving from the mainframe computer via the communications gear. The main loop of the terminal emulator repetitively performs four basic tasks:

1. The main loop calls the **charin** routine to process any incoming characters waiting in buffer **a**. If the character is a data character, it gets printed on the screen. If the character is the start of a terminal control sequence, it will cause special terminal behavior such as cursor movement, or window scrolling.

2. Next, the main loop calls the **charout** routine to send one of the waiting characters in the buffer **o** to the mainframe computer via the comgear. Later, when we discuss sending multiple-character sequences to the mainframe computer, it will become clear why there is a buffer between the **getc_noecho** and the **charout** routines.

3. Next, the main loop calls the **check_keyboard** routine to see if there is a character waiting, and if there is, it then calls the **getc_noecho** routine to fetch the waiting character. The fetched character is stored at the rear of the circular queue **o**. The **check_keyboard** and **getc_noecho** routines are the same ones developed in the earlier chapter on screen and keyboard management.

4. Finally, the main loop performs flow control. That is, if the mainframe is sending characters and the buffer is nearly full, then the emulator asks the mainframe to stop sending, by sending an XOFF character (i.e., control s) to the mainframe. Similarly, if the mainframe had previously been asked to stop sending characters, but now the buffer has sufficient space, the emulator tells the mainframe to resume sending, by sending an XON character (i.e., control q).

While all of this activity is being performed by the main program, the interrupt service routine is performing the real-time activities on a demand basis. That is, whenever a complete character is received in the Receiver Buffer Register (RBR), an interrupt is generated and the interrupt service routine moves it into the circular buffer **a**. Similarly, whenever the status of the 8250 changes, an interrupt is generated and the service routine updates global C variables so that the program can determine the status of the communications gear at any time. For example, when the Transmitter Holding Register (THR) becomes empty after sending a character, an interrupt is generated and the global C variable **thrfree** is set to 1, indicating to the main program that the THR register is now free.

It might seem odd that this design uses two buffers, but in each case the rationale is the same. That is, there are two activities to be coupled that are proceeding at different rates. The communications gear is sending characters at rates that, in theory, could be as high as 9,600 baud (approximately 1,000 characters a second) while the screen can be filled with characters at a maximum of something less than 1,000 characters per second, assuming that we use one BIOS call per character written to the display. In addition, the processing of intervening terminal control sequences may slow the display processing to well below 1,000 characters per second. While it may seem possible for tightly coded character processing to stay ahead of the incoming characters and therefore avoid the use of a buffer, we should not, in general, depend upon the speed of the code to protect against loss of data. The differing rates at which the producer and the consumer (i.e., the communication gear and main program, respectively) operate suggest the need for a buffer between them.

Similarly, the keyboard can generate multiple character sequences when a special key or function key is struck, but the communications gear can take only one character at a time. Once the communications gear has been given a character, the CPU must wait until that character has been serialized and sent to the modem before it can send another character. Thus, a buffer is required here as well.

Notice that in this design, characters that are typed at the keyboard are sent directly to the communications gear without the PC echoing them on the display screen. Data characters are written to the screen only after they have traveled to the mainframe computer, have been processed by the mainframe, and have been returned (echoed) over the communications lines. This mode of operation is called *full-duplex operation*[2] and is used by operating systems such as the UNIX operating system. A characteristic of this mode of operation is that the program on the mainframe is in complete control of the terminal behavior. It is the mainframe that decides exactly what gets written to the screen. A second characteristic of this mode of operation is that data is being sent in both directions simultaneously. There is no need for any protocol to decide which side is listening and which side is transmitting. In contrast, *half-duplex* mode of operation allows transmission in only one direction at a time and thus requires a protocol for deciding which side is listening and which side is transmitting. In half-duplex transmission, one side transmits while the other listens. When one side is done, the line is "turned around" via a handshaking protocol, and then the other side can transmit.

A general terminal emulator would provide options whereby the user could choose between full- or half-duplex communication, between local or remote echoing of characters, and so on. For simplicity, the example will allow only full-duplex operation without local echoing. The interested reader who wants to know more about these protocols should refer to McNamara[3] or Nichols et al.[4] It will be left as an exercise for the reader to extend the terminal emulator to allow half-duplex operation as a program option.

---

[2]Strictly speaking, the term *full-duplex* denotes only the fact that the communications gear is set up to simultaneously send and receive data. Informally, the term is often extended to connote the characteristics of the programs that communicate over a full-duplex circuit.

[3]John E. McNamara, *Technical Aspects of Data Communication*, Second Edition, Digital Press, 1982.

[4]Elizabeth A. Nichols, Joseph C. Nichols, and Keith R. Musson, *Data Communications for Microcomputers*, (New York: McGraw-Hill, Inc., 1982).

The Main Program

The terminal emulator main program is shown in Figure 5-3. It is a straightforward encoding of the data flow diagram shown in Figure 5-2. Figure 5-4 extends Figure 5-2, showing the detailed data flow relationships between C functions and global C variables. The reader should consult Figures 5-2 and 5-4 during the following discussion.

```
main(argc,argv)
        int argc;
        char *argv[];
        {
        unsigned char b[50];
        unsigned char inportb();
        unsigned char mcr,*s;
        _exittbc = 'A'  ;          /*dump stack on abnormal exit*/
        cls();
        counta = fronta = reara=0;
        counto = fronto = rearo=0;
        init_comgear();
        while(TRUE)
              {
/*tell user about parity or overrun errors*/
              report_errs();
/*print on screen or process any incoming character (i.e., char in buffer 'a')*/
              charin();
/*send to comgear any outgoing characters (i.e., char in buffer 'o')*/
              charout();
/*
   If we are not in pause mode (i.e., buffer is not close to full)
   and we are not sending a DTR signal to the modem,
   do the handshaking necessary to allow the reception of any
   incoming character.
*/
              if(!pause && ((mcr = inportb(MCR)) & 0x01)==0)
                    {
                    /*Tell Comgear that the data terminal is ready
                      (i.e., turn on DTR).
                      This is accomplished by writing a 1 into
                      bit 0 of Modem Control Register*/
                    outportb(MCR,(mcr | 0x01));
                    }
/*manage keyboard in polled mode*/
              if(check_keyboard())
                    {
```

Figure 5-3 Terminal Emulator Main Program

```
                                    *b = getc_noecho();
                                    *(b+1) = NUL;
                                    /* Typed chars may be:
                                            1. Local MSDOS command indicator
                                            2. A data character to be sent to the mainframe
                                            3. A special function key (e.g., up cursor)
                                    */
                                    if(*b == SOH) docommand(b);     /*Do a local command*/
                                    else if(*b != NUL) puto(*b);    /*Data character*/
                                        else dokey(b);              /*Function key*/
                                    }
/*Do flow control*/
                        if(pause && counta<almostempty)
                                {pause = FALSE; puto(XON);}
                        if(!pause && counto>half)
                                {pause = TRUE; puto(XOFF);}
                        }
            }
```

Figure 5-3 (Continued)

The main program starts out by clearing the screen (via **cls**) and then initializes the two circular buffers and the communications gear (via **init_comgear**). From then on until it terminates (within **docommand**), it simply traverses its main loop and services each item in turn.

Within this main loop, the first activity is to report any errors (via **report_errs**). Errors are signaled by the values of global variables that are set by the interrupt service routine (**asynch_intrpt**). There are four basic kinds of errors that are detected and cause the 8250 to generate interrupts. Each one of these error types is associated with a global C variable.

1. An overrun error is indicated by the global C variable **overerr**. An overrun occurs when the terminal emulator cannot process characters as fast as they are being received and a new character arrives before the terminal emulator can process the previous character.

2. A parity error is indicated by the global C variable **parityerr**. This may be a true parity error as, for example, might be due to line noise, or it may mean that the user has initialized the communications gear to expect the wrong kind of parity.

3. A framing error is indicated by the global C variable **framingerr**. This indicates that the stop bit is in an unexpected place. This can happen for a number of reasons. Among these reasons is the user initializing the communications gear to expect the wrong character length—for example, specification of 7-bit ASCII characters when the system is sending 8-bit characters.

4. A break interrupt is indicated by the C variable **brkint**. This indicates that

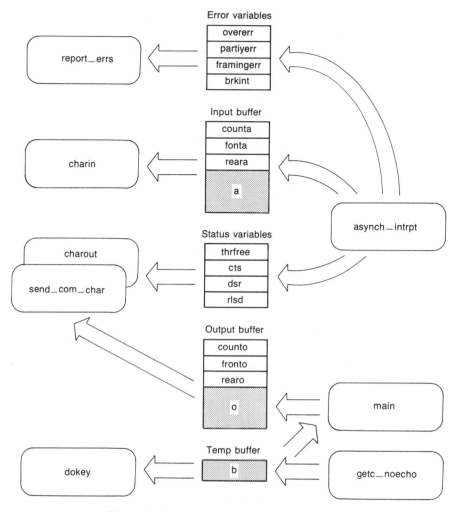

Figure 5-4 Data Management of Global Variables

the communications gear has received a break signal—that is, the Received Data Circuit is held at 0 (low) for longer that a full character transmission time.

The function of **charin** and **charout** should be generally clear from Figures 5-2 and 5-4. However, the code just following deserves some discussion. The objective of this code is to inform the modem[5] that the personal computer[6] is ready.

---

[5]The modem plays the role of the DCE or Data Communications Element as defined in the the EIA RS-232-C data communication standard.

[6]The computer plays the role of the DTE or Data Terminal Element as defined in the the EIA RS-232-C data communication standard.

This is accomplished by the 8250 turning on the DTR signal, bit 0 in the 8250's Modem Control Register.[7] The CPU gets access to this register, by reading and writing I/O port 3FC (the Modem Control Register).[8] If bit 0 is a 1, the 8250 is signaling the modem that the PC is ready to receive incoming characters. If bit 0 is 0, the 8250 is signaling that, for some reason, the PC is unable to receive characters. If for some reason the PC (via the 8250) is not sending DTR, the code just after the call to **charout** turns the DTR signal back on.

TABLE 5-1   I/O PORTS FOR 8250 ASYNCHRONOUS COMMUNICATIONS ELEMENT

```
            /* Asynch Communications Adapter IO Addresses*/
#define THR      0x3f8      /*Transmitter Holding Register, DLAB = 0*/
#define RBR      0x3f8      /*Receiver Buffer Register, DLAB = 0*/
#define DLL      0x3f8      /*Divisor Latch Least Signif Byte, DLAB = 1*/
#define DLM      0x3f9      /*Divisor Latch Most Signif Byte, DLAB = 1*/
#define IER      0x3f9      /*Interrupt Enable Register, DLAB = 0*/
#define IIR      0x3fa      /*Interrupt Identification Register*/
#define LCR      0x3fb      /*Line Control Register*/
#define MCR      0x3fc      /*Modem Control Register*/
#define LSR      0x3fd      /*Line Status Register*/
#define MSR      0x3fe      /*Modem Status Register*/
```

After assuring that the computer is sending DTR, the main program services the keyboard via the **check_keyboard** and **getc_noecho** functions. Keyboard management can be done in polled mode because BIOS has a built-in interrupt service routine that buffers characters coming from the keyboard. When this buffer becomes full, the computer beeps at the typist to inform him or her to slow down and let the computer catch up.

The details of processing the three different kinds of characters generated from the keyboard will be left as as exercise for the reader. The function **dokey** is simply a translation routine. It translates the character or characters typed into a sequence of characters to be sent to the mainframe. If this translation is based on a table of strings, the user can allow multiple definitions for the terminal by switching from table to table under user control. Alternately, the programmer can add commands by which the user can dynamically alter key definitions. The term *soft keys* is often used to characterize this capability.

The function **docommand** allows the terminal emulator user to execute MS-DOS commands or other local commands independently of the session with the mainframe. For example, the user may want to look at a floppy disk directory to search for a file to be sent to the mainframe computer. Certainly, he or she does

---

[7]For a detailed description of all of the 8250 registers relevant to the terminal emulator example, see Chapter 4 of this book or the *IBM Technical Reference Manual*, rev. ed. 2.02 (Boca Raton, Fla.: IBM, April 1983), pp. 1-234 to 1-248.

[8]See Table 5-1 for a complete listing of the C-preprocessor variables that have been set up to define the addresses of relevant I/O ports.

not want to exit the session with the mainframe, search the floppy, and then reestablish the session with the mainframe. The facilities within **docommand** are limited only by the programmer's imagination and the amount of memory on his or her PC.

Finally, the main loop does flow control. This uses the XON/XOFF control characters to manage the incoming character flow from the communications gear. When the buffer is nearly full, it sets the **pause** flag and sends an XOFF character to the host computer. When the PC catches up on its work and the buffer gets nearly empty, the PC resets **pause** and sends an XON character telling the host that it is OK to send more data.

Before we analyze the functions called by the main program, we will look at the structure of the interrupt service routine in order to better appreciate the interplay between the main program and the interrupt service routine.

The Interrupt Service Routine

The General Form

Interrupt service routines that run on an iAPX 86/88 family CPU, operating in conjunction with the Intel 8259A interrupt processor chip, must be designed to perform two tasks. They must re-enable the various pieces of interrupt hardware so that future interrupts can fire, and they must implement the processing logic required by the application program. These requirements result in the prototypical 8088 interrupt service routine design shown in Figure 5-5. The prototypical interrupt service routine design can be easily understood by following through the sequence of events that occur when an interrupt fires.

When a hardware interrupt fires, the CPU pushes the CPU **flags**, the **cs** register, and the **ip** register onto the stack; disables the CPU interrupt flag (**if**);

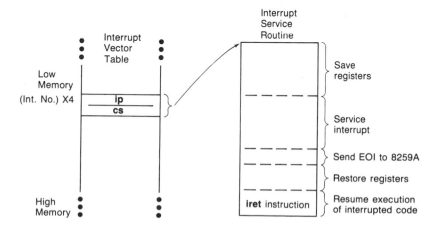

Figure 5-5 General Form of Interrupt Service Routine

reloads the **cs** and **ip** registers from the interrupt vector table,[9] and continues execution at the entry point of the interrupt service routine.

The service routine saves the registers it will use and services the interrupt with a minimum amount of processing, in order to allow other interrupts to proceed without being unduly delayed. This servicing must include actions which reset the various interrupt control mechanisms. For example, reading the 8250 I/O port associated with a specific type of 8250 interrupt, will reset the 8250 so that it can once again generate interrupts. Similarly, the 8259A must be informed when an interrupt has been fully serviced so that it can allow lower priority interrupts to proceed. The 8259A is informed of interrupt service completion by the interrupt service routine writing a special byte, called an 8259A End Of Interrupt command, to one of the 8259A's I/O ports (port 0x20). Finally, the service routine restores the registers it previously saved and performs an 8088 **iret** instruction, which reverses the initial effects of the interrupt. That is, the **iret** instruction loads the **ip** register, the **cs** register, and the CPU **flags** register from the top of the stack. Thus, execution will resume exactly at the point at which the CPU was interrupted.[10] Now that we have examined the general form and behavior of interrupt service routines on the PC, let us look at the details of the interrupt service routine for the asynchronous communications gear.

The Asynchronous Service Routine

Table 5-2, taken from the *IBM Technical Reference Manual*,[11] summarizes the various kinds of asynchronous interrupts that can occur, the Interrupt Identification Register (IIR) bit patterns that identify them, their priority levels, the source of the interrupt (e.g., data available), and the method of resetting the 8250 for that specific kind of interrupt (e.g., reading the Receiver Buffer Register I/O port). We will analyze each category in this table and describe the C code to handle it.

The first issue that the service routine must deal with is the determination of what caused the interrupt. This information is stored in an 8250 register called the Interrupt Identification Register, or IIR (0x3fa). One of the first things that the service routine will do is to read this register into a local C variable (**iir**), with the C code

```
iir = inportb(IIR);
```

---

[9]The absolute address from which the new values of the **cs** and **ip** registers are taken, is calculated by multiplying the interrupt vector number times 4. In the case of COM1, the associated interrupt vector number is 0C (hex), so that the interrupt vector is stored at absolute location 30 (hex).

[10]For an example of an interrupt service routine, the reader is referred to the keyboard interrupt service routine shown in Appendix A of the *IBM Personal Computer Technical Reference Manual*. This routine handles external (keyboard) interrupts generated on line IRQ1. Be sure to notice that there are two kinds of keyboard interrupt routines: the hardware interrupt generated by line IRQ1 and the software callable interrupt.

[11]*IBM Technical Reference Manual*, Edition 2.02, p. 1-242.

TABLE 5-2 INTERRUPT CONTROL FUNCTIONS

Interrupt ID Register			Interrupt Set and Reset Functions			
Bit 2	Bit 1	Bit 0	Priority Level	Interrupt Type	Interrupt Source	Interrupt Reset Control
0	0	1	—	None	None	—
1	1	0	Highest	Receiver Line Status	Overrun Error or Parity Error or Framing Error or Break Interrupt	Reading the Line Status Register
1	0	0	Second	Received Data Available	Receiver Data Available	Reading the Receiver Buffer Register
0	1	0	Third	Transmitter Holding Register Empty	Transmitter Holding Register Empty	Reading the IIR Register (if source of interrupt) or Writing into the Transmitter Holding Register
0	0	0	Fourth	Modem Status	Clear to Send or Data Set Ready or Ring Indicator or Received Line Signal Direct	Reading the Modem Status Register

where both **iir** and **inportb** have been declared as **unsigned char**, and **IIR**[12] is a C preprocessor symbol defined as

```
#define IIR 0x3fa  /*Interrupt Identification Register Address*/
```

Recall that **inportb** executes the 8088 **in** instruction, which reads the data at the I/O port address given by the parameter.

From Table 5-2, we see that **iir** will contain an even integer whenever there is an interrupt pending. There are four kinds of interrupts distinguished by the **iir**, which are prioritized according to the magnitude of the **iir** value. The higher priority interrupts fire before lower priority interrupts if the conditions they detect occur

---

[12]See Table 5-1 for a complete listing of relevant I/O port address definitions.

simultaneously. The highest priority interrupts are the Receiver Line Status interrupts. These interrupts notify the terminal of an emergency condition, such as an overrun error. In the terminal emulator, each of these errors is associated with a global variable, which is periodically checked by the main program (by calling **report_errs**). The C code that services these error interrupts is

```
lsr = inportb(LSR);
if(lsr & 0x02) ++overerr;
if(lsr & 0x04) ++parityerr;
if(lsr & 0x08) ++framingerr;
if(lsr & 0x10) ++brkint;
```

The bits in the Line Status Register or LSR (0x3fd) define what kind of emergency condition has occurred.[13] The interrupt is reset by reading the Line Status Register.

The second kind of interrupt occurs when a complete character has been received in the Receiver Buffer Register or RBR (0x3f8 & dlab = 0). This interrupt is serviced by the code

```
zero_dlab();
rbr = inportb(RBR);
puta(rbr);
```

The function **zero_dlab** zeroes the Divisor Latch Bit (DLB) in the Line-Control Register. This bit allows the I/O port address 0x3f8 to serve double duty. When the DLB is 0, reading 0x3f8 returns the RBR. When the DLB is 1, reading 0x3f8 returns the Least Significant Byte of the Divisor Latch, an integer that controls the baud rate of the 8250.

The service routine reads the waiting character from the RBR and stores it in the circular input buffer **a** via the routine **puta**. Reading the RBR resets the interrupt within the 8250.

The third kind of interrupt occurs when the Transmitter Holding Register, or THR for short (0x3f8 if DLAB =0)[14], becomes empty. This event informs the application program that the last character sent to the asynch gear has been moved out of the THR and the application program may now safely send another character. If the application program does not pay attention to this condition, it runs the risk of overwriting the previous character and thereby sending a garbage character to the mainframe. It is for this very reason that the outgoing characters are buffered in the array **o**.

[13]See the description of the main program for an explanation of the various global variables and their meaning. See the previous chapter for a detailed description of the Line Status Register.

[14]Although the THR and the RBR have the same I/O port address, they are distinct registers in the 8250 and are distinguished by whether the access is a write (THR) or a read (RBR).

The interrupt service routine communicates the status of the THR to the main program via the global **thrfree** flag. The code is

```
thrfree = 1;
```

The fourth and final kind of interrupt occurs when there is a modem status change. It is necessary to keep track of these status flags in order to ensure that all RS-232-C interface conditions are met for transmitting characters to and receiving characters from the modem. As with error interrupts and THR status interrupts, the emulator keeps track of the modem status within global C variables. The code that services modem status change interrupts is

```
msr = inportb(MSR);
if(msr & 1)    /*change in cts*/
        {cts = (msr & ctsmask) ? 1 : 0;
        ++intdcts;}
if(msr & 2)    /*change in dsr*/
        {dsr = (msr & dsrmask) ? 1 : 0;
        ++intddsr;}
if(msr & 4)    /*change in rlsd*/
        {rlsd = (msr & rlsdmask) ? 1 : 0;
        ++intdrlsd;}
```

The Modem Status Register or MSR (0x3fe) contains flags in the low-order nibble of the MSR that go high (1) when any one of the four status lines changes state. The actual state of the the associated line is contained in the high order nibble of the MSR. For example, bit 0 is the Delta Clear To Send flag (DCTS) and bit 4 is the actual value of Clear To Send (CTS). The global variable **ctsmask** is a constant used to mask out the CTS bit. The global variable **cts** is assigned the current state of the CTS line.

The other two signals, Data Set Ready or DSR and Received Line Signal Detect or RLSD, are similarly organized. We ignore the Ring Indicator signal, but if we were developing code for an auto-answer modem, it would have to be handled. The code would be similar to that of the other status lines.

The completed interrupt service routine is shown in Figure 5-6.

There are a few items that still require an explanation. Notice that the first thing the interrupt routine does is to mask off the asynch interrupts and then re-enable other interrupts. This allows higher priority system interrupts such as the system timer, interrupt IRQ0, and the keyboard, interrupt IRQ1, to proceed. We have set up the asynch interrupt service structure so that the service routine can be written in C. Due to the method used to set up the asynch interrupts, we cannot allow another asynch interrupt to fire until the current one is completely serviced, although we can allow other types of interrupts to proceed. If another asynch interrupt were allowed to fire before the current one is complete, we would rein-

itialize the interrupt stack and destroy any data currently residing there, such as
the pointer used to return from the function call.

The code for the **disable_asynch** function is

```
outportb(0x21,inportb(0x21) | 0x10);
```

This reads the 8259A interrupt mask register (I/O port 0x21) and ORs a 1 into bit
4, the bit associated with interrupt IRQ4. This masks the IRQ4 interrupt off.
enable_asynch, called at the very end of the service routine, reverses this process
by ANDing a zero into bit 4.

```
asynch_intrpt()
      /*this routine services the asynch comgear interrupts*/
      {
      unsigned char iir;     /*Interrupt Identification Register image
                                Address is 3FA.*/

      unsigned char rbr;     /*Receiver Buffer Register image.
                                Address is 3F8.*/

      unsigned char lsr;     /*Line Status Register image.
                                Address is 3FD.*/

      unsigned char imr;     /*Interrupt Mask Register.
                                Address 21.*/

      unsigned char msr;     /*Modem Status Register.
                                Address 3fe.*/

      unsigned char c,inportb();

      disable_asynch();      /*mask off asynch interrupt
                                so that we dont overwrite
                                interrupt stack*/

      enable_ints();  /*let other interrupts proceed*/

      /*Find out what kind of interrupt we have.*/

      iir = inportb(IIR);

      switch(iir)
            {
            case '\006':   /*Some kind of error, clear it and go on*/
                  ++interr;
                  lsr = inportb(LSR);
```

Figure 5-6 Asynchronous Interrupt Service Routine

```
              if(lsr & 0x02) ++overerr;
              if(lsr & 0x04) ++parityerr;
              if(lsr & 0x08) ++framingerr;
              if(lsr & 0x10) ++brkint;
              break;

      case '\004':    /*data available, put into circular buffer*/
              ++intdata;
              zero_dlab();
              rbr = inportb(RBR);
              puta(rbr);
              break;

      case '\002':    /*Transmitter holding register emtpy*/
              ++intempty;
              thrfree = 1;    /*trans holding reg is free*/
              break;

      case '\000':    /*Modem Status Change*/
              msr = inportb(MSR);
              if(msr & 1)    /*change in cts*/
                     {cts = (msr & ctsmask) ? 1 : 0;
                     ++intdcts;}
              if(msr & 2)    /*change in dsr*/
                     {dsr = (msr & dsrmask) ? 1 : 0;
                     ++intddsr;}
              if(msr & 4)    /*change in rlsd*/
                     {rlsd = (msr & rlsdmask) ? 1 : 0;
                     ++intdrlsd;
              /*Just ignore ring indicator*/
              break;

      default:/*This should never happen*/
              ++intdefalt;
              lsr = inportb(LSR);
              break;
      }

disable_ints();         /*Turn off all interrupts temporarily*/

outportb(0x20,EOI);     /* send OCW2 End of Interrupt Command to
                           port 20*/

enable_asynch();        /*Allow asynch interrupts to proceed after
                           return is executed. IRET instruction
                           re-instates flags, which will re-enable
                           all interrupts.*/

}
```

Figure 5-6 (Continued)

Notice that the **enable_asynch** call at the end of the service routine is executed with all interrupts disabled. This is to allow the interrupt routine to complete its work and return before another asynch interrupt can fire. It must restore the registers and restore the application stack before another asynch interrupt fires, otherwise the stack storage would get damaged. It also needs to execute an **iret** instruction to restore the CPU flags register, the **ip** register and the **cs** register to their pre-interrupt status. Having all interrupts disabled protects this restoration process.

There is an additional reason for turning off the interrupts at the end of the service routine. They should be off when the CPU sends the End Of Interrupt (EOI) code to the 8259A. An EOI is defined as the hexadecimal character 0x20 if written to port 0x20.[15]

Initializing the Asynchronous Interrupts

This section treats the subject of initializing the asynchronous communications interrupts so that the code developed earlier will execute properly. There are three tasks to be accomplished:

1. We must set up the data structures which vector the specific interrupt number to the interrupt service routine,
2. We must set up all of the enabling conditions for the various pieces of hardware with their variety of options, and
3. We must initialize global data used to communicate between the interrupt service routine and the main loop of the emulator.

Interrupt Data Structures

The basic problem with developing interrupt service routines in C is that we do not have as direct control over the machine's facilities as we do in assembler. For example, we do not have the ability to save registers directly or generate 8088 **iret** instructions easily. So therefore, we will achieve these requirements more indirectly than shown in the ideal interrupt service routine of Figure 5-5. The resulting interrupt service routine structure shown in Figure 5-7 is a bit more baroque but this structure is largely hidden from the casual user because the C86 library supplies two routines that do most of the dirty work.

The first routine is **intrinit**, which creates the structure shown in Figure 5-7. The user writes a C function that serves as the interrupt service routine and **intrinit** establishes the proper linkages. This includes creating a machine language (far) call to the C86 assembly language library function **intrserv**, followed immediately by the required **iret** instruction. Immediately following these two instructions is an·

---

[15]For the reader who would like to learn more about the 8259A, see the *iAPX 86,88 User's Manual*, AP-59, "Using the 8259A Programmable Interrupt Controller", pp. A-136 through A-174.

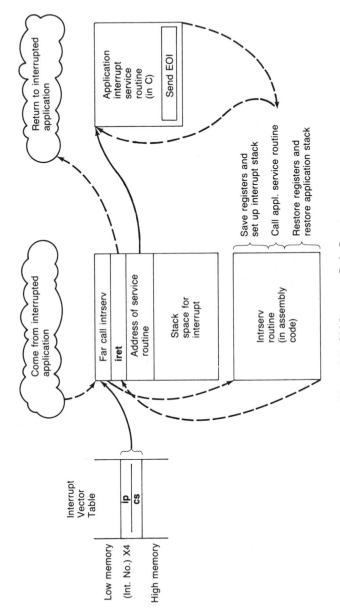

Figure 5-7 C86 Interrupt Code Structure

123

area reserved as stack space, for use by the user's interrupt service routine, as well as interrupt service routines of other, higher-priority interrupts.

intrserv, the second utility function provided in the C86 library, is an assembly language utility function that saves the registers, calls the user written C service routine, and restores the registers before returning to that **iret** instruction created by **intrinit**.

It will suffice to know that a call of the form

```
intrinit(&asynch_intrpt,500,0x0c);
```

will establish stack space of 500 bytes, and in addition, will establish the linkage to a user written C function named **asynch_intrpt**, which will be executed whenever interrupt number 0c (hex) fires.

Enabling the Communications Gear

Figure 5-8 summarizes the various enabling conditions that must be dealt with in order to get the previously described code to work. Let us start with the 8250.

Recall from Table 5-2 and from **asynch_intrpt** that the 8250 generates four different levels of interrupt, where each level is distinguished by an even integer stored in the Interrupt Identification Register (IIR). Each one of these levels can be individually enabled or disabled by setting or resetting bits in the Interrupt Enable Register or IER (0x3F9 if DLAB = 0).[16] The Data Available level is associated with bit 0, the Transmitter Holding Register Empty level with bit 1, the Receiver Line Status level with bit 2 and the Modem Status Change level with bit 3. Setting these bits to one enables the interrupt levels and resetting them to zero disables the interrupt level. For our design, we want all of these levels enabled. This is accomplished with the following code:

```
zero_dlab();         /*First zero divisor latch access bit*/
outportb(IER,0x0f);  /*Turn on asynch enabling bits*/
```

In order for the 8250 to send interrupts over the IRQ4 line, bit 3 of the Modem Control Register or MCR (0x3FC) must be set to one (high). Setting this bit low (0) disables all interrupt signals from the 8250.

While we are at it, we will turn on the DTR signal and turn off the RTS signal, telling the modem that the PC is ready to receive characters but has nothing to send at this instant. All of this is accomplished as follows:

```
outportb(MCR,0x09);
```

Next, we must tell the 8259A to signal the 8088 CPU when input signals appear on the 8259A's IRQ4 line. This is accomplished by resetting the appropriate

---

[16]See page 1-243 of the *IBM Technical Reference Manual* for a description of the Interrupt Enable Register.

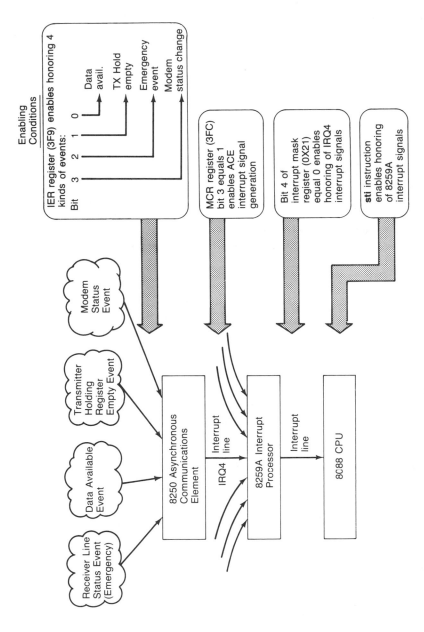

Figure 5-8 Enabling Conditions

bit in the interrupt mask register. In general, for an external interrupt IRQn, where n is an integer between 0 and 7, resetting (i.e., zeroing) bit n of the interrupt mask register enables external interrupt n. Setting bit n (i.e., setting bit n to 1) masks (i.e., turns off) external interrupt n.

The interrupt mask register is changed by writing a byte to I/O port 0x21. So that we do not disturb the state of the other external interrupts, we first read the interrupt mask register and zero only bit 4. It is recommended that interrupts be turned off when writing to the 8259A's I/O ports, so we will disable them before altering the mask register.

```
disable_ints();
outportb(0x21,(inportb(0x21) & 0xef));
enable_ints();
```

The final step is to enable the CPU interrupt flag so that it processes signals from the 8259A. This is accomplished with the 8088 sti instruction, which is executed by calling **enable_ints** in the last statement above. The interrupts will now fire and be processed by our interrupt service routine **asynch_intrpt**.

Initializing Global Data Variables

In order to assure that the global data variables used in the foregoing code start out with the proper initial values, we initially extract their values from the Modem Status Register:

```
msr = inportb(MSR);
cts = (msr & ctsmask)    ? 1 : 0;
dsr = (msr & dsrmask)    ? 1 : 0;
rlsd = (msr & rlsdmask)  ? 1 : 0;
ri =   (msr & rimask)    ? 1 : 0;
```

This code has the same structure as the code associated with the modem status interrupt processing within the interrupt service routine.

init_comgear

Putting all of this together, we produce the **init_comgear** routine shown in Figure 5-9.

```
init_comgear()     /*initialize comgear and comgear interrupts*/
     {

     unsigned char msr,dumy,inportb(),enable_bits;
     int asynch_intrpt();
```

Figure 5-9 Initializing and Enabling Interrupts

```
enable_bits = inportb(0x21);    /*read existing interrupt mask*/

printf("Port 21 mask currently set (one char in hex digits)=0x%x\n"
,(char) enable_bits);

/*initialize interrupt vector for comgear*/
intrinit(&asynch_intrpt,500,0x0c);

com_setup();

/*enable interrupts for receive line status (error)
  and data available.
  See Tech Ref Manual*/

zero_dlab();              /*First zero divisor latch access bit*/
outportb(IER,0x0f);    /*turn on asynch enabling bits*/
zero_dlab();
printf("Interrupt enable register (0x%x)\n",
        inportb(IER));

/*initialize communication flags per existing signals*/

msr = inportb(MSR);
cts = (msr & ctsmask)     ? 1 : 0;
dsr = (msr & dsrmask)     ? 1 : 0;
rlsd = (msr & rlsdmask)   ? 1 : 0;
ri =   (msr & rimask)     ? 1 : 0;

/*Operation Control Word1 (OCW1)-
  Unmask interrupt 4, where bit zero is rightmost bit*/

disable_ints();
outportb(0x21,(inportb(0x21) & 0xef));
enable_ints();
printf("Rereading, port 21 contains 0x%x\n", inportb(0x21));

/*Set bit 3 of modem control register to 1 to allow
  enabled interrupts to signal the 8259A.*/

/*While we are at it, tell Comgear
  that the data terminal is ready (DTR)
  and send 0 on rts line,
  by writing bits 0 and 1 of Modem Control Register*/

outportb(MCR,(unsigned char) 0x09);

printf("Waiting--");
scanf("%c",&dumy);
}
```

Figure 5-9 (Continued)

Initializing the 8250

One of the options of BIOS interrupt 14 allows the asynchronous communications gear to be "programmed." That is, the behavioral characteristics of this gear can be tailored to the user's needs. Specifically, the interrupt allows the following characteristics to be programmed:

1. The baud rate—from a low of 100 baud to a high of 9,600 baud
2. The character parity—even, odd, or none
3. The number of stop bits at the end of a character—1 or 2
4. The number of bits per character—7 or 8

Figure 5-10 shows two routines that initialize the 8250. **com_setup** queries the

```
unsigned int com_setup()
        {
        unsigned int baud, parity, stop, length;

        printf(
        "Baud rate: 0-100,1-150,2-300,3-600,4-1200,5-2400,6-4800,7-9600\n>");
        scanf("%d",&baud);

        printf("Parity:0-None,1-odd,2-even\n>");
        scanf("%d",&parity);

        printf("Stop bits: 0-1 bit, 1-2 bits\n>");
        scanf("%d",&stop);

        printf("Number of bits per character: 2-7 bits, 3-8 bits\n>");
        scanf("%d",&length);

        return(init_com(baud,parity,stop,length));
        }


unsigned int init_com(baud,parity,stop,length)
        unsigned int baud, parity, stop, length;
        {
        unsigned int al;
        unsigned char inportb();

/*      Declare structures which contain the register
```

Figure 5-10 Initializing the 8250

```
            values before and after a system interrupt
            executed by the C function sysint.
*/
            struct regval { int ax,bx,cx,dx,si,di,ds,es; };
            struct regval sreg ;
            struct regval rreg;

/*Initialize registers*/

            sreg.ax = sreg.bx = sreg.cx = sreg.dx =sreg.si =
                    sreg.di = 0;

/*Format data in al as required by BIOS interrupt*/

            al = 0;
            al = ((baud << 5) & 0xe0) | ((parity << 3) & 0x18) |
                ((stop << 2) & 0x04) | (length & 0x03);
            sreg.ax = al;      /* ah = 0*/
            sreg.dx = 0;       /*which rs232 card, 1 in this case*/
            return(sysint(0x14,&sreg,&rreg));

            }
```

Figure 5-10 (Continued)

user letting him or her specify the behavioral characteristics of the 8250. **init_com** issues the BIOS interrupt to set the user prescribed behavioral characteristics. **com_setup** is called from **init_comgear**.

Buffer Management and Critical Sections

Let us reconsider Figure 5-2. In both cases where we employ circular buffers, we have one producer process (e.g., keyboard management) that is responsible for putting characters into the buffer and we have a consumer process (e.g., character transmission to the mainframe) that is responsible for removing them. Further, the buffer is there for the very reason that the producer has the potential of occasionally producing characters faster than the consumer can consume them. Now let us consider a general design for the management of such a buffer structure.

We will construct three C functions:

1. The function **next()** is responsible for removing one character from the front of the circular buffer and returning that character as the value of the function.
2. The function **put(c)** is responsible for adding the character **c** to the end of the buffer.

3. The function **empty()** is responsible for determining whether the buffer has any characters in it or not, returning TRUE (nonzero) if it does not have any characters and FALSE (zero) if it does.

These functions will operate upon four C variables that, taken together, will constitute the implementation of the circular buffer.

1. The C variable **unsigned char buff[BUFFER_SIZE]** will serve as the actual buffer for the example.
2. The C variable **int front** will be the index of the next available character to be removed from the buffer, if there is one.
3. The C variable **int rear** will be the index of the next available empty storage position at the end of the buffer, if there is one.
4. The C variable **int count** will contain the number of data characters currently stored in the circular buffer.

Additionally, we will require the following invariant to be true both before and after the execution of any of the buffer management functions, although it may not hold for short periods of time during the execution of any of these functions.

```
rear = (front + count) % BUFFER_SIZE
```

where "**%**" is the modulo operator and **BUFFER_SIZE** is a **#define** symbol defining the size of the buffer. Notice that this equation implies that **front** = **rear** in exactly two situations: when the buffer is full (**count** = **BUFFER_SIZE**) and when the buffer is empty (**count** = 0).

These data structures plus the invariant lead to the implementation shown in Figure 5-11.

The reader should take a moment to analyze these functions and convince him- or herself that if the invariant is true upon entry to any one of these functions it will by necessity be true upon exit.

When implementing this design for the two arrays **a** and **o**, we could generalize these routines a step further and pass the name of the buffer as a parameter. As a general rule, such parameterization is a good idea, but in this case we prefer not to for two reasons. First, it means that each separate point of call must know the name of the buffer being operated upon. Rather than localizing such information, this would distribute the information throughout the program. Second, because of differing real-time constraints, we will design slightly different management functions for the **a** buffer and the **o** buffer. We will opt to localize usage of the names of the buffer and its associated variables inside the management functions.

The management functions for the **o** buffer are produced by a straightforward transliteration of the above design, by substituting the C variable names associated with the **o** buffer. Because the producer routine that is putting characters into **o** and the consumer routine that is removing characters from **o** are inherently syn-

```
unsigned char next()

        {       /*get next character & update circular buffer*/
        unsigned char current;
        if(count>0)
                {
                current = buff[front];
                --count;
                front = (front + 1) % BUFFER_SIZE;
                }
        else current = '\0';
        return(current);
        }

put(c)              /*put one character into the circular buffer*/
        unsigned char c;
        }
        if(count>=BUFFER_SIZE) return;   /*character lost, buffer
                                            overflow*/
        buff[rear] = c;
        rear = (rear + 1) % BUFFER_SIZE;
        ++count;
        }

empty()
        {
        if (count > 0) return (0);
        else return(1);
        }
```

Figure 5-11 Circular Buffer Implementation

chronized by the polling regime of the main program, there is no possibility of real-time interference between **next** and **put** executions. By the nature of the polling regime, we are assured that the invariant will always be true on entry to and exit from the **next** and **put** versions that manage **o**. However, the management functions for the **a** buffer require some modifications to assure the integrity of the buffer.

How do the requirements for managing the **a** buffer differ from those for the **o** buffer? Since the management of **a** has a real-time aspect, assuring buffer integrity (i.e., assuring that the invariant is always true) requires protective measures that arc not required for the management of **o**. Consider what is might happen without such measures.

Since **a** is managed by two totally unsynchronized processes, the operations of **next** and **put** could be interleaved in disastrous ways. That is, if used as specified above, these routines would allow the following sequence of events:

1. **next** fetches the value of **count**
2. An incoming character causes an interrupt
3. **put** is called from the interrupt handler and it adds one to the value of **count** and stores the new value
4. **next** is resumed, updates the old value of **count** (i.e., the value that existed before the call to **put**), and stores this value, destroying the value just stored by **put**

Given such a sequence, the invariant would no longer be true and ultimately, data would be lost.

The solution to this problem is to create versions of **next** and **put** that are synchronized so that the invariant is true both on entry and exit to either **next** or **put**. We synchronize **next** and **put** by disabling interrupts for the short sections of code that operate upon shared data. Regions of code that require such protection are called "critical sections."

This leads to the implementation shown in Figure 5-12. In these routines, **fronta**, **reara**, and **counta** are the analogs of the variables **front**, **rear**, and **count** in the general circular buffer design.

Sending Characters to the Comgear

When designing a routine to send characters to the 8250 for transmission to the mainframe, it is tempting to write a function that uses the BIOS interrupt number 14 (hex) and let BIOS do all of the work of sending the character. This method of sending characters has the undesirable side effect that it disables the 8250 interrupt system when BIOS sends DTR and RTS to the modem.[17] This causes the emulator to miss interrupts and, hence, miss changes in modem status. Therefore, we will transliterate the BIOS write comgear function into a C function named **send_com_char**, with minor modifications. The most important such modification is making sure that we leave the 8250 interrupt system on when we send DTR and RTS—that is, when we alter the bits in the Modem Control Register.

According to the RS-232-C standard, data terminal equipment (DTE) shall not transmit data to the data communications equipment (DCE) unless there is an ON condition for the following four signals:

1. Request To Send (RTS)

---

[17]See *IBM Technical Reference Manual*, App. A.

```
unsigned char nexta()

        {       /*get next character & update circular input buffer*/
        unsigned char current;
        disable_ints(); /*disable interrupts*/
        if(counta>0)
                {
                current = a[fronta];
                --counta;
                fronta = (fronta + 1) % BUFFER_SIZE;
                }
        else current = '\0';
        enable_ints();   /*enable interrupts*/
        return(current);
        }

puta(c)         /*put one character into the circular input buffer*/
        unsigned char c;
        {
        disable_ints(); /*disable interrupts*/
        if(counta>=BUFFER_SIZE) return;  /*character lost, buffer overflow*/
        a[reara] = c;
        reara = (reara + 1) % BUFFER_SIZE;
        ++counta;
        enable_ints();  /*enable interrupts*/
        }

emptya()
        {
        if (counta > 0) return (0);
        else return(1);
        }
```

Figure 5-12 Circular Buffer with Synchronized Access

2. Clear To Send (CTS)
3. Data Set Ready (DSR)
4. Data Terminal Ready (DTR)

That is, the proper handshaking for transmitting a character is that the DTE (i.e., the PC) signals the DCE (i.e., the modem) that it is ready (DTR) and, at the same time, that it wants to send a character (RTS). The DTE then waits until the modem (DCE) signals back that it also is ready (DSR) and that it is clear to send (CTS). This pattern is seen in Figure 5-13.

```
unsigned int send_com_char(c)
        unsigned char c;
        {
        unsigned int timeout;

/*This behaves much like the BIOS send character function except
  that it does not poll the Modem Status Register(MSR)
  and most importantly, does not turn off the 8250 interrupts
  by setting bit 3 of the Modem Control Register to zero. The
  MSR will change spontaneously via interrupts from the comgear.
*/

/*Turn on DTR and RTS signals, leaving the interrupt enable bit on*/
        outportb(MCR,0x0b);

/*Wait for DSR and CTS signals from modem.*/
        for(timeout=30000;(dsr==0|| cts==0) && timeout>0;--timeout);

        if(timeout==0)
                {
                printf("Time out waiting for DSR and CTS\n");
                return(0x8000);
                }

/*If the THR is not free wait on it*/

        for(timeout=30000;thrfree==0 && timeout>0;--timeout);
        if(timeout==0)
                {
                printf("Time out waiting for THR free\n");
                return(0x8000);
                }

/*Write character to comgear*/
        outportb(THR,c);
        return(0);       /*Successful*/
        }
```

Figure 5-13 Sending a Character to the 8250

Processing Incoming Characters

The function **charin** is responsible for processing incoming characters. There are several different classes of incoming characters and **charin** treats each slightly differently. For our example, we will distinguish three different classes of character:

1. Data characters, which will be written to the display without any further processing
2. Backspace, which causes cursor movement
3. The escape character ($\backslash$033), which signals the start of a terminal control sequence. Terminal control sequences (also called escape sequences) are discussed in detail in a later section, where we discuss the function **do_escape_seq**. Escape sequences typically cause the terminal perform local functions such as scroll the screen, clear the screen, insert a new blank line, and so forth.

The code for **charin** is shown in Figure 5-14.

```
charin()            /*process incoming characters*/
        {
        unsigned char c[2];
        unsigned char nexta();
        int row,col,mode;
        for (;!emptya();)
                {
                *c = nexta();

                switch(*c)
                        {
                        case ESC:
                                do_escape_seq();
                                break;
                        case BS:     /*backspace*/
                                read_cursor(&row,&col,&mode);
                                move_cursor(row,col-1);
                                break;
                        default:
                                fwrite(c,1,1,stdout);
                                break;
                        }
                }
        }
```

Figure 5-14 Processing Incoming Characters

Processing Outgoing Characters

The job of **charout** is to test to see if there are any characters to be sent and to assure that the last character transmission is sufficiently close to completion (i.e., the transmission holding register is free) that we can initiate the transmission of the next character. The code for **charout** is shown in Figure 5-15.

Controlling the Terminal

With the use of powerful microprocessors as the major component of many computer terminals, it has become possible to move more computations from the host to the terminal and, thereby, to speed up or otherwise improve the user interface. Terminal architectures have progressed from the dumb "glass tty," which could do little but display lines and scroll the screen, to intelligent terminals, which can perform sophisticated and extended computations locally. As such capability evolves,

```
unsigned int charout()   /*send outgoing characters*/
      {
      unsigned char nexto(),inportb();
      unsigned int send_com_char(),err;
      unsigned int timeout;
      /* Do not put the DCE into transmit mode, unless there is at least
         one character to send and the transmitter holding register is
         free.
      */

      if (!emptyo())
            {
            if(thrfree==0)
                  {    /*Wait on trans holding & shift reg to
                        become free*/
                  for(timeout=300;timeout>0 && thrfree==0;--timeout);
                  if(timeout==0)
                        {
                        printf("Timeout waiting on trans hold reg\n");
                        return(0x8000);
                        }
                  }
            err = send_com_char(nexto());
            return(err);
            }
      return(0xffff);
      }
```

Figure 5-15 Processing Outgoing Characters

it becomes advantageous to standardize the notions of what functions should be performed locally (i.e., at the terminal rather than at the host); how those functions are defined; and how those functions are invoked from the host. This section discusses a set of such functions as defined by the American National Standards Institute (ANSI)[18] and develops an implementation for some of the ANSI standard terminal control sequences (or escape sequences) that are sent by the host to cause the terminal to execute these local functions.

The motivation for adding this capability to the terminal emulator is to both extend the capability of the emulated "terminal" and to extend the set of host systems to which such a "terminal" can be connected. Not all terminals adhere to the ANSI standards, of course, but a large number of the most popular terminals do, either partially or completely, and this increases the likelihood that any given host system will support such terminals.

ANSI Standard Terminal Control

There are two classes of terminal control characters:

1. Single character controls, such as Backspace (Ctrl-H) and Return (Ctrl-M).
2. Multicharacter control sequences, such as those which clear some window on the screen, scroll a window on the screen, and move the cursor about the screen.

The single character controls are handled in **charin**. Their implementation is quite straightforward and should be easy to understand from a careful examination of the code discussed earlier. The most powerful and challenging functions are those invoked by the multicharacter control sequences. Consequently, this discussion will concentrate on the multicharacter control sequences. We will define a significant set of multicharacter control sequences, discuss the function of a few of the more interesting ones and finally, develop the code that handles a subset. The extension of this code to support the full set is largely straightforward and will be left as an exercise for the reader.

ANSI terminal control sequences have the general form:[19]

$$\langle ESC \rangle \ [\ \langle n \rangle \ ; \ \langle m \rangle \ ; \ \ldots \ \langle SPECCHAR \rangle$$

---

[18]ANSI Standard X3.64, "Additional Controls for Use with ASCII," Secretariat: CBEMA, 1828 L St. N.W., Washington, D.C.

[19]The notational conventions are: Symbols enclosed in angle brackets—i.e., "<>", are meta-symbols and represent some character sequence other than that between the angular brackets. Upper case and/or multicharacter metasymbols represent non-numerical ASCII character sequences—e.g., "H", and lower case, single-character metasymbols represent numerical ASCII character sequences, e.g., "15". Symbols not in angular brackets represent themselves. For example, "[" represents the ASCII character left square bracket (0x5B).

That is, the control sequence is introduced by the two character sequence "ESCAPE (0x1B) followed by LEFT BRACKET (0x5B)." Following this is an optional series of numerical parameters represented as ASCII numbers and separated by semi-colons. If omitted, these parameters will have default values, typically 0 or 1, depending upon the specific command. Finally, a single ASCII character, <SPEC-CHAR>—determines the specific escape sequence. A few sequences contain only the ESCAPE character followed by the SPECCHAR.

Consider the following example terminal control sequences. The sequence

```
<ESC>  [  <n>  ;  <m>  H
```

requests the terminal to position the cursor at line <n>, column <m>, while the sequence

```
<ESC>  [  <n>  S
```

requests the terminal to scroll up <n> lines. The standard is quite extensive and even goes so far as to allow the terminal screen to be broken into separate windows that can be managed separately. Indeed, many of the control sequences refer to the current window or to a specified window number in order to delineate the extent of their effect. For the sake of accuracy, we will define the terminal sequences just the same as the ANSI standard does, but for the exercise of this chapter, we will always consider any window specified by the standard to be the full screen. Given the screen management functions developed earlier, it is a straightforward task to extend the terminal emulator to manage subparts of the screen as discrete windows.

The following list specifies some of the ANSI terminal control sequences. We will implement a subset of these as an extension to the terminal emulator.

```
<ESC> [ <n> A          -Move cursor up <n> lines (default 1).
<ESC> [ <n> B          -Cursor down <n> lines (default 1).
<ESC> [ <n> C          -Move cursor right <n> columns (default 1).
<ESC> [ <n> D          -Move cursor left <n> columns (default 1).
<ESC> [ <n> E          -Move cursor to first column,
                        down <n> lines (default 1).
<ESC> [ <n> F          -Move cursor to first column,
                        up <n> lines (default 1).
<ESC> [ <n> G          -Move cursor to column <n> (default 1) of line.
<ESC> [ <n>;<m> H      -Position cursor to line <n>, column <m>.
<ESC> [ <n> I          -Move <n> tabstops to right (default 1).
<ESC> [ <n> J          -Erase to end of window (<n>=0), from beginning of
                        window (<n>=1), and entire window if <n>=2.
```

```
<ESC> [ <n> K          -Erase to end of line (<n>=0, default),
                        from beginning (<n>=1), or entire line if <n>=2.
<ESC> [ <n> L          -Insert <n> blank lines (default 1)
                        before current.
<ESC> [ <n> M          -Delete <n> lines (default 1) from current &
                        scrolls blanks into bottom of screen.
<ESC> [ <n> P          -Delete <n> characters (default 1)
                        starting from current position.
<ESC> [ <n> S          -Scroll current window up <n> lines (default 1).
<ESC> [ <n> T          -Scroll current window down <n> lines (default 1).
<ESC> [ <n> W          -Set tabstop in current column for <n>=0.
                        If <n>=2, any tabstop at current
                        column is cleared.
                        If <n>=4, all tabstops are cleared.
<ESC> [ <n> X          -Erase <n> character positions (default 1).
                        starting at current position.
<ESC> [ <n> Z          -Backtab: Move left <n> tabstops (default 1).
<ESC> [ <n><blank> @ -Scroll left <n> columns.
<ESC> [ <n><blank> A -Scroll right <n> columns.
<ESC> [ <n> @          -Insert <n> spaces (default 1) at current position.
<ESC> c                -Clear all, reset terminal.
<ESC> \                -Keyboard lock.
<ESC> b                -Keyboard unlock.
```

Processing Escape Sequences

Recall that **charin**, shown in Figure 5-14, calls a function named **do_escape_sequence** whenever it encounters an incoming escape character. **do_escape_seq** is shown in Figure 5-16 and definitions of the global data it uses are shown in Figure 5-17.

```
do_escape_seq(b)
        char *b;        /*working buffer*/
        {

        int j;
        int row,col,mode;
        int num,parms[16];
        char letters[5];

        parse_escape_seq(&num,parms,letters);
```

Figure 5-16 Processing Escape Sequences

```
      if(debug & PARSE_DEBUG)
            printf("parse returns num=%d,parms=(%d,%d),letters=%5c\n",
            num,*parms,*(parms+1),*letters);
      read_cursor(&row,&col,&mode);
      /* handle sequences of form ESC <letter>*/
      if(num<0)
            {
            if(*letters=='c')
                        {
                        /*clear screen*/
                        cls();
                        move_cursor(Y_HOME, X_HOME);
                        return;
                        }
            printf("Received unsupported escape sequence (ESC %c)\n",
                  *letters);
            return;
            }
      /*handle escape sequences of forms
            ESC [ <letter>
            ESC [ <n> <letter>
            ESC [ <n> ; <m> .... <letter>
            ESC [ <n> ; <m> .... <blank> <letter>
      */
      else
            {
            switch(*letters)
                  {
                  case 'A':     /*ESC [ <n> A --cursor up*/
                        move_cursor(row-MAX(1,*parms),col);
                        break;
                  case 'B':     /*ESC [ <n> B --cursor down*/
                        move_cursor(row+MAX(1,*parms),col);
                        break;
                  case 'D':     /*ESC [ <n> D --cursor left*/
                        move_cursor(row,col-MAX(1,*parms));
                        break;
                  case 'C':     /*ESC [ <n> C --cursor right*/
                        move_cursor(row,col+MAX(1,*parms));
                        break;
                  case 'K':     /*ESC [ <n> K --delete part of line*/
                        if((j = *parms) ==0)
                            /*erase to end of line*/
                            scroll_window(row,col,row,
                                        maxcol,0,NORM_ATTR,6);
                        else if(j==1)
                            /*erase from front of line*/
                            scroll_window(row,X_HOME,row,
```

Figure 5-16 (Continued)

```
                             col,0,NORM_ATTR,6);
                    else
                       /*erase whole line*/
                       scroll_window(row,X_HOME,row,
                                  maxcol,0,NORM_ATTR,6);
                    break;
        case 'J':    /*ESC [ <n> J --delete part of window*/
                    if((j = *parms) ==0)
                       /*erase to end of window*/
                       scroll_window(row,X_HOME,maxrow,
                                  maxcol,0,NORM_ATTR,6);
                    else if(j==1)
                       /*erase from front of window*/
                       scroll_window(Y_HOME,X_HOME,row,
                                  maxcol,0,NORM_ATTR,6);
                    else
                       /*erase whole window*/
                       scroll_window(Y_HOME,X_HOME,maxrow,
                                  maxcol,0,NORM_ATTR,6);
                    move_cursor(Y_HOME, X_HOME);
                    break;
        case 'M':    /*ESC [ <n> M --delete n lines*/
                    scroll_window(row,X_HOME,maxrow,maxcol,
                               MAX(*parms,1),NORM_ATTR,6);
                    break;
        case 'L':    /*ESC [ <n> L --open n lines*/
                    scroll_window(row,X_HOME,maxrow,maxcol,
                              MAX(1,*parms),NORM_ATTR,7);
                    break;
        case 'H':    /*ESC [ <n> ; <m>
                           --coords for new cursor position*/
                    move_cursor(*parms,*(parms+1));
                    break;
        default:
                    break;
        }
    }
}
```

Figure 5-16 (Continued)

Understanding the data structures is the key to understanding this function. There are three key data structures, the values of which are computed by **parse_ escape_seq**. These data structures are:

1. **parms** is an array of the integer parameters appearing in an escape sequence. For example, the escape sequence "<ESC>[14;25H" (i.e., move cursor to 14,25) would result in **parms** containing 14 and 25.

```
#define MAX_LINE 512              /*maximum length of any character string*/
#define BUFFER_SIZE 4096
#define TRUE 1
#define FALSE 0
#define MIN(I,J) (((I)<(J)) ? (I) : (J))
#define MAX(I,J) (((I)>(J)) ? (I) : (J))

/*cursor home position*/
#define X_HOME 0
#define Y_HOME 0

#define NORM_ATTR 0x07            /*normal or blank attribute*/
#define INV_ATTR 0x70            /*inverse video attribute*/
#define NORMBLNK_ATTR 0x87       /*normal blinking attribute*/
#define INVBLNK_ATTR 0xf0        /*inverse video blinking*/
#define NORMHLIT_ATTR 0x0f       /*normal with highlighting*/
#define INVHLIT_ATTR 0x78        /*inverse video with highlighting*/
#define NORMBLNKHLIT_ATTR 0x8f   /*normal,blinking,highlighting*/
#define INVBLNKHLIT_ATTR  0xf8   /*inverse, blinking,highlighting*/

int maxcol = 79;        /*max col number of screen*/
int maxrow = 24;        /*max row of screen*/
int maxcolp1 = 80;      /*max col of screen + 1*/
int maxrowp1 = 25;      /*maxrow + 1*/
```

Figure 5-17 Global Data Used by **do_escape_seq**

2. **num** is the number of integer parameters found in an escape sequence. In the foregoing example, **num** would have a value of 2. **num** is -1 in the case of degenerate escape sequences—that is, "<ESC> <LETTER>".

3. **letters** is a string of the letters that designate the function of the escape sequence. **letters** allows multiple characters only in the few cases where the function is designated by a blank followed by one other nonblank character. In the foregoing example, **letters** would contain the single letter "H."

This function makes extensive use of the screen management functions—for example, **move_cursor** and **scroll_window**, developed in an earlier chapter. Given a thorough understanding of these screen management functions, **do_escape_seq** is quite straightforward.

parse_escape_seq, shown in Figure 5-18, is a support function that computes **parms**, **num** and **letters**. This function processes through the escape sequence in a straightforward manner.

```
parse_escape_seq(num,parms,letters)
        int *num,*parms;
        unsigned char *letters;
        {
        unsigned char c,tmp[10],nexta();
        int i;
/* num(number of parms)           format
        -1                        <esc> <letters>
        1                         <esc> [ <n> <letters>
        2                         <esc> [ <n> ; <m> <letters>
        etc...
*/

        for(i=0;i<16;i++) parms[i]=0;
        if(!emptya() && (c=nexta()) =='[')
                {                       /* ESC [........  */
                *num = 0;
                /* throw away '['*/
                {
        else
                }                       /* ESC <letter>    */
                *num = -1;
                *letters = c;
                return;
                }

        i=0; *tmp='0';
        while (!emptya())
                {
                c = nexta();
                if(isdigit(c)|| isspace(c)) {tmp[i++] = c; tmp[i]='\0';}
                else
                        {
                        if(*tmp!='\0') parms[*num]=atoi(tmp);
                        ++(*num);
                        if(c==';') {i=0; *tmp='\0'; continue;}
                        if((*letters=c)!=' ') break;
                        *(letters+1)=nexta();
                        break;
                        }
                }
        }
```

Figure 5-18 Processing Escape Sequences

The first **if** statement recognizes "[" if there is one, or returns the degenerate escape sequence (i.e., <ESC> <LETTER>) if there is not one. The following **while** loop accumulates the integer parameters one at a time in the string **tmp**. Upon termination of a single string, it converts the integer parameter into internal form and stores it in **parms**. The **while** loop continues in this manner until a non-semicolon string terminator is found. Only then is the latter portion of the **else** clause ever executed, storing a single letter or a blank plus a single letter in **letters**. After that, the **while** loop is broken (via **break**) and the function returns.

There is a subtle potential problem with this function as it stands. It always assumes that once it sees an escape character, the rest of the escape sequence will be received and stored away in the buffer by the time **parse_escape_seq** is ready for it. In practice, this does not seem to cause problems. However, the routine would be more solid if it contained a timeout loop that waited for a few milliseconds whenever an empty buffer occurs in the middle of processing an escape sequence. It is likely that this would reduce the number of misinterpreted escape sequences.

EXERCISES

5.1. If you have access to a UNIX system, write a termcap definition of the terminal emulator and try using the **vi** editor running on the UNIX system. (One week.)

5.2. Write a version of **docommand** that allows the user to view the files in any local directory, to view any local file using the **more** program and to copy arbitrary local files. How might this facility be extended to allow any arbitrary DOS command?

5.3. Extend the implementation of **do_escape_seq** to incorporate the full ANSI standard. (Two months.)

5.4. Develop upload and download file transfer capabilities within the terminal emulator framework. What protocol will you use? Can your facility be used on any host without special programs that run on the host or must you install a program to run on the host and cooperate in the transfer? Discuss the tradeoffs. What will you do about data transmission errors? Detect, correct, or ignore? (This project will take from one month to a full quarter or more, depending on the sophistication of the target system.)

Chapter 6

Concepts
of Multitasking
and Window Interfaces

6.1 MULTITASKING

Multitasking is the capability for a computer to run more than one program at a time, such that, it appears to the user that the programs are running simultaneously. Each program operates as if it owned the whole computer, oblivious to any other programs running on the system and oblivious to the multitasking system itself. That is to say, programs that run on multitasking systems need have no special features designed into them to make them run on the multitasking system.

Why would one want multitasking, especially on a personal computer? After all, a personal computer is "personal," isn't it? One need not share it with others, at least not in the same sense or for the same reasons as the large-scale, expensive mainframes require sharing. Then why do I need more than one program running at once? Each user may have individual reasons for wanting to run more than one program, and typically those reasons grow out of the kind of job that the user performs. Indeed, some may never require general-purpose multitasking. If all that I ever do is word processing, then at most I might need only a specialized form of multitasking—that is, a special-purpose print spooling program that allows me to continue to compose my deathless prose, while my machine merrily drives the printer in the background. However, I both write text and develop programs, programs that often are quite large. It may take several minutes to perform a compile, object library update and target system relink. With a single processing system, I can only sit and twiddle my fingers, or find a ten-minute job that does not involve the computer while my compile is whirling away. I would prefer to be able to do something productive on the computer, even if that lengthened the

145

overall turnaround of my compile. And that's the rationale for generalized multitasking on personal computers. As PCs become faster and more powerful, the waste of having the user shut out by single-stream processing is no longer necessary. The capacity to perform several tasks at once is just waiting to be tapped, and multitasking is a mechanism to tap that extra capacity.

Now that we have a rationale, let's look at the technology underlying multitasking.

Processes (or Tasks)

We will be using the term *process*[1] in the following discussion and we will need a more precise notion of what a process is. Let us start by determining what a process is not.

Informally, we often use process and program synonymously, but formally they are not the same thing. A program, generally, is a block of code created by the linker, which is waiting to be executed. There is typically only one copy of a specific program, but when that program is combined with specific data and executed on a computer, there can be many instances of that program operating at any given time. Take the UNIX program, **wc**, which counts bytes, words, and lines in a file. At any one time, there can be a number of instances of **wc** executing on the computer, each counting the bytes, words, and lines of a different file. Each such actively executing instance of a program is a process.

A process sounds similar to a function (or procedure) in that a function is a combination of code plus data. Functions are combined with data to produce executable instances of themselves (on the stack). However, there is a critical difference that is revealed by considering flow of control. Only one function out of many possible functions within a single program can have control at a given time. Said another way, there is only one program counter per executing program instance and it can point to only one place in the program. Thus, even though there may exist many instances of a function at a given time, only one can be executing. By contrast, a set of *n* processes will have *n* independent flows of control—that is, *n* independent program counters. And not only are there *n* program counters, but those program counters are independent. That is, the flow of control in one process has no direct and necessary affect on the flow of control in another process.[2] This produces the salutary characteristic that each program can be designed without any consideration of other programs that may be running

---

[1]We will use the terms process and task synonymously, but because process is the more common term, we will use it in favor of task.

[2]There are indirect ways that one process may influence the flow of control of another process. For example, the two processes may be synchronized by one or more modes of interprocess communication—e.g., shared data or process-to-process messages. But such synchronization is at the discretion of the system designer, and is a different aspect of a process.

concurrently. Some consideration of other programs is necessary if interprocess communication is required, but this is a separate issue.

Let us consider another aspect of processes: They require resources in order to run, but the multitasking system, not the process, is responsible for managing those resources and arbitrating between competing processes. Suppose that we have two different processes that print their output onto the only printer in the system. Given no restrictions, we have the possibility of conflict if these two processes should happen to be executing at the same time on the same computer. The output of the two processes is likely to be interlaced on the system printer and probably would be useless. Of course, no multitasking system is going to allow this to happen. The system may take one of two approaches: either it assigns the printer resource to one or the other of the processes for as long as it needs it, suspending the execution of the other process in the meantime; or it will create two independent "virtual" printer resources (really just disk files) giving one to each process, and then sort out the physical order of printing later. The printer, real or virtual, is a resource needed by both processes in order to proceed. More generally, processes require a variety of different kinds of resources in order to be able to run. Processes variously require the CPU, memory, disk space, printers, plotters, and so forth. Without such resources a process cannot execute. It is the job of the multitasking system to manage these resources and assign them to the various processes so they can execute.

So far, we have described the essence of a simple process. However, sometimes we want more than just a simple process. For example, we may want the processes to cooperate with each other. That is, we may want each process to perform one part of a larger task. Let's consider the problem of two processes, A and B, both using the printer and plotter. Instead of allocating the physical devices to processes A and B, we could allocate virtual devices (really just processes) and make those virtual device processes emulate the behavior of the printer and the plotter. The process that plays the role of the printer (or the plotter) gathers up and stores the printer (or plotter) output on a file for later printing (or plotting).[3] However, the fact that each process is oblivious to other processes running in the system creates a problem. How do we get the signals and information between the generating processes, A and B, and the device spoolers? This is the problem of interprocess communication, which we will discuss in greater detail later. For now, suffice it to say that multitasking systems typically take one of two approaches to this problem. Either they provide a mechanism for two processes to share some part of memory, or they provide a message capability that allows processes to send streams of information explicitly to each other.

Now let us summarize the characteristics of a process.

1. A process is an instance of a program.

---

[3]Such a process is called a "spooler."

2. Each process has it own private data, which is independent of the private data associated with any other process.

3. A process is an active entity in the sense that either it is executing or it is in a state that it could execute, given the appropriate computing resources.

4. Each process has its own program counter—i.e., its own locus of control.

5. Each process requires a set of computing resources in order to execute.

6. A process may be allowed to communicate with other processes; for example, via shared memory or messages.

One of the most critical resources that a process needs to execute is the CPU. Scheduling the CPU is a rich and interesting subject, and one that is critical to the behavior of the multitasking system. The following section will consider alternative strategies for allocating the CPU to processes.

CPU Scheduling Strategies

In designing a scheduling strategy[4] for a multitasking system, one is faced with two basic questions that are not entirely independent. What is the strategy whereby the currently executing task relinquishes its control of the CPU, and what is the strategy for choosing the next process to run? Let's consider these questions in order.

The currently executing task can relinquish control of the CPU either involuntarily or voluntarily. These are called preemptive and non-preemptive scheduling, respectively.[5] With preemptive scheduling, control is seized from the executing process by forces beyond the control of that process. In the simple example developed in the following chapters, preemption is accomplished by a periodic timer interrupt routine. Thus, programs running on a system using preemptive scheduling need have no special features designed into them to give up control of the CPU. Any program that will run on a single-tasking system will in principle run on a multitasking system with preemptive scheduling, given that both systems accept the same set of system calls.

Programs that run on multitasking systems with non-preemptive scheduling must either be designed with explicit context switching mechanisms built into them or have the context switching mechanism buried within an operating system routine. For example, a system call to read or write a file may first check to see how long the current process has been running, and if it has exhausted its time slice, initiate a context switch. A drawback to non-preemptive scheduling that makes it prob-

---

[4]See also J. Peterson, and A. Silberschatz, *Operating System Concepts*, Addison Wesley, (1983), and Alan C. Shaw, *The Logical Design of Operating Systems* (Englewood Cliffs, N. J.: Prentice-Hall, Inc. 1974).

[5]Shaw discusses a third category, selective preemption, which is a variation on preemptive scheduling.

lematic for time-sharing systems is that one program may hold the CPU for a very long period of time.

Real systems tend not to be exclusively preemptive or non-preemptive. They generally contain a mix of methods for switching control from one process to another. In the example we will discuss, we will introduce several C functions that switch control non-preemptively: **resume**, **suspend**, **harikari** and **abort**. As the example system will illustrate, these functions are often buried within the operating system services and relinquish the CPU when it would be wasteful or futile to keep it.

In the forthcoming example, **resume** and **suspend** illustrate two differing flavors of this mode of relinquishing the CPU. **resume** relinquishes the CPU with the intention that the program be put on the ready list so that it can have another shot at the CPU whenever its next turn comes up. In other words, the resumed program is ready to run. All it needs to proceed is the CPU. In contrast to **resume**, **suspend** relinquishes the CPU when there is an explicit reason that it cannot proceed, such as a needed resource is currently unavailable. The use of **suspend** usually implies that some explicit action or event must occur before it makes any sense to **resume** the process. For example, a process may be suspended because the user issued a command to the window manager to change the currently active window to another window. Thus, the program in the formerly active window will be suspended when it tries to use the keyboard, which is now assigned to the newly designated current window. The event that would allow the suspended program to proceed is the reactivation of the suspended program's window by the user. Since a suspended program's forward progress is conditioned on an event, suspended processes do not go onto the ready list at the time of their suspension. They get back onto the ready list when the event that they are waiting for occurs.

The second scheduler design issue is the strategy for choosing the next process to run. Among the alternatives are the following:

1. *Priority Scheduling Strategy*. This strategy keeps a ready list of activity processes that is sorted based on a priority assigned to each process. Priorities are assigned either statically, based on some characteristic of the job (e.g., memory requirement or time estimate) or dynamically, based on a dynamic characteristic of the executing job (e.g., the number of I/O requests over a given period of time). Priority scheduling systems are typically batch job scheduling systems. For example, consider a system using static priorities for scheduling. The highest priority job will run to completion, unless a higher priority job enters the system in the midst of its execution. Priority scheduling algorithms may be either preemptive or non-preemptive.

   Two popular batch job scheduling strategies are varieties of priority scheduling with static priorities.

   1.1. *The First-Come-First-Served Strategy*. This strategy is basically a batch processing strategy. When a process (i.e., a job) is entered into the system, it is put at the end of the queue of jobs waiting for service. When the CPU becomes available, a job is chosen from the front of the queue, given the CPU, and it executes to completion.

    1.2. *The Shortest-Job-First Strategy.* This strategy schedules jobs based on their time estimates, often declared by the programmer on the job request record at the front of the job.

2. *Round Robin Strategy.* This strategy is often used in time-sharing systems. All active processes are kept on a circular queue, frequently called the "ready" queue. The scheduler proceeds around the queue and gives the CPU to each process in its turn. Round Robin schedulers can be either preemptive or non-preemptive, but they are typically preemptive.

3. *Multi-Queue Strategy.* With this strategy, the system contains a number of different queues that receive different classes of service. A simple example is a system that recognizes two kinds of jobs: interactive jobs and batch jobs, with each type having its own ready queue. The scheduler treats them differently in order to give the interactive jobs a responsive character at the expense of the batch jobs. A number of variations is used. Batch jobs may be blocked entirely while there are interactive jobs in the queue. Alternatively, the interactive jobs may get most of the time slices, with batch jobs allocated only a small percentage.

Interprocess Communication

In the discussion of processes, we noted that very often it is convenient to break a large job into a number of smaller pieces and implement each of those smaller pieces as a separate process. Such a strategy introduces the requirement for inter-process communication, the ability for processes to pass data and signals among themselves. There are two basic methods of interprocess communication: message passing and shared memory. For a good discussion of interprocess communication using message passing, see Peterson and Silberschatz[6] and for an implementation of message passing, see Comer.[7] Since message passing is beyond the scope of this book, we will not consider it further. But we will need to consider some of the problems associated with processes sharing memory.

    The implementation of memory sharing by processes takes a variety of forms. For example, some systems build the notion of processes into a programming language.[8] Typically, such systems achieve sharing of memory by sharing programming language variables among processes. However, such systems have a serious

---

[6]J. L. Peterson and A. Silberschatz, *Operating System Concepts*, pp. 329–340.

[7]Douglas Comer, *Operating System Design: The Xinu Approach*, (Englewood Cliffs, N.J.: Prentice-Hall, Inc. 1984), pp. 93–98.

[8]See P. Brinch-Hansen, "The Programming Language Concurrent Pascal", *IEEE Transactions on Software Engineering*, 1,2 (June 1975), pp. 199–207, and P. Brinch-Hansen, *Programming a Personal Computer*, (Englewood Cliffs, N.J.: Prentice-Hall, Inc. 1982).

drawback with respect to the kind of example system we want to develop in the following chapters. Because they are language based, they depend upon internal run-time structures that are typically only built by the compiler of their special programming language. For example, shared variables among processes are often implemented by a stack mechanism that takes the form of a tree, with the various branches containing the variable bindings that the various processes have access to. The implication of this is that all processes that are to run on such a system must be written in the programming language specific to that system. Or, at least, they must be developed in such a way that they have compatible internal run-time structures. This would mean that we could not run existing DOS applications on such a system, and this is far too limiting a condition.

Nevertheless, systems with shared variables and the example system that we will develop, have a common problem that they both must solve. Both must synchronize the access to the shared portions of memory. This is a problem that we have seen before. Recall the circular buffer example from Chapter 5. The buffer that handles incoming characters, **a**, is shared by two processes—the main program, which is removing characters from **a** to echo them on the screen, and the interrupt service routine, which is putting characters into **a** each time it gets a real-time interrupt from the comgear. In Chapter 5, we presented a possible interleaving of instructions that would cause data to be lost if we allowed it to happen. In the simple example that we will be developing, we will run into the same kind of problem.

This problem is called the "critical section" problem, which was first characterized by Dijkstra.[9] Simply put, this problem recognizes that processes sharing data contain certain "critical sections" of code that must not be allowed to access the shared data simultaneously. If a critical section associated with a variable is executing, no other critical section associated with that same variable in another process may be allowed to execute until the critical section currently executing is complete. Brinch-Hansen[10] suggests the following set of assumptions about critical sections sharing a common variable:

1. No more than one process at a time may be in its critical section.
2. A process cannot be indefinitely delayed from entering its critical section.
3. A process cannot remain inside of its critical section indefinitely.

Critical sections in the example to be developed will take the same approach that was used in the example of Chapter 5. We will use the interrupt system to assure mutual exclusion of critical sections. Actually, this solution does more than

[9]E. W. Dijkstra, "Cooperating Sequential Processes," Technical Report EWD-123, Technological University, Eindhoven, the Netherlands, 1965. Reprinted in F. Genuys (ed.), *Programming Languages*, (London: Academic Press, 1968), pp. 43–112.

[10]P. Brinch-Hansen, *Operating System Principles*, (Englewood Cliffs, N.J.: Prentice-Hall, Inc., 1973), p. 84.

just assure mutual exclusion of critical sections sharing the same variable. It assures mutual exclusion of all critical sections, which is really more than we need, but it is difficult to beat the efficiency of this solution because of its hardware implementation.

File System Management

File system management is an area that we have chosen not to consider. We will bypass the problem of developing a file management system in the simple example by using the file management system provided by DOS. For the most part, DOS provides everything we need in a file management system. There is, however, one critical element of a file management system for a single-user multitasking system that DOS does not provide, and that is file locking.

As long as processes are run to completion without preemption, one after the other, files cannot be simultaneously read and/or written by more than one process. Thus, DOS, as a single stream operating system, automatically protects files from damage that might be caused by accidental, concurrent operations upon them. However, as soon as we introduce the possibility of concurrent processes, that protection no longer exists. Thus, a multitasking system has the requirement for a file management mechanism that locks a file when first accessed by a process and prevents any other process from accessing that file until the lock has been released by the closing of the file, or the termination of the process. We will not address the problem of file locking in the forthcoming extended example, but will leave it as an exercise for the reader. See Exercise 8.4 in Chapter 8.

Sharing Code

In a multitasking system, code must be written so that it can be shared. Consider those functions within the system that provide operating system services to the processes running under the multitasking system. The routine that handles the keyboard will be invoked by many different processes, but we want to have only one copy of the code. What are the characteristics that make code sharable?

Sharable code must have the characteristic that two or more processes can be executing the code simultaneously without it affecting the results of any of the computations. Code that has this characteristic is called "reentrant" code. In order to assure reentrancy, the code must be non-self-modifying, and there must be a separate copy of the machine registers and data area for each separate process that will execute the code. For example, the DOS and BIOS keyboard service routines may be called from several of the processes running under the multitasking system. Since we cannot guarantee that each call to a keyboard service routine will run to completion without waiting (on the user), we must be able to interrupt the keyboard service routine and give the CPU to some other process that potentially can do some computation. Since the process that gets the CPU also may issue a keyboard service interrupt, we must assure that the DOS and BIOS keyboard service routines are reentrant. In the case of these keyboard service routines, we will replace much of their functionality with code that we have designed to be reentrant.

We cannot depend on all of the code in the system to be reentrant. In general, DOS and BIOS interrupts are unlikely to be reentrant. We certainly cannot depend on it. We can depend on their being "serially reusable"—that is, if we can be assured that they run from start to finish for any one interrupt request without being reentered, then we can assure that each interrupt request will operate as it is supposed to. We are guaranteed that these interrupts have the serial reusability property, because they must have that property to operate correctly in a single stream operating system.

In the forthcoming example, we will provide some mechanisms that prevent preemption of the CPU when a DOS or BIOS interrupt request is executing. This will be sufficient to assure the integrity of the DOS and BIOS interrupt operation and thus, assure the serial reusable property that we desire.

Deadlock and Its Prevention

Deadlock is the condition in a multitasking system, where some set of processes is blocked waiting on events that cannot occur. That is, every process in the set that could potentially be allocated the CPU is unable to run, because it lacks some resource held by some other member of the set. Let us see how this might happen.

Consider once again the situation in which we have two processes, A and B, that want to write their output to the system printer. Let us also assume that both want to use the system plotter as well, and further, that the multitasking system that they are running on does not have a virtual device facility. It only allocates real devices to processes. Now if process A starts out and writes some information to the printer, it will be allocated the printer resource. Next, suppose that process A is preempted and process B begins its execution by drawing a plot on the system plotter. Process B will be allocated the plotter. Now process B is ready to print on the printer, but when it issues its request, the multitasking system will suspend process B because the printer is already allocated to process A. Now process A is rescheduled and issues a plot request on the system plotter. Since the plotter is already allocated to B, process A is suspended—so we have a deadlock. Process A has the printer and cannot proceed until it is allocated the plotter. Process B has the plotter and cannot proceed until it is allocated the printer. Unless something is done, neither job can run to completion.

Peterson and Silberschatz[11] describe the conditions that must be simultane-

---

[11]Peterson and Silberschatz, *Operating System Concepts*, p. 261.

ously true in order for deadlock to occur. These conditions allow the potential for deadlock; they do not assure it. These conditions are:

1. *Mutual exclusion.* At least one resource on the system is not inherently sharable. As the printer in the example, such a resource, by its nature, needs to be allocated to a using process from the first moment the process requests the resource until it is done with the resource. If one process has such a resource, other processes are excluded from having it.

2. *Hold and wait.* Some process in the system must be holding some resources and waiting for other resources held by other processes. In the example, process A had the printer and was waiting for the plotter.

3. *No preemption.* The system will not preempt the resources in contention. In the example, our simple multitasking system has no mechanism for preempting the printer from process A so that process B could proceed.

4. *Circular wait.* There is a circular chain of processes holding one resource and waiting on another resource held by the next process in the chain. In the example, the circle contained only processes A and B. Process A held the printer and was waiting on the plotter, and process B held the plotter and was waiting on the printer.

Deadlocks are handled in three basic ways: prevention, avoidance and recovery. Prevention means that we structure our system so that one or more of the foregoing conditions cannot hold. For example, the keyboard and display management subsystems described in the following chapters use prevention to eliminate the possibility of deadlock. More specifically, the display is transformed into a sharable resource by the creation of virtual displays that the system maps onto the real display via the notion of windows. By this mechanism, each program deals with its own independent (virtual) display, which can never be requested by any other process. Of course, since we can accommodate only a finite number of windows, there is still the potential contention for allocation of virtual windows, but this is prevented by another method—a process cannot be initiated unless there is a window available for it. (See Exercise 6.1.)

In contrast, the keyboard, another inherently nonsharable resource, is handled by another method. The keyboard is time-shared, with the user deciding which process gets the keyboard, and when. That is, the user chooses a *current* window, thereby assigning the physical keyboard to the process running in that window. When the user decides to make some other window current, the keyboard becomes assigned to the new current window. Processes, running in windows other than the current window, that read the keyboard are suspended until the user decides to make their window current once again. This keyboard management scheme prevents deadlock by eliminating the no-preemption condition. It allows the keyboard to be preempted.

Prevention is not always adequate to handle deadlock. Sometimes it is better to avoid it by knowing enough about the behavior of a process before it executes. For example, if we know that two processes both will be using the system printer, we can simply delay the initiation of one of the processes until the other has completed it execution. In some systems, the user must declare resources before his or her job is initiated. This strategy is known as avoidance.

Deadlock recovery is the approach of letting deadlock happen and then trying to back out of it. Recovery can be quite difficult and is beyond the scope of this book.

For more on the subject of deadlock see Calingaert,[12] Peterson and Silberschatz,[13] or Shaw.[14]

6.2 WINDOW OR DISPLAY MANAGEMENT

The fundamental job of the window or display manager (DM) is to allow each concurrent application to interact with the shared resources (e.g., the display and the keyboard) as if it were the only application on the computer. This entails arbitrating between applications competing for nonsharable resources (for example, the keyboard) and mapping between the virtual resources and the real resources (for example, between windows and the physical display). An application program typically would assume that it alone had access to the whole display and therefore could write text anywhere on the display. The DM must map from this virtual video display assumed by the application program to the real video display, confining text written by each program to the window with which it is associated. Specifically, when the application program executes the BIOS interrupt to move the cursor to some arbitrary screen position, the DM must map from the coordinates supplied by the application program—that is, the virtual coordinates—to the appropriate absolute coordinates on the real video display. Similarly, when an application asks, via a BIOS interrupt, for the current position of the cursor, the display manager must return the virtual display coordinates of the current cursor position for the window associated with that application.

The DM establishes the regimen whereby many virtual screens are mapped onto the fixed space of the real display screen. Since the real display typically provides less total space than the sum of all of the simultaneous virtual displays possible, only a portion of each virtual display may be visible at a given time. The display manager accomplishes this mapping via the notion of a "window." A *window* is a rectangular area on the real display through which some portion of an associated virtual display screen can be seen. Figure 6-1 illustrates the format of

[12]Peter Calingaert, *Operating System Elements: A User Perspective*, (Englewood Cliffs, N.J.: Prentice-Hall, Inc., 1982), p. 105.

[13]James Peterson and Abraham Silberschatz, *Operating System Concepts*, p. 256.

[14]Alan Shaw, *The Logical Design of Operating Systems*, p. 203.

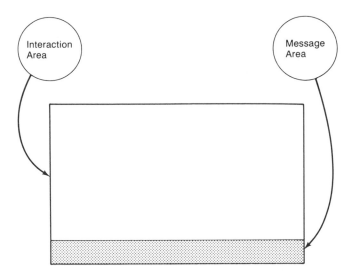

Figure 6-1　An Example Physical Layout of a Window

the windows to be used in our example DM. The term window motivates another commonly used term for the DM, *window manager*.

Text or Graphics

The rules that govern the behavior of windowing systems—that is, the window regimen—vary widely and each regimen has its own particular advantages and disadvantages. One major division arises based on whether or not the DM can handle graphical images. Graphical regimens typified by the Apple Macintosh or the Digital Research GEM interface allow the use of "icons"—that is, small pictures—to represent storage areas, menu options, and so forth. Such graphical regimens are quite popular and are widely believed to make the target system easier for the novice user to learn. These regimens also have their drawbacks: They are often slow and large because they typically have a more complex internal structure than text-based window regimens.

On the other hand, text-based window regimens allow only text characters to appear on the screen. This tends to reduce their internal complexity and thereby their memory requirements. On the downside, application programs that produce graphical output on the display will not run under text-based window regimens. The first release of IBM's Topview is a typical text-based window regimen.

Mouse input devices can be integrated into either regimen, but are more likely to be used in the graphic regimens and, indeed, are more likely to be needed there. Consideration of mouse devices, their handling, and the internal structures that they require is beyond the scope of this book.

Overlayed or Tiled

The second major method of categorizing window systems is based on whether the windows are "overlayed" or "tiled." Overlayed windows behave much like pieces of paper. Lay one on top and partially overlapping another, and part of the information on the bottom sheet is obscured by the top sheet. Just as with sheets of paper, a partially obscured window may be moved to the top of the stack, and the previously obscured information reappears, unaffected by its temporary elimination. Like pieces of paper, windows can generally be moved around the screen so that the windows in the set that the user is currently attending to do not obscure each other. Unlike paper, however, overlayed windows can generally be enlarged and contracted by the user in order to meet his or her needs of the moment.

In contrast, a tiling-based windowing system places windows adjacent to each other, like floor tile, with no part of any window overlapping any other. Typically, tiled windows, once established, cannot be moved, expanded, or contracted. Like overlayed windows, tiled windows usually allow the existence of virtual displays that are larger than that portion that shows through the window itself. Both systems typically provide some mechanisms for moving these virtual displays with respect to their window so that different parts of the virtual display may be moved under the window and thereby be viewable by the user.

The tradeoffs between overlayed and tiled windows revolve around issues of display manager complexity and the arguments take on something of a religious fervor. Neither system seems to be clearly better on all points, but overlaying window systems currently appear to be more popular.

Like text-based window systems, window systems based on tiling tend to be less complex and smaller because they do not require fully general window movement, growth, and contraction. In addition, fixing the position and size of the windows eliminates the need for window stacking logic and vastly simplifies the "clipping" algorithms that determine what information is showing through each window. Since tiling systems do not allow overlap, each clipping region is a simple rectangle, whereas with overlapping windows, the clipping regions can become complex polygons made up of many separate rectangles. The algorithms for clipping rectangles are relatively simple and fast. That is, with rectangles it is easier to decide what information can and cannot be seen through the window than it is with more complex polygons.

Tiling systems also simplify the algorithms that are required to track the cursor. If the window system allows a mode of cursor movement that does not confine the cursor to a single window, the DM must constantly keep track of the cursor position and decide with which window it is currently associated. Tracking algorithms map from a physical position on the screen to a logical position within the underlying data structures. This is similar to the clipping problem. It is simpler to determine whether a given coordinate position is within a rectangle than it is to determine whether it is within an arbitrary polygon made up of multiple rectangles. These characteristics tend to reduce the size and complexity of tiled systems. However, restricting the user to pre-placed, fixed-sized windows also reduces the flexibility of the system for the user.

Transcription and Image Buffers

Another variation among window systems is based on whether or not there is a buffer associated with the virtual display. Buffers are necessary with overlayed windows and typical with tiled windows. Only the simplest systems, such as the simple example shown in this book, do not keep some kind of buffer other than the video display buffer. For text-based systems, these buffers often are called "transcription buffers" and they can be quite large, at least in the vertical dimension. Window systems with transcription buffers usually provide facilities for scrolling the transcript backwards and forwards for the purpose of reviewing the record of interaction between the computer and the user, or for the purpose of copying complex commands to be edited and then reexecuted.

Why have buffers that are separate from the video display buffer? There are several reasons:

1. The user may want to keep more information than can be seen through the window.
2. The user may want to reduce temporarily the size of the window without losing information.
3. The user may want to put temporarily one window on top of another without losing information.

In each case, part of the information is temporarily hidden. Nevertheless, the user wants to reserve the option to redisplay that information in the window at some future time. While information of interest may be destroyed in the video display buffer, it is preserved in the image or transcription buffer, and is thus available for redisplay.

Process per Window

The final variation that we will discuss is based on the relationship between windows and processes. There are two basic architectures:

1. Many windows managed by one process
2. Many windows managed by the DM, such that each window is associated with one active process, also called the *process per window model*

First, consider the architecture providing many windows associated with a single process. Text editors are a good example of this mode of operation. The text editor that I use allows me to edit several files at once by providing a separate window for each file up to a maximum of four windows. It also provides up to twelve separate buffers and mechanisms for changing the relationship between buffers and windows. Therefore, I can edit up to twelve files at once. In this kind of a system, the application program (i.e., the editor) is responsible for managing the windows and the buffers, mapping keystrokes into the correct window, displaying portions of the files, and so forth. In other words, each such application program must incorporate many of the DM's functions in addition to providing the application logic.

An alternate philosophy, and the one used in the example presented, is that all window management functions—keyboard management functions and so on—are the province of the DM and should be largely invisible to the application program running under the DM. This often is called the one (active) *process per window* metaphor. We will incorporate this architecture into the simple example developed in the succeeding chapters.

Which mode of operation is preferable depends very much on the job that the user wishes to perform. In the near future, it is unlikely that I will give up my multiwindow text editor in order to perform word processing within a window-based multitasking system. On the other hand, there are times when I wish to perform more than one task at a time on my machine—for example simultaneous printing and compiling. Alternatively, I may want to run several applications and move information among them. In these latter two cases, a multitasking system with one process per window may be just what I need. Most users probably will want different modes of operation at different times. The facilities described in Chapter 3 provide the basic tools for building applications that create and manage several windows under control of a single application, and the example developed in the remaining chapters provides the basic functions for building display managers that provide the one process per window architecture.

EXERCISES

6.1. Consider the discussion of deadlock prevention. We described how the extended example (from the following chapters) alters the character of the display, an inherently non-sharable resource, in order to prevent deadlock. Indicate which of the four deadlock conditions cannot hold because of this window management system.

Chapter 7

A Multitasking
Window System

This chapter is dedicated to developing a general specification of the example window-based multitasking system that we will develop throughout the remainder of this book. We will present a set of requirements for the system, describe some of the key architectural features, and develop a few basic concepts and utility functions that will be required to understand the following chapters.

7.1 REQUIREMENTS

We want to develop a target multitasking system with one task (or process) per window. The target system will be complex enough to illustrate many important multitasking and windowing concepts, yet simple enough to be described in detail in a few chapters. Our objective is to develop an aid to the study of system software concepts, not to develop a production system. Therefore, we have omitted from the system, features and facilities that we felt were of a lesser pedagogical importance and were not necessary to produce a rudimentary working system. Similarly, we have omitted from the discussion those functions that are computationally straightforward or that present concepts of lesser importance.

The target system will run on top of DOS. This means that no special equipment, such as in-circuit emulators, or development environments are required to work with the system. Any user with a properly configured PC can begin to extend, modify, and experiment with the system.

What do we mean by a properly configured PC? We mean one that has:

1. DOS 2.0 or above

2. A hard disk (a floppy based system will work, but it is cramped)

3. A 256K memory is minimum, but more is better

4. A C compiler that handles full C per Kernighan and Ritchie,[1] allows memory models that exceed 64K, and allows the integration of functions written in assembler (we have used Computer Innovations C86 compiler for the functions shown in this book, but the Lattice C compiler is another strong candidate)

5. An 8086 assembler that is compatible with the DOS linker and the C compiler

6. A monochrome display, if you want to use the system as written; some minor modifications will allow a color monitor to be used (see the Exercises in Chapter 9)

The target system will run most existing DOS applications unaltered. The only ones that are excluded are those that do not use DOS or BIOS to access shared resources—for example, the display and the keyboard; those that alter the DOS system in ways incompatible with the multitasker—for example, replace interrupt 0x21; those that depend upon I/O redirection (see Exercises 8.3 and 8.4 in Chapter 8); or those that are based on the assumption that the full display is theirs—for example, programs using full-screen I/O. See the Exercises in Chapter 9 for modifications that would allow programs using full-screen I/O to run.

The target system will provide a text-based user interface. We do not require that it support graphics—for example, icons—or run programs that produce graphics on the display.

The target system will provide four fixed-position, fixed-size windows. See the Exercises in Chapter 9 for mechanisms whereby more windows, and windows that are adjustable, can be allowed.

The target system will be based on a one process per window user interface model. One of the windows is to be designated the current window and this is to be indicated by the fact that its border is highlighted. Fixed resources that are not inherently sharable—for example, the keyboard—are to be assigned to the current window. This provides a background/foreground style of operation. The current window will be the foreground process—that is, the one interactively involved with the user, and all other processes are background tasks, which are assumed to require no resources other than CPU, memory, disk, and display. Should a background task require the keyboard, as indicated by a keyboard read, it will be suspended. When a window containing a suspended process becomes the current window, execution of that process will be resumed.

The user will control the target system via interaction with the command processor, which runs as part of the scheduler process. To get the command processor's attention, the user must strike the Control-Break key combination. The

[1]Brian W. Kernighan and Dennis M. Ritchie, *The C Programming Language,* (Englewood Cliffs, N.J.: Prentice-Hall Inc., 1978).

command processor will provide facilities for suspending processes, resuming processes, initiating new processes, and changing the current window.

These requirements provide a target system that is rich enough to be interesting and yet is simple enough to be described in the remainder of the book.

7.2 ARCHITECTURE

In this section, we will make a few decisions that will affect the basic architecture of the example system. First, let us consider how we will schedule programs for execution.

Scheduling

We want programs to exhibit an interactive character, since they are to run in a personal computer environment rather than a batch environment. We also want to multitask the personal computer—that is, run several programs at once. Further, we want to be able to run existing DOS programs unaltered. Due to these three requirements, we are forced to choose a scheduling strategy similar to one used on time sharing systems: round-robin scheduling with preemption. Why? In order to get the interactive behavior within a multitasking environment, we must time share the CPU. In order to execute existing DOS programs unaltered, we must be able to preempt these programs when their time cycle is exhausted. Preemption will ensure that the interactive programs are not delayed indefinitely by some DOS program that is in the midst of a long, tight computing loop.

We will choose to run the scheduler as a process, process 0, and run it in its own window, window 0. The implication of the scheduler running as a process is that the scheduler process will receive control after each preemption.

We will organize the command processor (or "shell") as part of the scheduler, and therefore the interaction with the command processor will appear in window 0. In addition, this window provides a place for system traces, an invaluable aid in debugging the system.

The User Interface

An important design question is how does the user control the behavior of the multitasker? That is, how does the user indicate the desire to change windows, abort or suspend programs, start new programs, and so forth? Clearly, this must be at a level above the normal interaction with programs. While the user is interacting with the application programs, almost anything that is typed can be valid data for the program. We do not want to usurp any possible program data characters, and thereby prevent a perfectly legitimate program from running under the multitasker, or allow it to run but mask some of its functionality. DOS reserves one keystroke for exactly this kind of higher-level control function, and that is the Control-Break key. DOS provides only limited functionality with Control-Break. Generally, it just kills the current program. We will redefine Control-Break as the keystroke that gets the attention of the command processor (i.e., our shell program) and nest a rich set of functionality beneath it. This strategy will limit the potential conflict with the data expectations of application programs running under the multitasker.

The System Interface

Given that we have decided to run the multitasker on top of DOS, we have to establish an architecture for the interface between the multitasker and DOS. This is made more complex by the fact that we must run existing programs, and those programs are free to invoke DOS or BIOS functions. How do we establish this interface to DOS short of completely replacing DOS? Fortunately, many micro-computer operating systems, such as DOS, have chosen to establish operating system services and many machine-level services (BIOS) as software interrupts. This provides a flexibility that we would not have if the operating system services were supplied by system library routines that were loaded with the application programs. The set of operating system and machine-level services available to application programs is defined, at any moment, by the set of interrupt vectors associated with those services. Change those interrupt vectors and you have altered the functionality of the operating system and machine services. And that is exactly what we will do. We will completely replace certain vectors with our own code— for example, the program termination interrupt. Others—for example, the DOS function interrupt—we will simply intercept and alter to our purposes. As far as the application programs are concerned, they are interacting with unaltered DOS or BIOS. In a following section, we will describe in greater detail the method for accomplishing this interface redefinition.

7.3 SYSTEM OVERVIEW

Figure 7-1 presents an abstract view of the example multitasking system that we will develop in the remaining chapters. It is organized into three kinds of services:

1. *Software interrupt services*. These interrupt service routines either replace or modify the corresponding DOS and BIOS service routines. They represent the system interface that is seen by the application programs (processes) running on top of the multitasking system.
2. *Hardware interrupt services*. This is the system's software timer which is driven by the hardware clock. It includes the process preemption logic whereby the CPU is recaptured from executing applications when their time slice is exhausted.

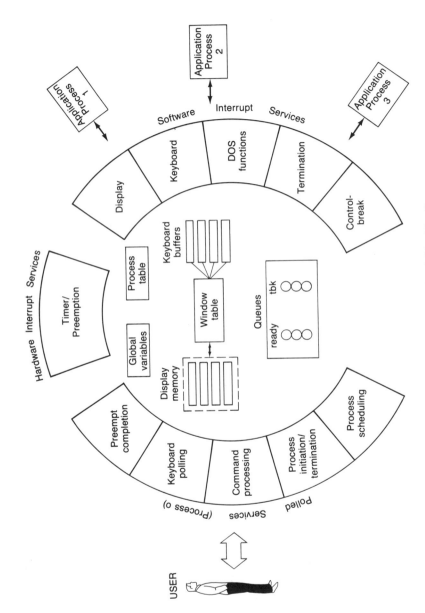

Figure 7-1 Organization of the Multitasking System

3. *Polled services.* These services are organized as part of process 0, the system process. These services include the processing of commands from the user, and other internal system services, the most important of which is process scheduling. When discussing scheduling, we will often refer to process 0 as the "scheduler."

Shown in the center of these services are the major data structures that tie the system together:

1. The global system variables, which provide information about which process is currently executing and how long it has been executing.
2. The process table, which contains information describing the state of each process in the system.
3. The window table, which contains description and status information for each of the windows on the display. Part of this status information is a keyboard buffer for each window in the system. The window table is the central structure involved in managing both the keyboard and the video display.
4. The queues, which keep track of which processes are in what state. The queues are central to the scheduler's task of deciding what it must do next.

7.4 BASIC DATA STRUCTURE CONVENTIONS

In order to understand the interface between the assembly language portions of the system and the C portions of the system, it is necessary to understand a number of conventions that are used throughout.

The DOS Interface

In our previous discussion of the multitasking system architecture, we asserted that the method by which we will interpose the multitasker between applications and DOS is replacement and interception of DOS and BIOS interrupts. Table 7-1 identifies the specific interrupt vectors affected, the name of the function that is invoked by the interrupt, and a short description of that function. Each one of these interrupt vectors corresponds to one of the abstract interrupt services shown in Figure 7-1.

The general pattern is that those DOS and BIOS functions that are not completely replaced, are relocated to interrupt vectors in the "user interrupt" area (interrupt vectors 0x60 through 0x67). This means that the C routine that emulates a DOS or BIOS function can still use the original DOS or BIOS function. For example, the keyboard software interrupt 0x16 emulator, **bios16**, can use software interrupt 0x63, containing the relocated pointer to the original BIOS keyboard interrupt routine, to read the physical keyboard in order to move characters from

TABLE 7-1 INTERRUPT ORGANIZATION FOR THE MULTITASKING SYSTEM

Interrupt Vector	Multitasker or DOS Function	Function Description
0x10	**capt10**	Intercept routine for BIOS video display functions. Calls multitasking routines **writeac, setpos, readpos,** and **scroll**.
0x16	**capt16**	Intercept routine for BIOS keyboard functions. Calls multitasking routine **bios16**.
0x1b	**kbbreak**	Intercept routine invoked if Control-Break has been struck. Calls multitasking routine **kbint**.
0x1c	**preempt**	Intercept routine for post timer interrupt processing. Will preempt processes that have exceeded their time slice.
0x20	**capt20**	Intercept routine for process termination interrupt. Calls multitasker's routine **wrapup** which calls **harikari**.
0x21	**capt21**	Intercept routine for DOS functions. Calls a variety of multitasker routines depending on the specific DOS function. Some functions are just passed through to the original DOS code.
0x60	------	Pointer to structure containing multitasker's global variables and process table.
0x61	DOS int 21	Pointer to original DOS function processing code.
0x62	DOS int 20	Pointer to original DOS termination processing code.
0x63	BIOS int 16	Pointer to original BIOS keyboard code.
0x64	BIOS int 10	Pointer to original BIOS video code.
0x65	DOS Cntrl-Brk	Pointer to original DOS Control-Break code.

the general BIOS keyboard buffer into the specific keyboard buffer associated with the current window. Then, when the application program issues a BIOS 16 interrupt, the C emulator routine **bios16** will fetch the character from the keyboard buffer associated with the window in which the reading application is running. Thus, the original BIOS interrupt service routine does the physical keyboard reads, while the BIOS interrupt 16 emulator, **bios16**, does the virtual keyboard reads. In general, the operation of **bios16** is typical of the way most of the interrupt emulators work. Of course, the details of each emulator differ, but the general pattern is much the same.

Interrupt intercept routines, which call the interrupt emulator routines, have a stereotypical structure; they

1. Save all registers on the stack.
2. Increment **lvlcalls** and set **noprmpt** to prevent preemption and then switch stacks to the temporary stack, if not yet done.
3. Sometimes analyze the registers to determine specifically what function is being requested, such as with interrupt 0x21, which has a rich set of subfunctions.
4. Set up the C register environment, set up the arguments to the C emulator routine, and call the emulator.

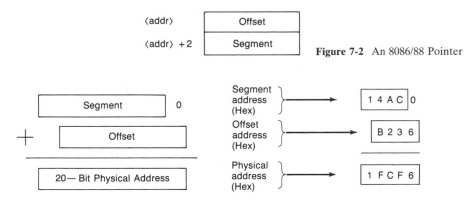

Figure 7-2 An 8086/88 Pointer

Figure 7-3a Physical Address Computation   **Figure 7-3b** Example of Physical Address Computation

5. Upon return from the emulator, reduce the level of preempt protection and, if returning to the application program proper and not just to a lower level of intercept code, restore the application program's stack.

6. Restore the registers from the stack and return.

Pointers

The 8086/88 can access up to one megabyte of storage with its addressing mechanism. Each 8086/88 address consists of two parts:

1. A 16-bit offset, which addresses bytes and can address up to 64K bytes

2. A 16-bit segment address, which addresses paragraphs[2] and can address up to 64K paragraphs.

Figure 7-2 shows these two parts stored as a pointer, with the offset stored in memory before the segment address. When the 8086/88 generates a physical address from a segment and an offset, it shifts the segment four bits to the left, filling the four bits with zeros. Then it adds the two quantities, resulting in a 20-bit physical address. Figure 7-3a illustrates the computation of a physical address. Figure 7-3b provides an example of this computation for a segment address of 0x14ac and an offset of 0xb236. This address will often appear in documentation as 14ac:b236. The machine will address byte 0x1fcf6.

The C86 compiler library provides two routines for mapping between the segment:offset form of an address and the 20-bit form of an address. **ptrtoabs** maps from a segment:offset pair to a 20-bit address, and **abstoptr** maps from the 20-bit address form to one of the many possible segment:offset pairs. We will need two additional address manipulation functions, **pfission** and **pfusion**. These functions are shown in Figure 7-4. **pfission** disassembles a pointer passed to it and stores the

[2]A paragraph is 16 bytes.

segment and offset portions in two C variables. **pfusion** performs the inverse operation, building a pointer out of a segment:offset pair.

In all of the code that will be shown in the remaining chapters, we will be working within a big memory model. Therefore, C pointers will use the 8086/88 pointer format.

Assembly Language/C Interface Conventions

In a number of examples that will be shown in later chapters, we will call C routines from assembly language routines. In order to make this work, we have to assure that the **es** register points to the Program Segment Prefix (PSP) of the multitasker

```
typedef char *pointer;
pfission(ptr,seg,off)           /*disassemble a pointer into segment and offset*/
        pointer ptr;            /*pointer to be disassembled*/
        unsigned int *seg,*off; /*segment and offset results of disassembly*/
        {
        union
                {
                pointer addr;
                unsigned int aparts[2];
                } lptr;
        lptr.addr = ptr;
        *off = lptr.aparts[0];
        *seg = lptr.aparts[1];
        }


pfusion(ptr2ptr,seg,off)        /*Fuse a segment and offset into a pointer*/
        pointer *ptr2ptr;       /*Pointer to the ptr to be fused*/
        unsigned int seg,off;   /*Segment and offset to be fused*/
        {
        union
                {
                pointer addr;
                unsigned int aparts[2];
                } lptr;

        lptr.aparts[0] = off;
        lptr.aparts[1] = seg;
        *ptr2ptr = lptr.addr;
        }
```

Figure 7-4 pfission and **pfusion**

and the **ds** register points to the multitasker's data area. Since control will often be coming (via interrupts) from application programs with different PSPs and data areas, we must restore the multitasker's **es** and **ds** register values so that global data references work properly. The assembly language code shown in Figure 7-5 restores the proper values for these registers. The double word _PSPSEG is a compiler generated pointer to the PSP of a C program.

```
        extrn   _PSPSEG:dword     ;pointer to multitasker's psp
        .   .   .
        .   .   .
        .   .   .

;       restore ds to SCHEDULER'S data group
        mov     ax,dgroup
        mov     ds,ax

;       restore es to SCHEDULER'S psp
        mov     ax,word ptr dgroup:_PSPSEG+2
        mov     es,ax
```

Figure 7-5 Restoring Registers

The second step of calling a C function is setting up the arguments. In order to transmit arguments to the C routines being called, we must put the arguments on the stack, with the first argument nearest the stack top and the last argument the farthest down in the stack. This is illustrated in Figure 7-6. Notice that a pointer argument is stored in the format discussed earlier, with the offset at the lowest address of the pair.

DOS Function Error Conventions

Many of the DOS functions indicate their success or failure by the state of the carry flag in the flags register on their return. If the carry flag is set, it indicates that an error occurred and the error code will be in the **ax** register. If the carry flag is clear, no error occurred. This convention frequently will be applied in the assembly code that follows.

Assembly Language Conventions

The assembly macros shown in Figure 7-7 establish a number of conventions that we will use throughout the remainder of the book.

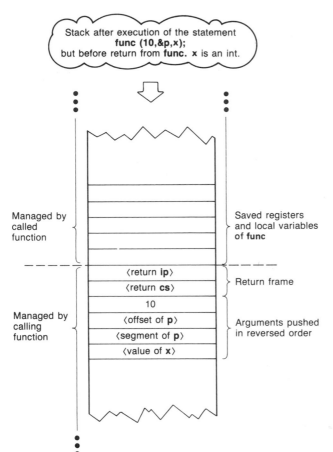

Figure 7-6 C Calling Convention Example

```
savesp    equ    0           ;offset of savesp field in proctbl entry
savess    equ    2           ;offset of savess field in proctbl entry
pspseg    equ    4           ;psp segment address for this process
windno    equ    6           ;window number associated with this process
mynoprmt  equ    28          ;noprmpt flag for this process
mylvlcal  equ    30          ;lvlcalls flag for this process
intstkss  equ    32          ;seg addr of temp stack for interrupts
prntr     equ    34          ;printer on flag
reserv    equ    36          ;reserved (2 words)
calllvl   equ    40          ;reserved
retproc   equ    42          ;reserved
retvalue  equ    44          ;reserved
waitsig   equ    46          ;reserved
msgbuf    equ    48          ;reserved
clock     equ    0           ;offset of clock in sched's global struct
procno    equ    2           ;offset of procno in sched's global struct
```

Figure 7-7 Assembly Macros

```
numprocs  equ      4          ;offset of numbprocs in sched's global struct
proctbl   equ      6          ;offset of proctbl in sched's global struct
tbk       equ      1256       ;offset of tbk queue in sched's global struct
ready     equ      1260       ;offset of ready queue in sched's global struct
doze      equ      1264
premptd   equ      1868       ;offset of preempted process number
noprmpt   equ      1870       ;offset of flag that prevents preemption of sys calls
lvlcalls  equ      1872       ;offset of variable with no. of lvls of sys calls

pentsize  equ      50         ;size of a process entry

blkszoff  equ      3          ;offset of block size in dos record preceding psps

eoi       equ      20h        ;end of interrupt code

;
;         MACROS FOR ASM ROUTINES
;

savreg    macro


;         save registers of current process on stack
;         in canonical order

          pushf
          push     ax
          push     bx
          push     cx
          push     es
          push     si

          push     dx
          push     di
          push     ds
          push     bp
          mov      bp,sp      ;set up access to arg
          endm

resreg    macro

;         restore registers

          pop.     bp
          pop      ds
          pop      di
          pop      dx
          pop      si
          pop      es
          pop      cx
          pop      bx
          pop      ax
          popf
```

Figure 7-7 (Continued)

```
        endm

;          access to registers stored in canonical form

bpreg     equ    0
dsreg     equ    2
direg     equ    4
dxreg     equ    6
sireg     equ    8
esreg     equ    10
cxreg     equ    12
bxreg     equ    14
axreg     equ    16
flgreg    equ    18
retip     equ    20
retcs     equ    22
retflg    equ    24

;          establish access to global variables via (es:si)

gaccess   macro  reg

          mov    reg,abs0                        ;segment containing pointer to globals
          mov    es,reg
          assume es:abs0
          les    si,dword ptr gcopy              ;load address of globals into (es:si)
          endm

saveint   macro reg

;          save flags and turn off interrupts

          pushf
          pop reg
          cli
          endm

resint    macro reg

;          restore interrupt status
          push   reg
          popf
          endm

;          increase and decrease level of software protection flags lvlcalls & noprmpt

protect   macro  globseg,globoff,reg
          mov    reg,true
          mov    globseg:noprmpt[globoff],reg
          add    word ptr globseg:lvlcalls[globoff],1
          endm
```

Figure 7-7 (Continued)

```
unprotec macro    globseg,globoff
         local    done
         sub      word ptr globseg:lvlcalls[globoff],1
         cmp      word ptr globseg:lvlcalls[globoff],0
         jg       done
         mov      word ptr globseg:noprmpt[globoff],0
done:
         endm
;
;        switch to upper (unused) portion of scheduler's stack for execution
;        of interrupt 21 functions in C

switchsk macro    globseg,globoff,sshold,sphold
         local    noswitch

;        dont switch if the scheduler is running
         cmp      word ptr globseg:procno[globoff],0
         je       noswitch

;        only switch at level 1 (already using stack for levels 2 and above)
         cmp      word ptr globseg:lvlcalls[globoff],1
         jg       noswitch

         push     ax                             ;temporarily save ax
         push     dx                             ;temporarily save dx

         mov      ax,globseg:procno[globoff]     ;currently executing process number

;        sphold   temporarily used to hold proc entry offset
;        sshold   temporarily used to hold proc tbl offset
;        globoff  temporarily used to hold temp stack segment

;        get process table entry for current process

         mov      sphold,pentsize ;size of a proctbl entry
         mul      sphold          ;proctbl entry size * index into proctbl(ax)
         mov      sphold,ax       ;sphold now offset of current process into proctbl
         mov      sshold,si       ;offset of global variables to sshold
         add      sshold,proctbl  ;(es,sshold) points to beginning of proctbl
         add      sshold,sphold   ;add proctbl offset to relative offset of entry
         mov      globoff,sshold  ;assure total offset in an index or base reg

         mov      globoff,globseg:intstkss[globoff]
                                  ;get temp stack's segment address

         pop      dx              ;restore dx value
         pop      ax              ;restore ax value

;        save current ss and sp regs

         mov      sshold,ss
         mov      sphold,sp
```

Figure 7-7 (Continued)

```
;         switch to ss and sp of temp stack (last 1000h bytes of program's region)
;         (no interrupts while switching stacks)
          cli

          mov     ss,globoff
          mov     sp,0ffeh                            ;point to last word

          push    sshold                              ;save ss & sp of old stack
          push    sphold

          sti
noswitch:
          endm

restorsk  macro   globseg,globoff,ssreg,spreg
          local   norestor

;         dont restore if the scheduler is running
          cmp     word ptr globseg:procno[globoff],0
          je      norestor

;         restore stack only if at level one (since we will be immediately
;         returning to level 0)
          cmp     word ptr globseg:lvlcalls[globoff],1
          jne     norestor


;         no interrupts while switching stacks
          cli

          pop     spreg
          pop     ssreg
          mov     sp,spreg
          mov     ss,ssreg

          sti
norestor:
          endm

;         set carry bit to indicate error or no error in DOS fnc
setcarry macro
          local noerr,alldone
;         Set carry bit to indicate results of DOS call
          pushf                                       ;save flags
          jnc     noerr
          or      word ptr retflg[bp],0001h           ;set carry bit in return frame
          jmp     alldone
noerr:
          and     word ptr retflg[bp],0fffeh          ;reset carry bit in return frame
alldone:
          popf                                        ;restore flags
          endm
```

Figure 7-7 (Continued)

```
setzero    macro
           local    nonzero,done
;          Set zero flag in return frame to indicate results of DOS call
;          (e.g., for DOS function 6)
           pushf                                        ;save flags
           jne      nonzero
           or       word ptr retflg[bp],0040h           ;set zero bit in return frame
           jmp      done
nonzero:
           and      word ptr retflg[bp],0ffbfh          ;reset zero bit in return frame
done:
           popf                                         ;restore flags
           endm
```

Figure 7-7 (Continued)

These definitions are contained in a header file, **process.h**, that is included in all assembly programs. It provides:

1. Macro variables that are initialized to the offsets of the variables in the multitasker's global variable block and the offsets of fields within the process table.

2. Macros to save and restore registers—**savreg** and **resreg**. Associated with these macros are a set of pre-initialized macro variables that contain the offsets of the various registers stored on the stack by **savreg**. These offsets simplify the job of setting up register return values for the various interrupt emulation functions. We just stick the return values in the proper place on the stack and **resreg** will automatically assure that the registers contain the proper values on return.

3. The macros **setcarry** and **setzero**, which set the carry and zero flag in the flags register image stored on the stack by **savereg**. See the section on DOS Function Error Conventions in this chapter.

4. The macro **gaccess**, which establishes the (**es, si**) register pair pointing to the multitasker's global variable block.

5. The macros **saveint** and **resint**, which save and restore the current flags to and from a register specified as an argument.

6. The macros **protect** and **unprotec**, which increment and decrement the multitasker's preemption protection call level counter, **lvlcalls**. The **noprmpt** preempt protection flag is set by **protect**, and reset by **unprotec** when **lvlcalls** becomes zero.

7. The macro **switchsk**, which switches to a temporary stack at the **lvlcalls** = 1 level and is a nop at **lvlcalls** > 1. The macro **restorsk** performs the inverse operation.

The following chapters will use these requirements and conventions in the creation of a simple multitasking system with a window-based display manager.

Chapter 8

Concurrency
Structures
and Their Management

8.1 DATA MANAGEMENT

A good way to understand a large and complex system is to start by studying its data structures. Data structure definitions represent abstract snapshots of the inputs and outputs of the various modules of a system. The following sections describe the family album for the example multitasking system.

Global Data Structures

The management of several processes running concurrently depends on global data structures that keep track of information about the state of the multitasking system in general, information about each process, and information about tasks that the multitasker must perform. These data structures are:

1. The multitasking state variables such as the multitasker's clock
2. The process table, which contains one entry for each process running
3. The queues of things for the scheduler to do—for example, terminate processes.

These global data structures are contained in a C structure that is global to the multitasker's main program. The definition of this structure in shown in Figure 8-1.

The scheduler keeps its own software clock, called **clock**, which is updated each time the hardware clock interrupt fires, 18.2 times per second. **clock** is updated

```
struct globals  /*Global variables providing status of the processes*/
        {
        unsigned int clock;             /*Scheduler's clock - used for preemption*/
        unsigned int procno;            /*Process number of currently executing process*/
        unsigned int numbprocs;         /*Number of currently active processes*/
        process proctbl[MAXPROCS];      /*Process tbl array*/
        queue   tbk;                    /*List of processes to be killed*/
        queue   ready;                  /*Ready list*/
        queue   doze;                   /*List of sleeping processes*/
        qentry qe[MAXQENTS];            /*Table of queue entries*/
        unsigned int preempted;         /*Number of process just preempted, else 0*/
        unsigned int noprmpt;           /*Flag indicating system call in progress,
                                           no preemption allowed.*/
        unsigned int lvlcalls;          /*No. of levels of systems calls in progress*/
        };
```

Figure 8-1 Multitasking System Global Variables

by a service routine called **preempt**, which is called by the BIOS system clock service routine when it completes its duties.

The variable **clock** is used mainly to measure the time slices of executing tasks. In the implementation described here, each time slice is nominally six ticks of **clock**, or about one-third of a second. Other factors, such as the user continually typing input characters to an active process, can alter the actual length of the time slice that any individual process receives. See the keyboard management section of Chapter 9 for more information on variation in time slices.

The variable **procno** is the process number of the currently active process. Process numbers are small integers that are assigned to a process upon its initiation. Each process number is unique and serves as an index to the process table entry associated with the specific process identified by that process number. Thus, process numbers can be thought of as unique names for the processes running in the system.

The multitasker always keeps track of which process currently is allocated the CPU (i.e., the currently executing process) by storing its process number in **procno**. This variable allows system interrupts to determine exactly which process is making the request and thereby determine which window is the target of messages and output. For example, the routine that writes a character to the display needs to know in which window to put the character.

The system keeps track of how many processes currently exist in the system via the variable **numbprocs**. Other simple variables indicate the number of the process just preempted (**preempted**) and the fact that the currently executing process cannot be preempted at this moment (**noprmpt** and **lvlcalls**). The flags **noprmpt** and **lvlcalls** prevent preemption of any process currently executing a DOS function, except under certain very special circumstances described in Chapter 9. More specifically, the flag **noprmpt** indicates that the process should not be preempted at this point. The integer **lvlcalls** indicates how many recursive call levels we have descended into DOS functions. It is incremented on each DOS call and decremented on each return. **noprmpt** will not be set to zero until we have returned all the way out of DOS—that is, until **lvlcalls** becomes zero. This mechanism is one of the prices that we pay for running the multitasking system on top of DOS.

Why not allow preemption within a DOS function? The basic reason is that the DOS functions are not reentrant. They were designed for a single-tasking system and, therefore, they assume that any one call to a DOS function will be completed before another is initiated. This assumption makes them "serially reusable" but not reentrant. It is a reasonable assumption for a single-tasking system. However, in order to be truly reentrant, DOS would have to have some data structure analogous to the process table and would have to execute each DOS function with respect to a specific process, in the sense that each execution of a DOS function would need to have its own local data storage area.

Other items within the global data are the process table (**proctbl**), which is discussed later; the scheduler's queues (**tbk**, **ready**, and **doze**); and an array (**qe**) of queue entry elements out of which queues are built. The queue **tbk** is a list of process numbers of processes that need to be terminated—that is, their storage returned to DOS, their entries removed from the process table, and so forth. The queue **ready** is a list of process numbers that are ready to run and the next process to get the CPU is chosen from this list. The scheduler, which is actually the main loop of the main program within the multitasking system, gets the CPU immediately whenever any other process gives it up. Among the actions that the scheduler performs each time it gets the CPU is to terminate all processes whose process numbers are on **tbk** and to choose the next process to run from those on **ready**.

For routines that are part of the multitasking system, a global variable **g** is provided to point to the structure of global variables. Application programs running under the multitasker also have limited access to the global variables through calls to process management functions such as **resume** and **suspend** that may be loaded as part of the application program's load module. This allows applications to be written that take greater advantage of the multitasking environment. For example, if a program is interacting with another program according to a "your turn, my turn, your turn" interaction protocol, the program could be designed to resume itself after its turn, since it knows that it can do no useful computation until the other program has performed its computation. By resuming itself, it gives the other program a shot at the CPU and does not waste a lot of "busy waiting" CPU cycles, which are performing little useful computation and preventing other processes from performing useful computation.

In order to allow application programs to use process management functions such as **resume**, the multitasker provides a pointer to the global structure at a fixed location in memory, address 0x180. This address is one of the interrupt vectors that the DOS system has designated as "user software interrupts." In order for an application program to use functions such as **resume** or **suspend**, it must declare a global variable **g**, and during its initialization, it must call a routine provided in the scheduler's library called "**access_globals**," whose only job is to transfer the pointer stored at 0x180 to the global variable **g**.

Programs that would need to take advantage of process management functions such as **resume** and **suspend**, in order to enhance their own operation or that of the system, are the exception rather than the rule. In general, it is not necessary for application programs to do anything special to run under the multitasking system.

The Process Table

The job of the process table, shown in Figure 8-2, is to keep information about each process. Some fields, such as the process name field, provide a convenient identifying mechanism for the user, but most fields provide important information about the state of the process or its location. For example, the fields **savess** and **savesp** are instrumental in saving the computational state of a stopped process. They provide a pointer to the top of the stack on which the registers of the stopped process are stored. Other fields are defined as follows:

1. The **windno** field provides the window table index of the window associated with the current process. (See Chapter 9 for a definition of the window table and a detailed discussion of its structure and management.)

```
typedef struct procentry          /*Process table entry*/
        {
        unsigned int savesp;                 /*Saved sp register*/
        unsigned int savess;                 /*Saved ss register*/
        unsigned int pspseg;                 /*Psp segment address of this process*/
        unsigned int windno;                 /*Window number assoc with this proc*/
        unsigned int procstate;              /*State of the process*/
        char procname[MAXPNAME+1];           /*Name of the process*/
        int pnum;                            /*Process number for this entry*/
        unsigned int mynoprmpt;              /*The noprmpt flag for this process*/
        unsigned int mylvlcalls;             /*The lvlcalls flag for this process*/
        unsigned int intstkss;               /*Seg of temp stack for dos 21 interrupt*/
        unsigned int prntr;                  /*Printer flag*/
        unsigned int reservd[2];             /*Reserved*/
        unsigned int calllvl;                /*Reserved*/
        unsigned int retproc;                /*Reserved*/
        unsigned int retvalue;               /*Reserved*/
        unsigned int waitsig;                /*Reserved*/
        unsigned int msgbuf;                 /*Reserved*/
        } process;
```

Figure 8-2 The Process Table Entry Definition

2. The **pnum** field contains the process number of the process table entry, which should be the same as the index of the process table entry. It is provided for validation and integrity checking.

3. The **procstate** field indicates the state of this process—that is, whether it is running, ready, suspended, or terminating.

4. The **pspseg** field provides the segment address, in paragraph form, of the Program Segment Prefix (PSP) of the program. This address is the start of the block of storage associated with the program.

5. The **intstkss** field is the segment address of a block of storage reserved at the end of the program for a temporary stack. The temporary stack is used during DOS interrupts that are intercepted by the multitasker and this helps protect against accidental overflow of the user stack. Some of the multitasker's routines that emulate DOS functions use more stack space than their DOS counterparts and without task switching this can cause trouble. The DOS function "tree," for example, uses part of the PSP area for its stack and this area is insufficient to handle the storage requirements of the multitasker's video output routines.

6. The **mynoprmpt** and **mylvlcalls** fields are for storing the global variables **noprmpt** and **lvlcalls** on those exceptional occasions when we allow a task switch in the middle of a DOS function. The exceptional occasion is when a keyboard read is issued by a process that is not currently allocated the keyboard. See the keyboard management section of Chapter 9 for more detailed information.

7. The **prntr** is the flag that determines whether or not a character being written to the video display should also be echoed on the printer.

8. The remaining fields are reserved for future enhancements and will not be required by the portions of the system described in this book.

Queues and Their Management

Queues are the way that the multitasker keeps track of items that it has to attend to. In the simple example described in this book, we have only two queues: the list of processes to be terminated, **tbk**, and the list of processes that are ready to run, **ready**. In a system with more capability, we would be likely to find a number of queues. For example, there would probably be a delay queue containing sleeping processes—that is, processes that are waiting some period of time before they begin execution.

A queue is just a pair of integers that index entries in the array **qe**. The C definition of a queue is shown in Figure 8-3. Queue entries, also defined in Figure 8-3, are made up of four integers. The integers **prev** and **next** are indexes into the array **qe** and represent links to the previous element of the queue (or zero, if there is no previous element), and the next element of the queue (or zero, if there is no next element). The field **pn** is for a process number, and the field **delay**, not used in the simple example, is projected to contain an integer that indicates when to awaken the sleeping process designated by the **pn** field of that entry. Figures 8-4 and 8-5 graphically show some example queues. By definition, a queue contains two elements, a header and a trailer, that do not contain queue entry data. They simply mark the top and bottom of the queue and are introduced to simplify the queue management algorithms.

For brevity, we will not present the definitions of the functions that manage queues but will only present their specifications in Figure 8-6.

Memory Management

One of the important jobs of the multitasking system is to manage the memory of the personal computer. When it needs to load and initiate a new program, it must find a sufficient amount of memory. Similarly, when a program terminates, the

```
typedef int qindex;      /*Index of a qentry record in the qentry table*/
typedef int pindex;      /*Index of a process record in the proctbl table*/

typedef struct qnt       /*Queue entry structure*/
        {
        qindex prev;             /*Previous queue entry*/
        qindex next;             /*Next queue entry*/
        int pn;                  /*Process number*/
        int delay;               /*Delay value (if delay queue)*/
        } qentry;

typedef struct que       /*Queue head and tail structure*/
        {
        qindex qhead;            /*Index of head entry of queue*/
        qindex qtail;            /*Index of tail entry of queue*/
        } queue;
```

Figure 8-3 Definition of **queue** and **qentry**

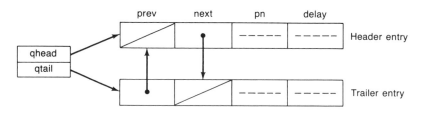

Figure 8-4 An Empty Queue

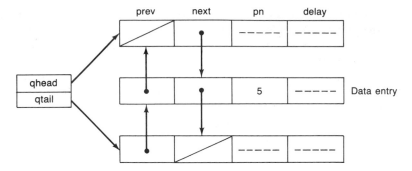

Figure 8-5 A Queue Containing One Element

```
qindex allocqe()
        This function searches the array qe looking for an available qentry
        cell. An entry is considered to be available if both the next and
        prev fields are zero. It returns the index of the available entry,
        or ERROR (-1) if none is available.

queue *createqueue(q)
        queue *q;

        The variable q is a C pointer to a queue location. This function
        creates an empty queue like that shown in Figure 8-4 and
        initializes the integers at location q to the indexes of the
        queue header element and trailer element, respectively.
        It returns q.

dump_any_queue(r,who)
        queue *r;
        char *who;

        This trace function prints out the contents of a queue pointed to
        by the C pointer r. The character array who contains the name
        of the routine that asked for the dump. The name is used as a title
        of the dump to identify the context.


int empty(q)
        queue *q;

        This function returns TRUE if the queue pointed to by the C pointer
        q contains no elements, else it returns FALSE.


int enqueue(item,tail)
```

Figure 8-6 Specification of Queue Management Functions

```
        int item;
        qindex tail;

        This function adds an element at the end of a queue, putting the value
        item in the pn field of the added entry.
        The variable tail is the index of the
        trailer entry for the target queue. It returns item.

qindex find(item,head)
        int item;
        qindex head;

        This function searches for the first element on the queue whose pn
        field contains item and returns the index of the queue entry, or
        zero if there is no such item in the queue.

int push(item,head)
        int item;
        qindex head;

        This function creates a new queue entry at the front of the queue
        whose header element is indexed by head. It puts item in the
        pn field of the entry and returns item.

int pop(head)
        qindex head;

        This function removes the first element of a queue whose header element
        is indexed by head and returns the pn field of the removed entry.
        If the queue is empty, it returns EMPTY (-1).

int remove(item,head);
        int item;
        qindex head;

        This function removes the queue entry whose pn field contains item
        and returns item.
```

Figure 8-6 (Continued)

system needs to return the memory used by that program to the pool of available
memory so that it can be reused. Typically, this is accomplished by the operating
system, which keeps a list of blocks of memory with a few bytes of prefix information
that indicates (1) whether the memory is available or in use, (2) how big the block
of memory is, and (3) a link to the next block of memory if there is one. This is

```c
#include <stdio.h>
#include "errno.h"                /*C86 Error codes*/
#include "proc.h"                 /*Global definitions*/
unsigned get_mem(nbytes,rbytes) /*Get nbytes of memory from DOS*/
        long nbytes;      /*Number of bytes requested*/
        long *rbytes;     /*Number of bytes actually returned*/
        {
        struct regval sreg ;
        struct regval rreg;
        unsigned flags;

        if(tracef)
                printf("get_mem: Requesting %lx bytes of memory from DOSn",nbytes);

        sreg.bx = (unsigned) (nbytes / PARASIZE + 1);
        sreg.ax = 0x4800;

        /*now call dos function dispatcher*/
        flags = sysint21(&sreg,&rreg);
        *rbytes = ((long) rreg.bx) * PARASIZE;  /*Actual no of bytes found*/

        if(((flags & CARRY_BIT) && rreg.ax == ENOMEM) || *rbytes < nbytes)
                printf("get_mem: Insufficient memory to load program\n");
        if ((flags & CARRY_BIT) && rreg.ax == ECNTLBLK)
                printf("get_mem: DOS Memory control blocks destroyed\n");

        if(tracef)
                printf("get_mem: Returning %lx bytes of memory at segment %x\n",
                       *rbytes,rreg.ax);

        return(rreg.ax);
        }


unsigned ret_mem(segpsp)              /*Return memory starting at segpsp to DOS*/
        unsigned segpsp;              /*Segment address of the block*/
        {
        struct regval srv ;
        unsigned flags;

        if(tracef) printf("ret_mem: Returning memory at %x to DOS\n",segpsp);

        srv.es = segpsp;
        srv.ax = 0x4900;

        /*now call dos function dispatcher*/
        flags = sysint21(&srv,&srv);
        if(tracef)
                printf("ret_mem: Results-- flags=%x, ax= %x\n",
                       flags,srv.ax);
```

Figure 8-7 get_mem, ret_mem and memsize

```
        return(srv.ax);
        }


unsigned int memsize()
/*      This function reads the memory size using BIOS interrupt 0x12.
        On return ax contains the number of 1K contiguous blocks of memory
        on the system.
*/
        {

        struct regval rreg;

        /*now call bios*/

        sysint(0x12,&rreg,&rreg);
        return(rreg.ax);
        }
```

Figure 8-7 (Continued)

exactly what DOS 2+ does and it provides interrupt 0x21 functions for application programs to allocate, de-allocate, and modify blocks of memory. For the details of DOS data structures and memory management scheme, see Redmond, 1984.[1]

We will use the DOS memory management functions to allocate memory for new programs to be loaded. This is in keeping with our philosophy to let DOS perform system functions whenever possible.

DOS provides three memory management functions. Function 0x48 allocates a block of memory, 0x49 de-allocates a block of memory—that is, returns it to DOS—and 0x4A modifies a block of memory by growing it or shrinking it. We will incorporate functions 0x48 and 0x49 into the functions **get_mem** and **ret_mem**. These functions are used by the multitasker for program creation and termination, respectively. Figure 8-7 contains the definitions of these functions plus an associated function, **memsize**, a function to read the size of memory using a BIOS 0x12 interrupt. Figure 8-8 contains the definition of **errno.h**, a header file containing definitions required by **get_mem**. The **errno.h** header file is part of the C86 compiler distribution and is reprinted with permission of Computer Innovations, Inc. Appendix B contains the **proc.h** header file which includes additional definitions required by these functions.

8.2 PROCESS MANAGEMENT

The process management functions that have been implemented in the simple example include context switching, scheduling the next process to run, process creation, program loading, and process termination.

[1]William J. Redmond, "Managing Memory: A Guided Tour of DOS 2.0 Memory Management," *PC Tech Journal*, 2, No. 2 (August 1984), 43–62.

```
/*       error return definitions for math functions
*/

extern int errno;                /* contains the error indicator */
#define EDOM 33                  /* arg not in domain of function */
#define ERANGE 34                /* result too large */

/*       error return definitions for system function calls
*/

#define EFNUM 1                  /* invalid function number */
#define ENOENT 2                 /* File not found */
#define EPNFOUND 3               /* Path not found */
#define EMFILES 4                /* Too many open files (no handles left) */
#define ENACCESS 5               /* Access denied */
#define EHANDLE 6                /* Invalid Handle */
#define ECNTLBLK 7               /* Memory Control Block Destroyed */
#define ENOMEM 8                 /* Insufficient memory */
#define EMBA 9                   /* Invalid memory block address */
#define EENV 10                  /* Invalid Environment */
#define EFORMAT 11               /* Invalid Format */
#define ECODE 12                 /* Invalid access code */
#define EDATA 13                 /* Invalid Data */
#define EDRIVE 15                /* Invalid drive was specified */
#define ECDIR 16                 /* Attempt to remove the current directory */
#define EDEVICE 17               /* Not same device */
#define EFILES 18                /* No more files */

/* CI-C86 I/O error codes
*/

#define EFULDSK 119              /* Full disk */
#define ESKCDEV 120              /* Seek on Character Device */
```

Figure 8-8 errno.h

Context Switching

Context switching is the process of saving the state of the currently executing process, initializing the computer with the state of the next process to chosen run, and then transferring control to that process. The multitasker must perform a number of housekeeping tasks during a context switch. For example, it must keep track of which process is running, and it must reset the clock.

The multitasker establishes a canonical form for the state of a stopped process, shown in Figure 8-9. This canonical form captures all of the information necessary to restart the process in exactly the same state it was in when a context switch occurred. New processes are initialized in exactly this canonical form so that they can be treated like any other stopped process. See the discussion of the function **startstate** later in this chapter.

The canonical form chosen for saving the state of a stopped process is a design issue. Where do we store the register values, and what are the tradeoffs of the various options? There are two basic design options. One can choose to store all of the register values in the process table proper, or one can just store a pointer to the place where the registers are stored. The design tradeoffs between the two options are multitasker space requirements and convenience versus application stack overflow risks. If we choose to store all of the registers in the process table, we must pre-allocate enough space to handle the maximum number of processes. This increases the space requirements of the multitasker. It also makes the storing and reloading of the registers somewhat more clumsy. It is easy just to push values on the stack and later pop them off. On the other hand, storing registers on the stack may cause stack overflow in programs that have cut their stack requirements

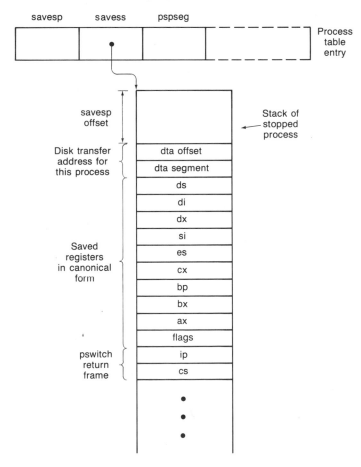

Figure 8-9 Canonical Form of a Stopped Process

down to the bare minimum. While this is certainly a risk, it is not as bad as it first sounds. Most interrupt service routines temporarily store some or all of the registers on the stack; so to run at all, application programs must provide enough stack space to accommodate these interrupts. This small amount of space for register saving plus a strategy of switching to a temporary stack during DOS functions (discussed later) are enough to make the risk of stack overflow minimal. Given a low risk and considering the advantages of space minimization and convenience, we have chosen to store all of the registers, except the **ss** and **sp** registers, on the stack. The **ss** and **sp** registers are stored directly in the process table on a context switch, and they provide the link to the remaining registers.

All context switches are effected by a function named **pswitch**, which stores the register values on the stack as shown, retrieves and stores the disk transfer address (a DOS mechanism providing a fixed position buffer for disk transfers), and then stores the stack segment and offset registers in the process table fields **savess** and **savesp**, respectively. **pswitch** then reloads the stack segment and offset registers from the process entry of the process to be restarted and performs the inverse of the save operation. The definition of **pswitch** is shown in Figure 8-10.

Context switches occur in one of two ways. Either the executing process explicitly gives up the CPU, say by calling **resume** or **suspend**, or the executing process runs out of time in its time slice and is preempted. Both situations ultimately cause the context switch by a call to **pswitch**, but the route by which they arrive at that call is quite different. There is nothing unusual or unconventional about explicit context switches, but preemptive context switches involve an unusual and interesting set of mechanisms. In order to explain these mechanisms, we will need to describe the clock mechanism used by the BIOS system.

Recall in Chapter 4 our discussion of the structure of the hardware interrupts. Various pieces of hardware—the timer, keyboard, asynchronous communications gear, and so on—are tied to the 8259A interrupt processor chip. Each time one of these pieces of gear sends an electrical signal to the 8259A, it causes an interrupt to occur in the 8088, and if properly enabled, the 8088 halts whatever it is doing to process the interrupt. The highest priority hardware interrupt is the timer interrupt, interrupt 0x8. It fires 18.2 times per second on the PC and each time it fires the BIOS interrupt service routine updates the PC's time of day clock and times out the diskette motor. This service routine supplies one other important service. Just before it returns from the interrupt, it performs a software interrupt on vector 0x1c allowing for a user service routine that will get called 18.2 times per second independent of what else is happening within the system. This is exactly the mechanism that we need to grab control from an executing process.

The 0x1c vector is initialized to an **iret** instruction when the system is booted, so most of the time it is just a no-op. The multitasker replaces this no-op with a pointer to an interrupt service routine called **preempt**, shown in Figure 8-11.

It is **preempt**'s job to decide whether or not to stop the currently executing process and switch control to the scheduler so that it can schedule another process

```
        include model.h
        include prologue.h
@code   ends

abs0    segment at 0h
        public  gcopy
        org     180h
gcopy   dw      ?                       ;pointer to scheduler's global variable struct
abs0    ends


@code   segment
        include process.h

a1      equ     @ab+6                   ;offset of argument on the stack

        public  pswitch
pswitch proc    far


;       save registers of current process on stack
;       in canonical order
        pushf
        push    ax
        push    bx
        push    bp
        mov     bp,sp                   ;set up access to arg
        push    cx
        push    es
        push    si

        push    dx
        push    di
        push    ds
;       get and save (on the stack) the dta of the current process

        mov     ax,2f00h
        int     21h
        push    es
        push    bx

;       allow access to scheduler's global data via (es:si)
        mov     ax,abs0                 ;segment containing pointer to globals
        mov     es,ax
        assume  es:abs0
        les     si,dword ptr gcopy      ;load address of globals into (es:si)
```

Figure 8-10 pswitch

```
        mov     ax,es:procno[si]          ;currently executing process number

;       get process table entry for current process

        mov     di,pentsize     ;size of a proctbl entry
        mul     di              ;proctbl entry size * index into proctbl(ax)
        mov     di,ax           ;di now offset of current process into proctbl

        mov     bx,si
        add     bx,proctbl      ;(es,bx) points to beginning of proctbl

;;;;;;;;;;;;;;;;;;;;;;; start of basic process switch ;;;;;;;;;;;;;;;;;;;;;;;;;;;;;

;       save flags and turn off interrupts

        pushf
        pop dx
        cli


;       save sp and ss in proctbl entry

        mov     es:savesp[bx+di],sp
        mov     es:savess[bx+di],ss

;       save noprmpt and lvlcalls flags

        mov     ax,es:noprmpt[si]
        mov     es:mynoprmt[bx+di],ax
        mov     ax,es:lvlcalls[si]
        mov     es:mylvlcal[bx+di],ax

;       get process table entry for next process and switch processes

        mov     ax,a1[bp]       ;get target process number from stack
        mov     di,pentsize     ;size of a proctbl entry
        mul     di              ;proctbl entry size * index into proctbl(ax)
        mov     di,ax           ;di now offset of current process into proctbl

        mov     bx,si
        add     bx,proctbl      ;(es,bx) points to beginning of proctbl

        mov     ax,a1[bp]                 ;get arg pno again before resetting ss
        mov     es:procno[si],ax          ;reset currently executing procno

;       restore sp and ss
```

Figure 8-10 (Continued)

```
        mov       sp,es:savesp[bx+di]
        mov       ss,es:savess[bx+di]

;       restore noprmpt and lvlcalls flags

        mov       ax,es:mynoprmt[bx+di]
        mov       es:noprmpt[si],ax
        mov       ax,es:mylvlcal[bx+di]
        mov       es:lvlcalls[si],ax

;       restart scheduler's clock

        xor       ax,ax                     ;zero accumulator
        mov       es:clock[si],ax

;       restore dta of new current process

        pop       ax                        ;retrieve offset of dta
        pop       ds                        ;retrieve seg of dta
        push      dx                        ;save flags temporarily
        mov       dx,ax                     ;ds:dx contains pointer to dta
        mov       ax,1a00h
        int       21h                       ;set dta address

;       restore interrupts
        popf

;;;;;;;;;;;;;; end of basic process switch ;;;;;;;;;;;;;;;;;;;;;;;;;;;;;;;;;;;;;

;       restore registers

        pop       ds
        pop       di
        pop       dx
        pop       si
        pop       es
        pop       cx
        pop       bp
        pop       bx
        pop       ax
        popf
        ret                   ;restart the target process code
pswitch endp
        include epilogue.h
        end
```

Figure 8-10 (Continued)

```
        include model.h
        include prologue.h
@code   ends

abs0    segment at 0h
        extrn   gcopy:far        ;pointer to scheduler's globals
abs0    ends

@code   segment
eoi     equ     20h              ;end of interrupt signal

        extrn   pswitch:far      ;function which switches contexts
        include process.h

SCHEDLER equ    0                ;procno for scheduler

        public  preempt
preempt proc    far

;       delete from stack the interrupt return frame pointing to system timer.
;       Preempt will complete timer's functions.

        cli             ;allow no interrupts while fooling with global data

        pop     ax                      ;remove ip
        pop     ax                      ;remove cs
        pop     ax                      ;remove flags

;       save registers

        push    bx

        push    bp
        mov     bp,sp                   ;set up access to arg
        push    cx
        push    es
        push    si
        push    dx



;       allow access to scheduler's global data via (es:si)

        mov     ax,abs0
        mov     es,ax
        assume  es:abs0
        les     si,dword ptr gcopy      ;(es,si) now points to beg of globals
        mov     ax,es:procno[si]        ;currently executing process number
        mov     cx,es:clock[si]         ;scheduler's clock
        add     cx,1                    ;tick clock
        mov     es:clock[si],cx         ;store new clock value
        cmp     ax,0                    ;is scheduler running
```

Figure 8-11 preempt

```
        je      current                 ;if so, resume scheduler regardless of clock
;       scheduler not running

;       assure that we don't preempt a DOS system call

        mov     ax,es:noprmpt[si]
        cmp     ax,0
        jg      current                 ;return to current (DOS interrupt) program
;       ok to switch processes if enough clock ticks have passed



        cmp     cx,6                    ;have there been more than 6 ticks of clock
        jg      resched
;       scheduler not running and clock <= 6
;       resume current process


current:
        pop     dx
        pop     si
        pop     es
        pop     cx
        pop     bp
        pop     bx

;       finish up system timer code
        mov     al,eoi
        out     20h,al                  ;send end of interrupt to 8259a
        pop     dx                      ;restore registers saved by system timer.
        pop     ax
        pop     ds
        iret

resched:                                ;Since scheduler not running & clock > 6,
                                        ;switch to scheduler
                                        ;who will reschedule next process


;       reset clock

        xor     ax,ax
        mov     es:clock[si],ax
```

Figure 8-11 (Continued)

```
;          note number of preempted process so scheduler will put it on ready queue

           mov      bx,es:procno[si]        ;put number of preempted process
           mov      es:premptd[si],bx       ;in global vbl for scheduler

;          Send an eoi so succeeding timer interrupts may proceed.
;          We send the eoi before the call to pswitch because we do not
;          know how long it will be before we return to complete the
;          last few instructions of preempt.

           mov      al,eoi
           out      20h,al                  ;eoi to 8259a

;          switch to the scheduler's context

           mov      bx,SCHEDLER
           push     bx                              ;push arg to pswitch (process # of scheduler)
           call     pswitch
           pop      bx

;          restore registers

           pop      dx
           pop      si
           pop      es
           pop      cx
           pop      bp
           pop      bx

;          restore regs saved by system timer
           pop      dx
           pop      ax
           pop      ds

           iret                ;go back to process that was interrupted by the system timer
preempt endp
           include epilogue.h
           end
```

Figure 8-11 (Continued)

for execution. **preempt** will stop the currently executing process only if three conditions hold:

1. The current process is not the scheduler.
2. The current process has been running for more than six clock ticks, or about one-third of a second.
3. The current process is not in a nonpreemptable state. That is, it is not in the middle of a DOS call.

Upon entry, **preempt** removes from the stack the interrupt return frame pointing back to the system timer service routine. This effectively lets **preempt** return not to the timer code, but to the code that was interrupted by the timer in the first place. The rationale for this is based on the requirements of the hardware, specifically the 8259A. In case **preempt** decides, later in the algorithm, to switch contexts, it could be a long time before control would return to this point in the currently executing process, and therefore, it could be a long time before the system timer service routine sent the 8259A an EOI (End Of Interrupt). The system timer service routine sends the EOI *after* control returns from the user service routine. Since the interrupt system is effectively disabled until the 8259A receives its EOI, the EOI must be sent before contexts are switched, which means that it must be sent from **preempt** and not from the system timer. Since we must assure that only one EOI gets sent, we cannot let the system timer service routine finish up its code. **preempt** must do that. It must send the EOI, restore the registers saved by the system timer, and when control returns to **preempt**, if ever, return directly to the code that was executing when the timer interrupt occurred.

If **preempt** decides to stop the currently executing process, it will call **pswitch** to perform the actual context switch and will designate the scheduler (process 0) as the new process. This allows the scheduler to go once around its main loop, doing housekeeping as required, before it context switches to the next process to execute.

The choice of the size for the time slice should be based on experimentation and on how the system is to be used. The designer wants to choose a time slice that is big enough so that the overhead of context switching is small in comparison to the time spent doing real work. A good rule of thumb is that context switching should take no more than 10 percent of the computational time. On the other hand, the designer wants to choose a time slice that is small enough to retain the user's sense of simultaneous execution. The choice of a time slice of six clock ticks (one-third of a second) for the example system is somewhat arbitrary. Try other time slices and see how they alter the feel of the system.

The Scheduler

The multitasker's scheduler, which is the main loop of the multitasker's main program, runs as process 0 in the system, but it is a special process that can never be preempted because it is a part of every preemption. Whenever an executing process is preempted, **preempt** switches context to the scheduler and lets it schedule the next process to execute rather than scheduling the next process itself. This means that the overhead to change from one executing application process to the next consists of two context switches plus some scheduler computation. If the scheduling were done from within **preempt**, we could eliminate one context switch and reduce the number of times the scheduler executes its main loop. We chose to make the scheduler a special process in order to reduce the possibility of user stack overflow, to simplify the actual context switching process, and to make the timer service routine as short as possible. Since the **preempt** routine is executed on the user stack, we must take care to keep the number of function calls and the number of local variables to be stored on the stack at a minimum. Also, **preempt** and all of the functions that it calls must be run with interrupts off, or we must be sure that no logic path reachable from **preempt** is longer than 55 milliseconds. Should such a path exist and the interrupts be enabled, say by a DOS call, the timer service routine could be called before the previous call to the routine returned. While this is not likely, it is possible given that a lot of complex scheduling activity were organized as part of the system timer function. Therefore, we are careful to keep the amount of computation possible in the timer service logic to a minimum. (See Exercise 8.5.)

The multitasker's main program is shown in its entirety in Figure 8-12, but the discussion will center on the main loop of this program. See Appendix B for global definitions germane to the scheduler. The scheduler is an infinite loop that repeatedly performs five basic tasks.

1. It checks the global variable **gbl.preempted** to determine whether it received control as a result of a preemption, and if so, it puts the number of the preempted process on the ready queue by calling **makready**. This also could have been done by a call within preempt, but performing this housekeeping function at this point is part of the effort to reduce the amount of code to be executed from the timer service routine.

2. It calls **terminate** to complete the termination of any programs on the **tbk** queue. **terminate** returns the program's memory area to DOS, zeros the process table entry, and marks the associated window table entry as not in use.

3. It checks the status of the keyboard. This will result in a call to the keyboard BIOS intercept routine and will cause any characters that are waiting in the BIOS buffer to be put into the keyboard buffer associated with the current window. See Chapter 9 for more details on keyboard management.

4. It invokes **command**, the program that handles interaction between the multitasker and the user, if the Control-Break key has been struck. This interaction is described in detail in Chapter 9.

5. It schedules the next program to be executed.

The scheduling of the next process is a variation on round-robin scheduling. The variation is that the process in the current window—that is, the window to which the keyboard is currently allocated—will be the next process to run if it was interrupted in the midst of a keyboard read and there are characters waiting in the keyboard buffer associated with this process. This tends to eliminate delays between the time a character is typed and the time it is echoed on the screen. If the condition does not hold, the user is probably not typing and tasks are chosen on a pure round-robin basis.

```
#include          <stdio.h>
#include          "proc.h"
#include          "window.h"
#include          "load.h"
#include          "globdefs.h"
#include          "globinits.h"
#include          "_default.c"
#include          "prefmain.c"
main()
        {
        unsigned keyboard_char();
        int jj;
        int i;
        int wpno;
        unsigned int flags;

        extern char _exittbc;

        /*Set up for stack trace on abnormal exit, when exit() is
          called with a non-zero value*/
        _exittbc = '\020';

        disp_level = 0;

        display = abstoptr((unsigned long) 0xb0000);
        cls();
        printf("Printer on value (0-off, 1-on)>");
        scanf("%d",&printer_on);

        initsched();    /*Initialize scheduler's structures*/

        for(i=0;i<5;i++) beep();

        initwindow(1,7,0,5,78);
        initwindow(2,14,0,5,78);
        initwindow(3,21,0,2,78);
        dump_window(1);
        dump_window(2);
        dump_window(3);

        disable(&flags);
        gbl.preempted = 0;
        restore(flags);

        while(TRUE)
                {
                if(gbl.preempted != 0)
                        {
                        if(traceb)
                                printf("Scheduler recognizes process no %d as preempted\n",
                                        gbl.preempted);
                        makready(gbl.preempted);
                        if(traceb)
                                dump_queues("Scheduler after preempt");
```

Figure 8-12 The Main Program

```
                            disable(&flags);
                            gbl.preempted = 0;
                            restore(flags);
                            }

/*Release proc tbl storage and memory for processes on tbk queue*/

            terminate((g->tbk).qhead);

/*Check keyboard to allow any characters waiting in bios buffer to
  migrate into the appropriate window buffer*/

            keyboard_char();

/* The following if statement handles scheduler meta command mode */

            if(break_cmd)
                    {
                    command();
                    }

            if(!empty(&(g->ready)))
                    {
                    /*If non-scheduler process in current window is
                      reading & its buffer
                      is not empty, let it have control first*/

                    wpno = wintbl[cwin].pnumb;
                    if(wpno!= SCHEDULER
                      && ((g->proctbl)[wpno].mylvlcalls > 0)
                      && !emptykeybuf(cwin))
                            {
                            remove(wpno,(g->ready).qhead);
                            jj = wpno;
                            }
                    else    /*Just take processes in round-robin order*/
                            jj = pop((g->ready).qhead);

                    if(traceb)
                            printf("Calling restart on process number %d\n",jj);
                    restart(jj);
                    }
            if(traceb)
                    {
                    dump_queues("scheduler");
                    dump_ptbl("scheduler",2);
                    dump_wins("scheduler");
                    }
            }

      }
```

Figure 8-12 (Continued)

The computation of this special condition is not completely obvious. The scheduler computes the process number of the process running in the current window and assures that it is not the scheduler, since the scheduler cannot be rescheduled. Given that the scheduler is not the process associated with the current window, it then checks the process table variable **mylvlcalls**, which indirectly indicates whether or not the process is reading the keyboard. A keyboard read is the only DOS call that can be interrupted with a context switch before it is complete. Therefore, if **mylvlcalls** is greater than zero, the process is in the middle of a keyboard function. Finally, the scheduler uses the function **emptykeybuf** to check the keyboard buffer associated with the current window. If all of these conditions are true, the process number **wpno** is removed from the ready queue and the process associated with it is restarted.

Process State Change

A process can be in one of four states in our simple example: RUNNING, READY, SUSPENDED, or TERMINATING. The **procstate** field in the process table entry contains an integer code defining the state of the process associated with that table entry. The definitions of these state codes are:

```
#define RUNNING         0       /*Process is running */
#define READY           1       /*Process is ready to run*/
#define SUSPENDED       2       /*Process is suspended*/
#define SLEEPING        3       /*Process is sleeping*/
#define WAITMSG         4       /*Process is waiting for a message*/
#define WAITSIG         5       /*Process is waiting for a signal*/
#define TERMINATING     6       /*Process is being terminated*/
```

We have included some additional states with the expectation of system extensions. (See Exercise 8.6.)

If a process is in the RUNNING state, it has the CPU. If it is READY, it is waiting for the CPU and will be found on the ready queue. If a process is SUSPENDED, it cannot run for some reason. Perhaps it wants to read the keyboard, but the keyboard is currently associated with another window. Finally, a process that is TERMINATING has been stopped and is waiting on the **tbk** queue to have its memory and table resources returned to the system. The valid transitions between these states are defined in the Process State diagram in Figure 8-13. The transition arcs are labeled with the functions that effect those transitions.

A basic utility function that is used by several of the transition functions is **restart**, shown in Figure 8-14. **restart** performs the necessary housekeeping to make the **pno** process the currently executing process. That is, it removes **pno** from the ready queue, sets its state to RUNNING, and does a context switch by calling **pswitch**. It also writes a message to the scheduler's window message area indicating that a process is being restarted. Notice that **restart** turns interrupts off and does

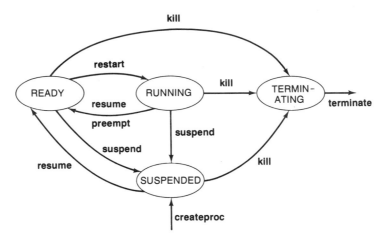

Figure 8-13 Process State Diagram for Example

not turn them back on until after the return from the context switch. This will not of course affect the process that is being restarted since it will have its own state of the interrupt flags saved in its register block. The reason for the interrupts being off is to ensure integrity of the transition. All of the housekeeping involved in transition must be done without any preemptions.

When switching the CPU from one process to another, both processes need to change state. **restart** has half of the responsibility. It is responsible for changing the state of the **pno** process to make it the currently executing process. The other half of the state transition—that is, the transition of the currently executing process to a non-RUNNING state, is more complex and is the responsibility of some higher-level function, such as **resume**. Once the higher-level function has completed its half of the transition process, it calls **restart** to complete the second half.

makready is another utility function used in the process of state transitions. **makready**, shown in Figure 8-15, assures that the specified process number, **pno**, is valid and that it is not the scheduler's process number. Once this is verified, it changes the **procstate** field in the process table and adds **pno** at the end of the ready queue. **outrange** is the function that checks for bad process numbers.

resume, shown in Figure 8-16, handles the change of state of the current process to the READY state. Like **restart**, it writes a message in the scheduler's window message area noting that a process number **pno** is being resumed. It also performs some integrity checks, assuring that **pno** is a valid process number, that the indicated process table entry is in use (because the **pspseg** field is nonzero), and that the process number **pno** agrees with the process number in the window table entry derived from **pno**. If any of these tests fail, a message is written to the scheduler's window message area, and **resume** returns indicating failure. Given that **pno** passes all of the integrity checks, **resume** calls **makready** to change the state of **pno** to READY and put it on the ready queue, and then restarts the scheduler so that it can decide on which process to next schedule for the CPU.

```
#include          <stdio.h>
#include          "proc.h"
int restart(pno)
        int pno;
        {

        extern struct globals *g;
        process *nxt;
        int flags,curpno;

        /*Change the state of the new process to RUNNING and remove it
          from the ready list. */

        strcpy(s,"Restarting pno  (      )");
        converti2s(pno,&(s[17]));
        errormsg(SCHEDULER,s);


        disable(&flags);            /*Disable interrupts while changing globals*/
        curpno = g->procno;
        if(pno!=SCHEDULER) remove(pno,(g->ready).qhead);
        nxt = &((g->proctbl)[pno]);
        nxt ->procstate = RUNNING;


        /*pswitch does the actual process switch*/
        pswitch(pno);
        restore(flags);
        return(NOERROR);
        }
```

Figure 8-14 restart

The method of composing the error message used by **resume** is somewhat unusual and, indeed, quite ugly. Why don't we just use **sprintf** to generate the string and be done with it? Alternately, why not just **printf** the error message to the scheduler's window and be done with it? The second question is easier so, let us answer it first. **resume, suspend** and related routines are embedded deeply within the multitasking system. They must be callable from within any system routine, including the multitasker's low level I/O routines. Therefore, these routines must not try to perform I/O via the C runtime I/O system—for example, via **printf**—because the C runtime I/O system ultimately calls multitasker's low level I/O routines—for example, **displayc**—to perform physical I/O. Now, if a low level I/O routine such as **displayc** should call one of these routines such as **suspend**, we have an infinite loop.

The reason we do not use **sprintf** in these deeply embedded routines is a bit

```
#include <stdio.h>
#include "proc.h"
int makready(pno)
        int pno;
        {

        extern struct globals *g;
        process *curr;

        if(outrange(pno)) return(ERROR);              /*Bad process number*/
        curr = &((g->proctbl)[pno]);

        if (pno!=SCHEDULER)
                {
                curr->procstate = READY;
                enqueue(pno,(g->ready).qtail);
                }
        return(NOERROR);
        }

int outrange(pno)
        int pno;
        {
        if(pno < 0 || pno > MAXPROCS) return(TRUE);
        return(FALSE);
        }
```

Figure 8-15   makready and outrange

more subtle. Basically, we want to avoid the possibility of a **sprintf** operation destroying the state of an incomplete **printf** operation. There are places within the scheduler where we allow **printf**s to be used because we are assured that the scheduler cannot be preempted and therefore these **printf**s will run end-to-end without interruption. However, remember that these **printf**s will ultimately invoke the low level I/O routines and if a low level I/O routine should use **sprintf** or call a function that uses **sprintf**, we would run the risk of altering the state of the incomplete **printf**. Even though in many places it may be safe to use **sprintf** in deeply embedded system routines, our policy is not to because the safety of the I/O should not be dependent upon the particular structure of a particular routine. Therefore, we keep the two I/O subsystems separate. (See Exercise 8-9.)

    suspend, shown in Figure 8-17, handles the change of state of the current process to the SUSPENDED state. It first assures that the specified process is a

```
#include <stdio.h>
#include "proc.h"
#include "window.h"
#include "globdefs.h"
int resume(pno)
        int pno;
        {
        extern struct  globals *g;
        int flags;
        unsigned win;

        strcpy(s,"Resuming pno (     )");
        converti2s(pno,&(s[14]));
        errormsg(SCHEDULER,s);

        win = (g->proctbl)[pno].windno;
        disable(&flags);          /*Disable interrupts while changing globals*/
        if(outrange(pno) ||(g->proctbl)[pno].pspseg == 0
                ||wintbl[win].pnumb != pno)
                {
                strcpy(s,"resume: bad process entry (     ). State = (     )");
                converti2s(pno,&(s[27]));
                converti2s(((g->proctbl)[pno].procstate,&(s[44]));
                errormsg(SCHEDULER,s);
                restore(flags);
                return(ERROR);
                }
        makready(pno);
        if(g->procno!=SCHEDULER) restart(SCHEDULER);
        restore(flags);
        return(NOERROR);
        }
```

Figure 8-16 resume

candidate for suspension. Only RUNNING or READY processes can be suspended. It changes the state of the **pno** process to SUSPENDED. Next, it writes a suspension message to the window message area of the process being suspended. If the **pno** process is in the READY state, it is removed from the ready queue. If the **pno** process is not in the READY state, it must by default be in the RUNNING state—that is, the currently executing process is suspending itself. (See the section in Chapter 9 on keyboard management.) In this case, the scheduler is restarted, unless **pno** is the scheduler, in which case **suspend** is just a no-op. When nonscheduler processes are restarted, **suspend** will change the current window to the scheduler if the process to be suspended is running in the current window. It is then the user's responsibility to decide which window should be the current window. As with **restart** and **resume**, the process state changing takes place with the interrupts

```
#include <stdio.h>
#include "proc.h"
#include "window.h"
int suspend(pno)
        int pno;
        {
        extern struct  globals *g;
        process *curr;
        int flags,cstate;
        unsigned win;
        disable(&flags);            /*Disable interrupts while changing globals*/

        curr = &((g->proctbl)[pno]);
        cstate = curr->procstate;
        win = curr->windno;
        if(outrange(pno) ||(cstate != RUNNING && cstate != READY))
                {
                restore(flags);
                return(ERROR);
                }

        if(pno!=SCHEDULER) curr -> procstate = SUSPENDED;

        strcpy(s,"suspend: suspending procno (    ) in window (    ) cstate (      )");
        converti2s(pno,&(s[29]));
        converti2s(win,&(s[46]));
        convertx2s(cstate,&(s[60]));
        errormsg(pno,s);

        /*If the process being suspended is ready (and therefore, not running),
          assure that it is not on the ready queue*/
        if(cstate == READY) remove(pno,(g->ready).qhead);

        /*If running process suspending self and is in current window,
          must associate keyboard with SCHEDULER*/
        else if(g->procno!=SCHEDULER && pno == (g->procno))
                {
                errormsg(SCHEDULER,"suspend: restarting scheduler");
                if(win==cwin) change_window(0);
                restart(SCHEDULER);
                }
        restore(flags);
        return(NOERROR);
        }
```

Figure 8-17 suspend

off, for the same reason. We cannot tolerate preemptions when only part of the necessary updates are complete. To ensure integrity of the system, state change updates must be atomic operations. All information in the process table and window table must be consistent before we can allow preemptions.

```
#include <stdio.h>
#include "proc.h"
#include "window.h"
int kill(pnum)  /*kill process number pnum*/
        {
        int flags;

        extern struct   globals *g;

        strcpy(s,"kill (      ) called with procno       running");
        converti2s(pnum,&(s[6]));
        converti2s((g->procno),&(s[32]));
        errormsg((g->procno),s);

        if(pnum==SCHEDULER) return(ERROR);        /*can't kill scheduler*/

        if(outrange(pnum) || ((long) (g->proctbl)[pnum].pspseg) == NULL)
                {
                strcpy(s,"kill: attempt to kill a non-existent process (#      )");
                converti2s(pnum,&(s[47]));
                errormsg((g->procno),s);
                return(ERROR);
                }

        disable(&flags);            /*disable interrupts while changing global vbls*/

        (g->proctbl)[pnum].procstate = TERMINATING;

        push(pnum,(g->tbk).qhead);        /*scheduler does actual termination*/

        remove(pnum,(g->ready).qhead);   /*remove it from ready list if there*/

        --(g->numbprocs);

        if((g->proctbl)[pnum].windno == cwin) change_window(0);

        if(g->procno != SCHEDULER)
                {
                restart(SCHEDULER);
                }

        restore(flags);

        /*After scheduler has killed process pnum, control will return here
          (sooner or later), unless this process is the one being killed*/

        return(pnum);
        }
```

Figure 8-18 kill

kill, shown in Figure 8-18, handles the change of state of the current process to the TERMINATING state. Like **suspend**, **kill** performs some integrity checking to assure a good process number and an active process table entry. It changes the state of the process in the process table; pushes the process number, **pnum**, onto the **tbk** queue; removes the process from the ready queue (if it is there); and decrements the number of active processes. If the process being killed is associated with the current window, the scheduler's window is made the the current window. Finally, the scheduler is restarted unless it is already running.

Process Creation

Up to this point, we have been discussing processes that are already running or that are at least ready and able to run. In the next two sections, we will consider the process of creating, loading, and initiating a new process. Let's start with process creation.

The requirement of process creation is to transform a string of characters containing a command, much like a DOS command line, into a loaded process that is in the state SUSPENDED. This is accomplished by the function **createproc**, shown in Figure 8-19. **createproc** and most of the other functions discussed in this section depend on the definitions in the header file **load.h**, shown in Figure 8-20.

```
#include <stdio.h>
#include "proc.h"
#include "load.h"
#include "window.h"
int createproc(prog,wno)
        unsigned char *prog;      /*Pointer to command line*/
        unsigned int wno;         /*Window number for process*/
        {
        process *pt;
        int pno,i,flags;
        pindex allocpe();
        extern int *_PSPSEG;
        extern pblock parmb;
        char msg[128];
        int doserror,loadprog();

        if(tracef) printf("Entering createproc(%s,%d)\n",prog,wno);
        disable(&flags);                 /*Disable interrupts while
                                           changing global vbls*/

        /*Find an empty process table slot*/
        pt = &(g->proctbl);
        i = allocpe();

        if(i<0)
                {
                errormsg(SCHEDULER,"createproc: Too many processes");
```

Figure 8-19 createproc

```
                 restore(flags);
                 return(ERROR);
                 }
if(wno <= 0 || wno > numwindow)
        {
        sprintf(msg,"createproc: Invalid window number (%d) for process %.32s",
                wno,prog);
        errormsg(SCHEDULER,msg);
        restore(flags);
        return(ERROR);
        }

++(g->numbprocs);
pt[i].procstate = SUSPENDED;
pt[i].pnum = i;
strncpy(pt[i].procname,prog,MAXPNAME);

/*Associate process with window wno*/
wintbl[wno].pnumb = i;
pt[i].windno =wno;

/*Set up parmb*/
parmb.cline = (char *) prog;
parmb.fcb1 = 0;
parmb.fcb2 = 0;

/*Inherit environment from multproc*/
parmb.env_seg = ((unsigned int *) _PSPSEG)[ENVOFFSET/2] ;
doserror = loadprog(prog,&parmb,i);

/*If loadprog failed, clean up*/
if(doserror)
        {
        sprintf(msg,"createproc: loadprog failed on command '%.21s', error no. %x",
                prog,doserror);
        errormsg(SCHEDULER,msg);
        delete_window(pt[i].windno);
        zeroarray(&(pt[i]),sizeof(process));
        restore(flags);
        return(ERROR);
        }
else
        {
        sprintf(msg,"createproc: command '%.58s' loaded",prog);
        errormsg(SCHEDULER,msg);
        sprintf(msg,"%.78s",prog);
        errormsg(i,msg);
        }
clear_window(wno);
restore(flags);
if(tracef) dump_ptbl("createproc",5);
return(i);
}
```

Figure 8-19 (Continued)

```
/*** Parameter block used to load overlays (without immed. execution) *******/

typedef struct povblk
        {
        unsigned int env_seg;    /*Segment at which to load file*/
        unsigned int reloc;      /*Relocation factor*/
        }
        poverblock;


/***************** Parameter block used to load and exec progs *************/

typedef struct pblk
        {
        unsigned int env_seg;
        char *cline;
        char *fcb1;
        char *fcb2;
        }
        pblock;


typedef struct fhdr             /*Fixed part of exe file header*/
        {
        unsigned signature;       /*"0x4d5a"-signature of an exe file*/
        unsigned image_len;       /*Load module image size mod 512*/
        unsigned filesize;        /*No. of 512 byte pages in file*/
        unsigned nreloc;          /*No. of relocation table items.*/
        unsigned hdrsize_para;    /*No. of paragraphs (16 bytes) in header*/
        unsigned min_xmem;        /*Minimum number of paragraphs req'd above prog*/
        unsigned max_xmem;        /*Maximum no. of para. req'd above prog*/
        unsigned stackoff;        /*Offset of stack segment in module (para. addr)*/
        unsigned stacksp;         /*Sp register value at start of execution*/
        unsigned checksum;        /*Negative sum of all words in file*/
        unsigned startip;         /*Value of ip register at start of execution*/
        unsigned startcs;         /*Value of cs register at start of execution (para. addr)*/
        unsigned firstreloc;      /*Offset of first reloc item in file*/
        unsigned overlayno;       /*Overlay number*/
        } header;


typedef struct                  /*Program Segment Prefix structure -- psp*/
        {
        unsigned int20;              /*Interrupt 20 instruction for termination purposes*/
        unsigned top_mem;            /*First available segment of memory (paragraph form)*/
        unsigned char dummy;         /*Dummy spacing byte*/
        unsigned char longcall[5];   /*Long call to DOS function dispatcher*/
        unsigned *termaddr;          /*Terminate exit address*/
        unsigned *ctrlbreak;         /*Control-Break Exit address*/
        unsigned *criterror;         /*Critical error Interrupt vector*/
        unsigned char resrved[0x46]; /*Reserved for use by DOS*/
        unsigned char pspfcb1[0x10]; /*Fcb area for first parameter*/
        unsigned char pspfcb2[0x14]; /*Fcb area for second parameter*/
        unsigned char parmlen;       /*Length of command line*/
        unsigned char parmarea[0x80]; /*Unformatted parameter area (default DTA)*/
        } *psp;
```

Figure 8-20 load.h Header File

```
typedef struct dir        /*Directory entry description returned by DOS fnc 4E*/
         {
         char dosarea[21];                    /*Reserved for DOS use*/
         char fattrib;                        /*File attribute*/
         unsigned ftime;                      /*File time stamp*/
         unsigned fdate;                      /*File date stamp*/
         unsigned lowfsize;                   /*Low word of file size*/
         unsigned highfsize;                  /*High word of file size*/
         char filen[13];                      /*File name and extension*/
         } direntry;

typedef struct            /*File control block*/
         {
         char drive;                          /*Drive number*/
         char name[8];                        /*File name*/
         char exten[3];                       /*File extension*/
         unsigned block;                      /*Current block number*/
         unsigned record_size;
         unsigned long file_size;
         unsigned date;
         char resrv[10];
         unsigned char record;                /*Current record number in block*/
         unsigned long random;                /*Random record number*/
         } fcb;
```

Figure 8-20 (Continued)

   creatproc starts by finding an available slot in the process table via the function **allocpe**. If there is no slot available, it writes a message to the scheduler's window area and returns an error (-1). On success, **creatproc** will return the process number of the created process. Next, it validates the window number it has been given. **creatproc** could search for an available window, but we do not want that to happen. The calling routine may be starting a program in an already allocated window, as would happen if one application program issued a DOS function call to execute another application program. (See Exercise 8.7.) Next, **creatproc** sets up the process table and the window table with information about the process. It still has not gotten the program loaded into memory from disk, but it will use the function **loadprog** to perform that operation. **loadprog** requires a parameter block in the format required by DOS function 0x4b. See the **pblock** typedef in Figure 8-20. **creatproc** sets up the parameter block and calls **loadprog**, who does all of the hard work. If the load succeeds, **creatproc** writes a success message to the window message areas of both the scheduler and the target process, clears the window of any residual information left by the last user, restores the flags, and returns the process number. If the loading process fails, it writes a message to the scheduler's window message area, deletes the entries in the process and window tables, restores the flags, and returns ERROR.

Program Loading and Initiation

In a single-user DOS system, program loading and initiation is handled by the DOS function 0x4b, subfunction 0. For the multitasking system, this will not work because we cannot depend on this function to be reentrant. That is, this function is designed to load the target program, give it control allowing it to execute to completion, and then receive control back from it. In other words, it is designed to behave like a function call. The question is: What will happen if another program is loaded in the middle of execution of the target program? What will happen when one of the programs terminates? Which one will actually get terminated, if any? Without seeing the code for DOS function 0x4b, the answers to these questions are indeterminate. Since DOS was not designed to be a multitasking system, we have no cause to expect it to behave like one. Therefore, we will have to develop our own functions for loading programs and assure that they allow independent loading, initiation, and termination of programs.

Our strategy is to use the DOS function that loads overlays, DOS function 0x4b, subfunction 3. DOS will do the code relocation for us, but it will return control immediately after loading and not try to execute the module. One minor problem is that this will require the multitasker to capture and process all program terminations. Should one of these "overlays" terminate without the multitasker capturing the termination, DOS would terminate the multitasker.

We will start by explaining how to load **.exe** files and then generalize the notions to include **.com** files. The basic difference between **.exe** files and **.com** files is that the code image in the **.exe** file must go through a relocation step that the **.com** file does not. A **.com** file is said to be "code segment relocatable"—that is, the only relocation necessary is the proper setting of the **cs** register. All offsets are relative to the **cs** register. An **.exe** file, on the other hand, starts off with a header record containing a list of offsets within the load module that must be relocated relative to the segment address of the start of the program code.

We will start by discussing the relationship between the **.exe** file header record information (defined as the **typedef header** in Figure 8-20) and the loaded program, shown graphically in Figure 8-21. Figure 8-22 contains some definitions that we will use in this discussion and later in explaining the code.

From the standpoint of our loader, a loaded program consists of six basic regions. The first is a 0x100 byte region called the Program Segment Prefix (or PSP). This is a DOS-defined region that contains the run-time information about the program. We will discuss more about this region later. The second region is the program proper—that is, the program code and data. The C compiler puts the start of the stack well above the end of the program code plus data region, leaving a region that is used as heap space. Next is the stack region, followed by a region of memory above the program proper that is suppose to be reserved. Some programs will relocate their stack space into this region, so do not depend on it. Finally, we have added a region for use by the multitasker as a temporary stack

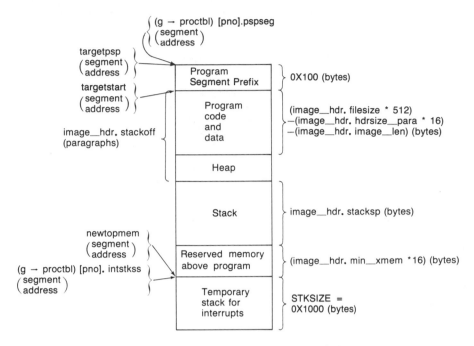

Figure 8-21 Load Image as Defined by **.exe** File Header Fields

region while it is emulating DOS interrupts. This keeps the multitasker from overflowing the stacks of programs that have particularly small stacks.

The information in the header record of an **.exe** file defines the size of the middle four regions, the offset of the program's stack segment and, by implication, the start of the temporary stack. **loadprog** receives the **.exe** header in a record structure named **image_hdr**, and in order to make a stronger connection between this discussion and the later discussion of **loadprog**, we will refer to the **.exe** header record structure by that name throughout this discussion. Let's look at the fields in **image_hdr**.

The first field is the signature field. If a file with a **.exe** extension contains "0x4d, 0x5a" in the signature field, it is highly likely that that file is a legal **.exe** file. Three of the next four fields (excluding **image_hdr.nreloc**) provide the information necessary to compute the region of the load module containing the program code and data. **image_hdr.filesize** is the number of 512 byte pages in the **.exe** file. **image_hdr.hdrsize** contains the number of paragraphs of the **.exe** file that are taken up by the header record and **image_hdr.image_len** is the number of bytes that the last page of the **.exe** file is short of a full page. Thus, the C code

```
image_size = (((long) image_hdr.filesize) * LOADPGSIZ)
            - (((long) image_hdr.hdrsize_para) * PARASIZE)
            - ((long) image_hdr.image_len);
```

```
#define FALSE           0
#define TRUE            1
#define MAXPNAME        15      /*Maximum length of a process's name*/
#define MAXPROCS        25      /*Maximum number of processes*/
#define MAXQENTS        75      /*Maximum number of queue entries*/
#define STKSIZE         0x1000  /*Size of interim stack (bytes)*/
#define BUFFER_SIZE     128     /*Size of keyboard buffer*/
#define EXEHDRLEN       0x1c    /*Size of fixed portion of exe file header*/
#define EXESIG          0x5a4d  /*Signature word of an exe file*/
#define LOADPGSIZ       512     /*Page size (in bytes) used by linker-loader*/
#define PARASIZE        16      /*Paragraph size in bytes*/
#define HEAPSIZE        512     /*Minimum heap size allocated to loaded prog*/
#define CMD_AREA_LEN    126     /*Max length of command line (+ '\0') in psp*/
#define START_DTA_OFF   0x80    /*Offset within psp of starting DTA*/
#define ENVOFFSET       0x2c    /*Environment field offset (in bytes) within psp*/
#define PGPSPLEN        0x10    /*Length of the psp in paragraphs*/
#define BPSPLEN         0x100   /*Length of the psp in bytes*/
#define INTR_ON_BIT     0x0200  /*Interrupt bit in flags register*/
#define TRAP_ON_BIT     0x0100  /*Trap bit in flags register*/
#define CARRY_BIT       0x0001  /*Carry bit in flags register*/
#define SIGN_BIT        0x0080  /*Sign bit in flags register*/
#define DIRECTION_BIT   0x0400  /*Direction bit in flags register*/
#define ZERO_BIT        0x0040  /*Zero bit in flags register*/


/*Special Interrupt Vectors*/

#define INTERCEPT16     0x16    /*Bios interrupt 16 vector*/
#define INTERCEPT10     0x10    /*Bios interrupt 10 vector*/
#define KEYBOARDBRK     0x1b    /*Keyboard break function executed on ctrl_brk key*/
#define POSTTIMER       0x1c    /*Post timer interrupt*/

#define DOSTERM         0x20    /*Address of DOS termination handler*/
#define DOSFNC          0x21    /*Address of DOS function handler*/
#define TERMADDR        0x22    /*Termination address for program*/
#define CNTRL_BRK       0x23    /*Control Break address for this program*/
#define ERRORINT        0x24    /*Address of critical error handler for this program*/

#define GLOBALS         0x60    /*Address of Global variables for SCHEDULER*/
#define REALDOSFNC      0x61    /*New location of vector to the
                                  real DOS FUNCTION (int 21) code*/
#define DOSINT20        0x62    /*New location of vector to real DOS int 20 code*/
#define BIOS16          0x63    /*New location of vector to real BIOS int 16 code*/
#define BIOS10          0x64    /*New location of vector to real BIOS int 10 code*/
#define ORIGCTLBRK      0x65    /*New location of vector to original ctl brk code*/
#define USERINT6        0x66    /*Reserved as user interrupt*/
#define USERINT7        0x67    /*Reserved as user interrupt*/

/* DOS and BIOS variable locations*/

#define BIOSBREAK_OFF   0x71    /*Offset of bios_break flag, used by keyboard
                                  bios to signal DOS that the break key has
                                  been depressed*/
```

Figure 8-22 Definitions from **proc** Header File

```
#define BIOSBREAK_SEG    0x40      /*Segment of bios_break flag*/

/* DOS and BIOS function codes */

#define BIOSREADCODE     0x0000    /*BIOS int 16 function to read a char from keyboard*/
#define BIOSCHECKCODE    0x0100    /*BIOS int 16 function to check status of keyboard*/
#define BIOSKEYBRDINT    0x16      /*BIOS keyboard interrupt*/
#define DOSPRINTCHAR     0x0500    /*DOS print character function*/

/* Process states */

#define RUNNING          0         /*Process is running (one one process)*/
#define READY            1         /*Process is ready to run*/
#define SUSPENDED        2         /*Process is suspended*/
#define SLEEPING         3         /*Process is sleeping*/
#define WAITMSG          4         /*Process is waiting for a message*/
#define WAITSIG          5         /*Process is waiting for a signal*/
#define TERMINATING      6         /*Process is being terminated*/

#define SCHEDULER        0         /*Process number of the scheduler task*/
#define MAXDELAY         0x7fff    /*Maximum delay value*/
#define MINDELAY         0x0       /*Minimum delay value*/
#define EMPTY            -1        /*Empty queue signal*/
#define NOERROR          0         /*Non error return value (actually any val > -1)*/
#define ERROR            -1        /*Error return value*/

/*Macros*/

#define ABS(x)           ((x < 0) ? -(x) : (x))

#define MAX(A,B) ((A) > (B) ? (A) : (B))        /*Maximum of two numbers*/
#define MIN(A,B) ((A) < (B) ? (A) : (B))        /*Minimum of two numbers*/

/******* Scheduler Control Characters (follow Ctrl-brk character) ***********/

#define ABORT      'a'    /*Abort program(s) in current window*/
#define BOUNDARY   'b'    /*Redraw window boundaries*/
#define COMMAND    'c'    /*Make scheduler's window current to give command*/
#define DUMP       'd'    /*Dump globals and process table*/
#define HELP       'h'    /*Show help screen*/
#define HELP2      '?'    /*Show help screen*/
#define LOOK       'l'    /*Look at window table*/
#define NEXT       'n'    /*Associate keyboard with next window*/
#define PRINTER    'p'    /*Toggle printer flag for current process*/
#define QUIT       'q'    /*Quit Scheduler*/
#define RESUME     'r'    /*Resume program(s) associated with current window*/
#define SUSPEND    's'    /*Suspend program(s) associated with current window*/
#define TRACE      't'    /*Toggle one of the trace flags*/
#define WINDOW     'w'    /*Go to window n*/
#define REALCTLBRK 'x'    /*Execute the real control break code*/
```

Figure 8-22 (Continued)

will compute the number of bytes in region one of the load module. The paragraph offset of the stack relative to the start of the program code is defined by the field **image_hdr.stackoff**. Notice that the start of the stack does not necessarily have to be at the end of the program plus data region. Typically, it is not for C86 programs because the compiler allocates the region after the end of the program plus data region and up to the reserved memory area above the program as the heap plus stack space. There is no fixed boundary between the heap and stack. The only requirement is that the upward-growing heap and the downward-growing stack never meet.

For **.exe** programs in general, we will take the larger of the program code plus data region and the stack offset; then we add to that the stack **sp** value to provide enough memory for the program proper. To this we will add the number of paragraphs specified in **image_hdr.min_xmem** as reserved space above the program and 0x100 bytes for the PSP. Computation of this figure is one of **loadprog's** main tasks.

Now, let us leave the remaining fields in **image_hdr** for the discussion of the starting state of the loaded program and turn to a discussion of the PSP, which must be properly set up by **loadprog**. The C definition of the **psp** struct is shown in Figure 8-20. The PSP starts with an interrupt 0x20 instruction stored in the **int20** field. This field provides one of the several methods for terminating a DOS program. If the program transfers to the zeroth word of its PSP, it fulfills the DOS requirement to have the **cs** register set to the PSP starting address and invokes the DOS termination function. This is an older method of termination that is no longer the recommended method, but programs still exist that use it and therefore we will have to intercept this interrupt and perform our own termination processing. We will discuss termination in a later section.

The next field, **top_mem**, is the top of memory field. It contains the segment address of the first paragraph after the program. In the case of the multitasker's loader, this is the first paragraph of the temporary stack. Many programs use this field to determine just how much memory that they can use. Consequently, to keep such programs from usurping the temporary stack area, we put the temporary stack outside of the program proper by setting this field to the first word of the temporary stack.

The next field, **dummy**, is reserved by DOS. It is followed by a long call to the DOS function dispatcher, **longcall**. The next three fields are pointers to the termination exit address, **termaddr**; the Control-Break exit address, **ctrlbreak**; and the critical error handler vector. DOS program termination logic restores these three fields to the values that they had on entry to the program. This provides a mechanism for one program to call another and to specify where control should go to on return from that program. When a program terminates, DOS will pass control to the address specified in the program's **termaddr** field. Thus, in order for a program to execute another program, it must set **termaddr** to the address that the subprogram should return to and then execute the DOS load function. This should be considered in the design for Exercise 8.7.

The next 0x46 bytes, **resrved**, is reserved by DOS. One field in this area, at offset 0x2c, contains the segment address of the program's environment string. We will make use of the environment string in searching for the file to load. More about this when we discuss the function **lfsearch.**

The next two fields, **pspfcb1** and **pspfcb2**, are reserved for the file control blocks (fcbs) of the first two parameters in the command line. The format of an fcb was defined earlier. These fcbs are created by compiler functions and there is no need for us to examine their format.

The final field, **parmarea**, is a multiuse area. Initially, the loader puts a copy of the command line at this location. This gives the program a mechanism to extract information from its command line. It is also established as the default Disk Transfer Area (DTA)—that is, the default buffer for disk transfers. This can be changed by the program, of course. Those are the formal uses for this area. In addition, some programs, such as "tree," appear to relocate their stack to this area so that they can use upper memory as a buffer.

Now that we understand what information is available from the linker via the header record for **.exe** files, and we know what fields are required in the PSP, we are ready to take a look at **loadprog** (see Figure 8-23). In the interest of brevity, we have removed the trace statements from **loadprog.**

```
#include <stdio.h>
#include "proc.h"
#include "load.h"
#include "errno.h"
#include "globdefs.h"
int loadprog(cmd,parmb,pno)
        char *cmd;                      /*Command line typed by user*/
        pblock *parmb;                  /*Load and execute style parameter block*/
        pindex pno;                     /*Process number for the program being loaded*/
        {
        char filen[128];                /*File name from command line*/
        extern poverblock overlay_parm; /*Load overlay style parameter block*/
        extern header image_hdr;        /*Header record structure for exe file*/
        extern int _MAXFMEM;            /* MAXIMUM STACK+HEAP REQUIRED */
        char *parmfcb1;                 /*FCB for parmfile1*/
        char *parmfcb2;                 /*FCB for parmfile2*/
        char *makefcb();
        unsigned ax_value;              /*Initial ax val giving drive validity*/
        unsigned * numbytes;            /*Pointer to number of bytes in segment*/
        char resfname[128];             /*Buffer for a filename with drive,
                                          path + extension*/

        long image_size;                /*Number of bytes of memory req'd to
                                          execute this program*/

        long ret_size;                  /*Number of bytes actually obtained
                                          from DOS*/

        unsigned get_mem();             /*Call DOS to get a chunk of memory*/
        unsigned newpspseg;             /*Start segment of new psp for program*/
        extern unsigned startseg;       /*Point to start loading new code*/
        extern psp newpsp;              /*Pointer to psp of new program*/
        unsigned newtopmem;             /*Value of top of memory for new program*/
```

Figure 8-23 loadprog

```
unsigned doserror;                    /*DOS error code*/
unsigned long startstack;             /*Offset of stack in segment*/
extern char * abstoptr();
int i,j;
int filetype;                         /*Type of file found-com, exe or not found*/
direntry fdes;                        /*Description of file found by lfsearch*/
char msg[128];

/*Extract file names from command line*/
parsecmd(cmd,filen,parmfile1,parmfile2);

/*Search for file name returning full file name +path, and file description*/
filetype = lfsearch(filen,resfname,&fdes);

if(filetype == FILENOTFOUND)
        {
        sprintf(msg,"loadprog: file '%s' not found",filen);
        errormsg((g->procno),msg);
        return(FILENOTFOUND);
        }
if(filetype == COMFILE)
        /*Create a header record for the com file*/
        create_com_hdr(&image_hdr,&fdes);
else

        /*Read exe header into memory*/
        if(read_exe_hdr(&image_hdr,resfname)<0) return(FILENOTFOUND);

/*Compute the amount of memory required for this program*/

/*First overall filesize minus the size of the header information*/
image_size =  (long) image_hdr.filesize * LOADPGSIZ -
              (long) image_hdr.hdrsize_para * PARASIZE;

/*Reduce imagesize by no. of bytes the actual image length is below
  than an even page boundary (except if field is set to dummy value of 4)*/
if(image_hdr.image_len != 4)
        image_size -= image_hdr.image_len;

/*Add in the size of the psp*/
image_size += 0x100L;

startstack = ((unsigned long) image_hdr.stackoff) * PARASIZE;
image_size = MAX(image_size,startstack);

if(filetype==EXEFILE) /*Stack seg follows prog seg for EXE files*/
        image_size += image_hdr.stacksp;

else                  /*Stack seg overlaps prog seg for COM files*/
        image_size = MAX(image_size,(unsigned long) image_hdr.stacksp);

/*Add in the minimum number of paragraphs required above the program*/
image_size += (image_hdr.min_xmem * PARASIZE);

/*Add an extra STKSIZE bytes for interrupt stack at top of memory*/
image_size += STKSIZE;

newpspseg = get_mem(image_size,&ret_size);
```

Figure 8-23 (Continued)

```
if(ret_size < image_size || newpspseg == ECNTLBLK
        || newpspseg == ENOMEM) return(-1);

newpsp = (psp) abstoptr(((unsigned long) newpspseg) << 4);

/*Create a program segment prefix for program to be loaded*/
create_psp(newpspseg);

parmfcb1 = makefcb(parmfile1);
parmfcb2 = makefcb(parmfile2);
ax_value = 0;
if(parmfcb1)
        {
        movmem(parmfcb1,&(newpsp->pspfcb1),0x10);
        }
if(parmfcb2)
        {
        movmem(parmfcb2,&(newpsp->pspfcb2),0x14);
        }
if(parmfcb1) free(parmfcb1);
if(parmfcb2) free(parmfcb2);

if(filetype == COMFILE) /*Reduce number of bytes in segment by 100 hex*/
        {
        numbytes = (unsigned *) &((newpsp->longcall)[1]);
        *numbytes -= 0x100;
        }

/*Increment newpspseg by 0x10 paragraphs (0x100 bytes) to account
  for the psp */
startseg = newpspseg + 0x10;

/*Set environment segment address in target program's psp*/
((unsigned int *) newpsp) [ENVOFFSET/2] = parmb->env_seg;

/*Load program as if it were an overlay*/
overlay_parm.env_seg = startseg;
overlay_parm.reloc = startseg;

/*Use full filename created in lfsearch*/
doserror = (unsigned) loadexec(resfname,&overlay_parm,3);
if(doserror != 0)
        {
        printf("loadprog: Dos error %d (decimal) on loading %s\n",
                doserror,cmd);
        switch(doserror)
                {
                case 1:
                        errormsg(SCHEDULER,"loadprog: Invalid DOS function number");
                        break;
                case 2:
                        errormsg(SCHEDULER,"loadprog: File not found");
                        break;
                case 5:
                        errormsg(SCHEDULER,"loadprog: Access denied");
                        break;
                case 8:
                        errormsg(SCHEDULER,"loadprog: Insufficient memory");
                        break;
```

Figure 8-23 (Continued)

```
                            case 10:
                                    errormsg(SCHEDULER,"loadprog: Invalid environment");
                                    break;
                            case 11:
                                    errormsg(SCHEDULER,"loadprog: Invalid format");
                                    break;
                            default:
                                    errormsg(SCHEDULER,"loadprog: Indeterminant DOS error");
                                    break;
                            }
                /*Clean up storage structures*/
                ret_mem(newpspseg);
                return(doserror);
                }

    /*Exclude temporary interrupt stack from memory program can access*/
    newtopmem =  newpspseg + ((unsigned) (image_size / PARASIZE))
                - (STKSIZE/PARASIZE);

    /*Change top of memory for the new program*/
    newpsp -> top_mem = newtopmem;

    /*Put command line into psp*/
    strncpy(&(newpsp -> parmarea),parmb -> cline,CMD_AREA_LEN);
    newpsp->parmlen = (unsigned char) strlen(parmb->cline);
    (g->proctbl)[pno].pspseg = newpspseg;

    /*Set segment ptr to temp stack, for use during interrupts*/
    (g->proctbl)[pno].intstkss = newtopmem ;

    /* Set up stack ss and sp register values in process entry and
       initialize stack so that the program will be resumed starting at
       its entry point.
    */
    startstate(pno,filetype,&fdes,ax_value);
    return(doserror);
    }
```

Figure 8-23 (Continued)

If for the moment the reader takes it on faith that the functions called by **loadprog** perform their assigned missions, we will delay detailed discussion of those functions until later.

loadprog starts out by parsing the command line in order to get the name of the file to be loaded and the name or names of the parameter files, which must be turned into fcbs and put into the PSP. Next, **lfsearch** searches for a **.exe** or a **.com** file, first in the current directory and then in each directory on the PATH variable list in the program's environment. Given that it found the file to be loaded, the full file name including path will be returned in **resfname** and the directory description of that file will be returned in the structure **fdes**. See the **typedef direntry** in Figure 8-20. Next, it creates the **image_hdr** record. For **.exe** files this is the header record we discussed earlier and is read directly from the file by **read_exe_hdr.** For .com files, this structure is computed by **create_com_hdr.** This allows us to use the same code, for the most part, in loading the two kinds of files.

loadprog computes the load image size in a **image_size** according to the formula we established in the earlier discussion and invokes **get_mem** to get the memory from DOS. It stores the new memory segment address in **newpspseg**, and also converts it into a full pointer called **newpsp**. It calls the function **create_psp**, which uses DOS function 0x26 to set up many of the PSP's fields. It creates fcbs and moves them into the PSP. It sets the variable **startseg** to the segment address of the start of the program, the first paragraph following the PSP. It puts the address of the environment string inherited from the multitasker at offset 0x2c in the PSP. It then sets up the parameter block required for loading overlays and invokes the C library function **loadexec**, which will issue the DOS function 0x4b, subfunction 3. Assuming no loading error, the segment address of the top of memory is computed and stored in the **top_mem** field of the PSP. The command line is moved to offset 0x80 of the PSP, the process table fields **pspseg** and **intstkss** are set, and the function **startstate** is called to set up the program to look like a stopped process.

startstate is defined in Figure 8-24. We have used local variables that correspond to register names to make clearer the intended destination of the items that are put onto the stack. It may be useful to refer to Figure 8-8, which illustrates the canonical form of a stopped process, to better understand this function.

startstate adjusts the initial value of sp provided by the linker to allow 32 bytes of information to be put onto the stack. These 32 bytes make the program look like our standard stopped process with the "return frame" pointing to the first executable instruction in the program, as passed by the linker. Recall that for real stopped processes the return frame points back to the middle of the function that is called **pswitch**. The **ss** register value for **.exe** files is just the segment address of the program code, offset by the linker generated value **image_hdr.stackoff**. For **.com** files, all four segment registers (**ss**, **cs**, **es**, and **ds**) are set to the start of the PSP. The **ss** and **sp** values are put into the process table emulating **pswitch**'s behavior when saving the state of a process. Although not required by the DOS loading specification, we set **bx** and **cx** to the size of the file, as does the debugger. Next, **startstate** overlays that portion of the user's stack to be initialized, with the array **tstacktop**. It then puts the various values into their proper location in **tstacktop**.

Now, let's analyze **lfsearch**, the function that finds the directory containing the load file (see Figure 8-25).

In order to understand **lfsearch**, we need to discuss the environment string that is supplied to each program by DOS (or by **loadprog**, in the case of programs running under the multitasker). Figure 8-26 shows an example environment string. The environment string is a mechanism whereby system-level variables describing the computing environment can be set by the user and tested by various programs in order to tailor the program's behavior to the computing environment. The **PATH** variable is a good example. Its value (on the right side of the = symbol) is an ordered list of directories separated by semicolons that are the places where the user keeps executable files. Whenever DOS is asked to load a file that it does not find in the current directory, it will check the directories listed in the **PATH** var-

```
#include <stdio.h>
#include "proc.h"
#include "load.h"
#include "globdefs.h"
startstate(pnum,filetype,fdes,ax)
        int pnum;                /*Process number of process to initialize*/
        int filetype;            /*EXE or COM file being initialized*/
        direntry *fdes;          /*File directory entry record*/
        unsigned ax;             /*Initial value of ax indicating drive validity*/
        {
        unsigned long stkaddr;   /*Stack address as a long integer*/
        unsigned *tstacktop;     /*Pointer to target stack top area*/

        process *pt;             /*Points to process entry of pnum in proctbl*/
        unsigned targetpsp;      /*Segment address of psp*/
        unsigned targetstart;    /*Segment address of start of code*/

        extern header image_hdr; /*exe file header record*/
        unsigned long prog_size; /*size of program for .exe files*/

        unsigned sp,ss,flags,es,cs,ip,ds,cx,bx;
                                 /*Key registers*/
        unsigned sp0;            /*sp value assigned by loader*/
        extern int pswitch();
        unsigned i;

        pt = &(g->proctbl);      /*Get pointer to proctbl*/

        disable(&flags);         /*Disable interrupts while changing global data*/

        targetpsp = pt[pnum].pspseg;
        targetstart = targetpsp + PGPSPLEN;

        sp0 = image_hdr.stacksp;
        sp = sp0 - 32;           /*Relocate sp to account for initial values on
                                    stack*/

        pt[pnum].savesp = sp;

        /*Store stackseg, relocated relative to the start of the code
          (i.e., pspseg address + 0x10 paragraphs or 0x100 bytes) for EXE files,
          but pointing at the psp for COM files*/

        pt[pnum].savess = ss =
                (filetype==EXEFILE) ? (image_hdr.stackoff + targetstart)
                                    : targetpsp;

        restore(flags);
        cs = (filetype==EXEFILE) ? (image_hdr.startcs + targetstart) : targetpsp;
        ip = image_hdr.startip;
        es = targetpsp;
```

Figure 8-24 startstate

```
ds = targetpsp;

if(filetype==COMFILE)
        {
        bx = fdes->highfsize;
        cx = fdes->lowfsize;
        }
else
        {
        /*Program size is (the no. of 512 byte pages) * 512
                        - (the no. of 16 byte paragraphs in header) *16
                        - (the no. of bytes the last page is short of 512)
        */

        prog_size = (((long) image_hdr.filesize) * LOADPGSIZ) -
                    (((long) image_hdr.hdrsize_para) * PARASIZE)
                    - image_hdr.image_len;

        pfission(prog_size,&cx,&bx);
        }

/*Set up access to top of stack area so that it may be initialized*/
pfusion(&tstacktop,ss,sp);

zeroarray(tstacktop,32);          /*Default for registers is zero*/
/*Last word of stack (tstacktop[14]) is left zeroed to accommodate .com
   files*/

/*Set up return frame (from pswitch) that points to start of code*/

tstacktop[13] = cs;
tstacktop[12] = ip;

/*Use existing flags register with interrupts turned on and other
   flags off*/
tstacktop[11] = (flags | INTR_ON_BIT)
                & (~SIGN_BIT) & (~CARRY_BIT)
                & (~DIRECTION_BIT);

tstacktop[10] = ax;
tstacktop[6] = es;
tstacktop[2] = ds;

tstacktop[7] = cx;
tstacktop[9] = bx;

tstacktop[0] = START_DTA_OFF;
tstacktop[1] = (g->proctbl)[pnum].pspseg;

return;
}
```

Figure 8-24 (Continued)

```
#include <stdio.h>
#include "proc.h"
#include "load.h"
#include "errno.h"
#include "globdefs.h"
int lfsearch(filename,pathname,filedes)
        char *filename;         /*Name of file to be loaded*/
        char *pathname;         /*Pointer to full path name constructed by lfsearch*/
        direntry *filedes;      /*Pointer to description returned by search*/
        {

        int i,doserror,l;
        int findfile();
        char *envfind();
        char *ptrtoenv;         /*Pointer to my environment string*/
        char *paths;            /*Pointer to paths as specified in environment*/
        char *savepaths;        /*Pointer to start of the string returned by envfind*/
        char otherpath[128];    /*Buffer for paths from environment*/

        char *curdir,*gcdir();  /*Current directory name*/


        /*First search current directory*/
        curdir = gcdir("");

        /*if the filename does not explicitly contain .com, try .exe files*/
        if(!extension(filename,".com"))
                {
                assembfile(curdir,filename,".exe",pathname);
                doserror = findfile(pathname,filedes,0);
                if(doserror==0)
                        {
                        free(curdir);
                        return(EXEFILE);
                        }
                }

        /*If the filename does not explicitly contain .exe, try .com files*/
        if(!extension(filename,".exe"))
                {
                assembfile(curdir,filename,".com",pathname);
                doserror = findfile(pathname,filedes,0);
                if(doserror==0)
                        {
                        free(curdir);
                        return(COMFILE);
                        }
                }


        free(curdir);
        /*Not in current directory, use PATH specifications in environment*/
```

Figure 8-25 lfsearch

```
savepaths = paths = envfind("PATH");

if(paths==NULL) return(FILENOTFOUND);

while (paths)
        {
        for(i=0;i<strlen(paths) && i < 127 && paths[i] != ';'
           && paths[i]!= '\0'; ++i)
               {
               otherpath[i]=paths[i];
               }
        otherpath[i]='\0';        /*terminate path string*/

        /*Update paths to null if we just found the last path expression
          or to the start of the next path expression*/
        if (paths[i] == '\0') paths = NULL;
        else paths = (paths + i + 1);


        /*if the filename does not explicitly contain .com,
          try .exe files*/
        if(!extension(filename,".com"))
               {
               assembfile(otherpath,filename,".exe",pathname);
               doserror = findfile(pathname,filedes,0);
               if(doserror==0)
                      {
                      free(savepaths);
                      return(EXEFILE);
                      }
               }

        /*Did not find an .exe file, try a .com file*/

        /*If the filename does not explicitly contain .exe, try .com files*/
        if(!extension(filename,".exe"))
               {
               assembfile(otherpath,filename,".com",pathname);
               doserror = findfile(pathname,filedes,0);
               if(doserror==0)
                      {
                      free(savepaths);
                      return(COMFILE);
                      }
               }
        }

free(savepaths);
return(FILENOTFOUND);
}
```

Figure 8-25 (Continued)

```
assembfile(directory,filename,ext,resfile)
        char *directory;
        char *filename;
        char *ext;
        char *resfile;
        {
        char dummy[128];
        strncpy(dummy,directory,126);
        strcat(dummy,"\\");              /*Add backslash after directory name*/
        strcat(dummy,ext);
        makefnam(filename,dummy,resfile);
        return;
        }
extension(filename,ext) /*Does filename contain the extension ext*/
        char *filename;
        char *ext;
        {
        int l;
        l = strlen(filename);
        if (l <= 4) return(0);
        if(strcmp(&(filename[l-4]),ext)) return(0);
        return(1);
        }
```

Figure 8-25 (Continued)

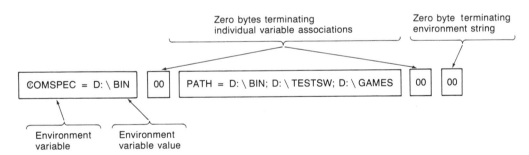

Figure 8-26 Example Environment String

iable's value string. The Unix convention is to keep most production programs in a top-level directory named "**bin**." I have followed this convention on my system, adding the "**D:**" disk designation because my bin directory is on my hard disk, which is my **D**: disk.

lfsearch searches according to the following rules:

1. In every directory searched, if the file extension is not specified, search first for an **.exe** file and failing to find one, search for a **.com** file.

2. Search the current directory first.

3. If not found in the current directory, search the directories listed in the value list of the environment variable **PATH**.

The name of the current directory is returned by the C library function **gcdir** and the list of paths associated with the environment variable **PATH** is returned by the C library function **envfind**. **lfsearch** is relatively straightforward.

   read_exe_hdr and **create_com_hdr** are shown in Figures 8-27 and 8-28. The major differences in loading an **.exe** file and a **.com** file are:

1. For **.com** files, all segment registers are by default initialized to point to the

```
#include <stdio.h>
#include "proc.h"
#include "load.h"
#include "errno.h"
int read_exe_hdr(hdr,filename)    /*Read header of exe file*/
        header *hdr;               /*Header structure*/
        char *filename;           /*Name of file containing load image*/
        {
        int fd;                   /*File descriptor*/
        int readres;              /*Result returned from read*/
        int closeres;             /*Result of close operation*/
        int i;

        fd = open(filename,BREAD);
        if(fd<0) return(fd);

        readres = read(fd,hdr,EXEHDRLEN);
        closeres = close(fd);

        if (readres <=0)                        /*EOF or error on read*/
                {
                return(readres);
                }
        else if (readres != EXEHDRLEN ||
                closeres < 0 ||
                hdr->signature!=EXESIG)         /*Short header record or
                                                 close error or
                                                 bad exe file signature*/
                {
                return(-1);
                }
        else return(readres);
        }
```

Figure 8-27 read_exe_hdr

```c
#include <stdio.h>
#include "proc.h"
#include "load.h"
#include "errno.h"
int create_com_hdr(hdr,fdes)      /*Create a header for a com file*/
        header *hdr;              /*Header structure*/
        direntry *fdes;          /*Name of file containing load image*/
        {
        unsigned long fsize;                  /*Actual size of com file in bytes*/
        unsigned long modulsize;              /*Total size of loaded module including
                                               stack + heap*/
        unsigned int sp;

        pfusion(&fsize,fdes->highfsize,fdes->lowfsize);
        hdr->image_len = fsize % LOADPGSIZ;
        hdr->filesize = (fsize + LOADPGSIZ - 1) / LOADPGSIZ;     /*File size in pages, ceiling*/
        hdr->nreloc = 0;
        hdr->hdrsize_para = 0;
        hdr->min_xmem = 1;
        hdr->max_xmem = 0xffff;


        /*Stack segment starts at end of program, allow a stack of 2000*/
        hdr->stackoff = 0;

        /* 64K  - 0x1000 bytes for interrupt stack
                - 0x20 bytes free mem above prog*/
        hdr->stacksp = (unsigned) 0xefe0;

        /*Execution starts at paragraph 0, offset 100*/
        hdr ->startip = 0x100;
        hdr ->startcs = 0;


        hdr ->firstreloc = 0;
        hdr ->overlayno = 0;

        }
```

Figure 8-28   create_com_hdr

start of the PSP. For **.exe** programs, the values for the **cs** and **ss** are determined by the linker, and only the **ds** and **es** registers default to the start of the PSP.

2. The first instruction of a **.com** file must be the first byte following the PSP—that is, offset 0x100 from **cs** register. The first instruction of an **.exe** file is determined by the linker.

3. The stack size for **.com** files defaults to 0x100 at the end of the program's segment. The stack size and placement for **.exe** files is determined by the linker, based on information supplied by the compiler.

4. A **.com** program is limited to a 64K segment and usually gets a full segment if possible. An **.exe** program is not so limited.

Termination

A DOS process can terminate in a variety of ways including executing an interrupt 0x20, jumping to offset 0 of its PSP (where an int 0x20 is stored), issuing an int 0x21 with DOS function of 0 or 0x4c, or calling location 0x50 of its PSP with **ah** set to either 0 or 0x4c. In all cases except the DOS function 0x4c, DOS requires that the **cs** register contain the segment address of the PSP when the termination function is issued. DOS also supplies another special-purpose termination function, 0x31, which is "terminate and stay resident". A spooling program is a typical example of a program that would employ this kind of termination.

If we left the DOS termination system alone, the termination of any process running under the multitasker would cause termination of the multitasker. Our strategy to avoid this problem is to replace interrupt 0x20 with our own routines **wrapup** and **harikari**. **wrapup** is the interrupt intercept function and **harikari** performs the actual termination. We will intercept the DOS termination functions with **capt21** and transform them into interrupt 0x20s. Figures 8-29 and 8-30 show the definitions of **wrapup** and **harikari**, respectively.

```
        include model.h
        include prologue.h
        include process.h
        public wrapup
@code   ends

abs0    segment at 0h
        extrn   gcopy:far        ;pointer to scheduler's globals
abs0    ends


@code   segment
wrapup  proc    far
        extrn   harikari:far     ;pointer to C routine that does actual wrapup
        extrn   _PSPSEG:dword    ;pointer to multitasker's psp
;       save flags and turn off interrupts

        pushf
        pop dx
        cli


;       set up (es:si) to access globals and increase software protection flag
        gaccess di
```

Figure 8-29 wrapup

```
        protect es,si,di

;       switch to temporary stack (unless it has already been done in capt21)
        switchsk es,si,di,cx

;       restore ds to SCHEDULER'S data group
        mov     ax,dgroup
        mov     ds,ax

;       restore es to SCHEDULER'S psp
        mov     ax,word ptr dgroup:PSPSEG+2
        mov     es,ax

        call harikari

;       Control should never return to here. A call to kill within harikari
;       will cause a context switch to the SCHEDULER and this process will
;       never again be a candidate for execution.

        iret
wrapup  endp
        include epilogue.h
        end
```

Figure 8-29 (Continued)

```
#include <stdio.h>
#include "proc.h"
harikari()
        {
        unsigned int flags;

        if(g->procno==SCHEDULER) return(ERROR);

        disable(&flags);

        /*Assure no preemptions until termination is complete*/
        (g->noprmpt) = 1;
        ++ (g->lvlcalls);
        (g->clock) = 0;

        restore(flags);

        kill(g->procno);

        /*harikari never returns. Kill will resume the scheduler, which will
```

Figure 8-30 harikari

```
        destroy all vestiges of this process*/

/*If we get to here, oh-oh*/

strcpy(s,"harikari: unable to kill process number Aborting system. Type>");
converti2s((g->procno),&(s[40]));
errormsg((g->procno),s);
getchar();
/*Restore interrupt vectors*/
termsched();
exit(1);
}
```

Figure 8-30   (Continued)

Recall that **kill** will put the process number onto the **tbk** queue and the scheduler will call **terminate** the next time it goes around its loop. **terminate**, shown in Figure 8-31, will eradicate all vestiges of the process.

```
#include <stdio.h>
#include "proc.h"
int terminate(head)
      qindex head;
      {
      process *proc;
      int *stack,pop(),pno;
      unsigned int flags;
      qindex find();
      char msg[128];

      disable(&flags);
      while((pno=pop(head))!=EMPTY)
            {
            if(pno == SCHEDULER || outrange(pno)) continue;

            if(find(pno,((g->ready).qhead))!=NULL)
                  {
                  sprintf(msg,"terminat: Found killed process %.15s (%d) on ready list",
                  (g->proctbl)[pno].procname,pno);
                  errormsg(SCHEDULER,msg);
                  }

            /*Remove procno from ready queue, to be safe*/
            remove(pno,(g->ready).qhead);

            /*Return memory to DOS*/
            ret_mem((g->proctbl)[pno].pspseg);
```

Figure 8-31   terminate

```
        clearkeybuf((g->proctbl)[pno].windno);


        /*Delete the window associated with this process*/
        delete_window((g->proctbl)[pno].windno);


        /*Remove proctbl entry*/
        proc = &((g->proctbl)[pno]);
        zeroarray(proc,sizeof(process));/*zero process entry*/
        }

    restore(flags);

    return(NOERROR);
    }
```

Figure 8-31 (Continued)

EXERCISES

8.1. Explain why the **qentry** array **qe** is preallocated storage and part of the multitasker's globals. [Hint: Consider the consequences of using heap storage via **alloc** or **calloc**, and allowing an application running under the multitasker to invoke a process management routine such as **resume** (loaded with the application program) that manipulates the ready queue.]

8.2. The simple multitasking example described here does not implement the "pipe" operator that allows the output of one program to be directed to another program. Design an extension that implements the pipe operator. Discuss the tradeoffs of implementing the buffer connecting the two programs as a file or as an in-memory buffer. What happens when a reading process reads an empty pipe? If you suspend such a process, what signals it to be resumed? What happens if one of the processes in a pipe chain terminates? What if the last process terminates (say, abnormally) before the first? What if the first process terminates first?

8.3. Extend your design from the previous problem to implement the ">" and "<" operators.

8.4. The simple example developed contains no file protection scheme. It depends on the honor and good faith of the programs running under the multitasker. In a production system, no file protection scheme is unsatisfactory at best and a disaster at worst. Design a file protection scheme extension to the simple example that locks files so that a file being used by one process is inaccessible to another process. What should be done when there is a conflict? If a process is suspended trying to open a locked file, what signals its resumption? What information must be kept in such a scheme? What data structures are required? What is the relationship to the process table entries? What interrupts (if any) must be intercepted?

8.5. Suggest a redesign of the preemption logic that eliminates the extra context switch when changing from one executing application to another. Make sure that your design will work for applications with small stacks. If you decide to switch to the temporary stack during preemption, what other routines will have to be changed? What is the interaction between this logic and the logic to switch stacks on intercepted interrupts?

8.6. Suggest a design extension that allows processes to sleep and wake up at a predefined time. Do you need a new queue? A new state? Who checks the queue?

8.7. The example shown has made no provision for application programs that execute a DOS function 0x4b, load or execute a second program. Suggest a design that will handle this. Use the typedefs **pblock** and **poverblock** in your design and think about how **creatproc** might be used. Does its existing calling sequence need to be changed? Should the multitasking system keep track of which processes invoked which other processes, or should we just leave it up to the application programs to manage? Frame an argument for why we might want the system to keep track of the "call chain." Explain why the existing DOS functions will not work within the framework of the simple example.

8.8. DOS load specifications indicate that the **ax** register is initialized to reflect the validity of the drive specifiers on the two parameters specified on the command line. 0xff indicates an invalid drive and 0x00 indicates a valid drive. The low-order byte (**al**) is associated with drive 1 and the high-order byte (**ah**) with drive 2. The multitasker defaults them to valid. Suggest the logic necessary to set them per the DOS specification. How can the loader determine what drives are valid on any system?

8.9. Why would it be a bad idea for **suspend** to use **printf** (or any of the C runtime I/O library) to write a trace message from deep within the multitasking system? Consider the "ugly" code used to create window messages in **resume**, **suspend** and so on. Design a **sprintf**-like function for doing this job that does not use any part of the C runtime library. As a simplication, this function needs to handle only decimal integers, hexidecimal integers and strings. How will you handle a variable number of arguments? Where does the working storage for constructing the string come from?

8.10. Consider alteration to the preemption conditions so that if there is only one process running on the system other than the scheduler, it would not be preempted. Why might this be desirable? What functions are affected? Is there deadlock potential in such an extension? If so, explain how to avoid it? Develop a design for such an extension.

Chapter 9

The User Interface

9.1 WINDOW MANAGEMENT

A Simple Display Manager

In this chapter, we will develop and explain a simple display manager. To keep the example simple, we will choose to tile the screen with windows that are almost as wide as a real monochrome display. Figure 9-1 illustrates the format of the windows to be used in our example DM. This will eliminate the need to introduce

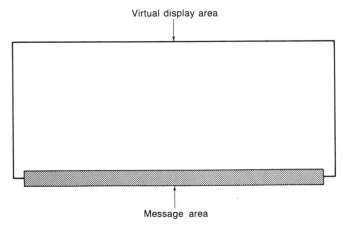

Virtual display area

Message area

Figure 9-1 Physical Layout of a Window

transcription buffers and all of the complexity involved in mapping the information between the buffer and the window. In this simple example, the only buffer is that provided by the monochrome display buffer. This example incorporates much of the structure and functionality found in the more complex DMs with transcription buffers and movable windows, and can be transformed into a more complex DM with relative ease. That is to say, there are no major architectural inconsistencies that would require a major redesign of the example DM.

Window Table Definition

The window table is the data structure that is central to window management, as well as keyboard management. The C definition is shown in Figure 9-2:

```
typedef struct win
        {
        unsigned int inuse;       /*Is this window being used*/
        unsigned int rorg;        /*Row of upper left corner of window*/
        unsigned int corg;        /*Column of upper left corner of window*/
        unsigned int h;           /*Usable height of window--boundaries extra*/
        unsigned int w;           /*Usable width of window*/
        unsigned int crow;        /*Current row of cursor for this window on real screen*/
        unsigned int ccol;        /*Current column of cursor for this window on real screen*/
        unsigned int vrow;        /*Current row of cursor for this window on virtual screen*/
        unsigned int vcol;        /*Current column of cursor for this window on virtual screen*/
        unsigned int pnumb;       /*Process number associated with this window*/
        unsigned int (*keybuf)[];/*Pointer to keyboard buffer for this window*/
        unsigned int kbcount;     /*Number of characters in keyboard buffer*/
        unsigned int kbrear;      /*Index of rear of buffer, where next char goes*/
        unsigned int kbfront;     /*Index of front of buffer, where next char
                                    to be read comes from*/
        } window;

extern window wintbl[];           /*Window table*/
extern unsigned int cwin;         /*Current window number. I.E. The window the
                                    user is talking to*/
extern unsigned int numwindow;    /*Number of active windows*/

extern unsigned int printer_on;   /*Control PrtSc has toggled the printer on*/
```

Figure 9-2 The Window Table

Each entry in this table contains information about one window, and it keeps track of several kinds of information:

1. The allocation state of the window
2. The position and size of the window on the real screen (see Figure 9-3)
3. The position of the cursor in absolute coordinates and in virtual coordinates (see Figure 9-3)

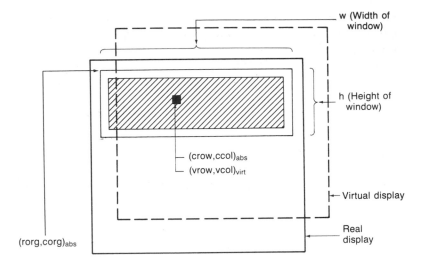

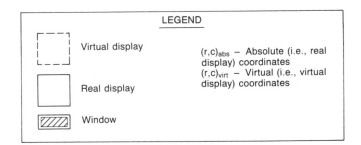

Figure 9-3 Relationship of a Window to Real and Virtual Displays

4. The process number currently associated with this window
5. The characters typed from the keyboard for this window that have not yet been fetched by some form of a read operation

The actual declaration of **wintbl** is in the global variables associated with the main program of the multitasker. Thus, **wintbl** exists in the multitasker's global variable area. In addition to **wintbl**, **cwin** is the index of the current window, **numwindow** indicates how many usable windows are available on the display (including windows in use and windows not in use), and a global printer flag allows characters that are written to the display to be echoed on the printer.

Some of these fields require a bit more explanation. The **h** and **w** fields represent only the usable height and width of the window. They do not include the borders. Therefore, the actual space required by the window on the screen is (**h** + 2) by (**w** + 2), and the upper left corner of the the writable portion of the window is at absolute coordinate position (**rorg** + 1, **corg** + 1). The offset of the virtual display with respect to the real display is defined by the difference between the virtual cursor position and the real cursor position. It is therefore critical that the virtual and real cursor position fields never become unsynchronized. If one gets changed in the window table, the other also must be changed.

The use of the window table fields and associated variables in the following sections will clarify their meaning and constraints.

Emulating DOS Display Functions

Since one of the requirements of our multitasking window system is to run existing programs unaltered, we must be able to handle the DOS functions that write the screen and cause those functions to write within the appropriate window. This requires that we intercept interrupts on vector 0x21; sort out which DOS functions the multitasker needs to emulate and dispatch control to the emulator functions; and finally, dispatch control to all other DOS functions that we have no need to intercept. **capt21** in Figure 9-4 is the mechanism for intercepting DOS interrupt 21. It captures several types of DOS functions in addition to those that write the display, but for the moment we will concentrate just on those DOS functions that write the display—that is, functions 2 and 6 (when **dl** is not equal to 0xff).

```
            include model.h
            include prologue.h
@code       ends

abs0        segment at 0h
            extrn   gcopy:far           ;pointer to scheduler's globals
abs0        ends

@code       segment
            include process.h
            extrn   strngout:far
            extrn   cptioctl:far
            extrn   wrapup:far
            extrn   charout:far
            extrn   keyin:far
            extrn   _PSPSEG:dword        ;pointer to scheduler's psp

            public  capt21
capt21      proc    far
            cld                          ;clear direction flag for DOS
;           save registers
            savreg
```

Figure 9-4   capt21

```
;         set up (es:si) to access globals and increase software protection flag
          gaccess di
          protect es,si,di

          sti                      ;allow interrupts
;         intercept characters going to screen
          cmp      ah,2            ;dos function 2?
          je       chrout
          cmp      ah,6            ;dos function 6?
          jne      ne1
          cmp      dl,0ffh         ;dos fnc 6 is output only if dl not ffh
          je       ne1
          jmp      chrout
ne1:      jmp      notout
chrout:
;         switch to temp stack at end of process's region
          switchsk es,si,ax,di

          push     bp              ;save access to argments
          mov      dh,0
          push     dx              ;push argument
          call     charout
          pop      dx
          pop      bp              ;restore access to arguments

;         reaccess scheduler's global variables and decrease
;         software protection flags by one level
          gaccess cx
          restorsk es,si,di,dx
          unprotec es,si

;         Reset carry bit to indicate no error result for DOS call
          and      word ptr retflg[bp],0fffeh      ;reset carry bit in return frame
          mov      axreg[bp],ax                     ;puts results in ax on stack
          resreg
          iret
notout:
          cmp      ah,44h          ;ioctl device function
          jne      not44
          cmp      al,3            ;write bytes to device
          jne      ne2             ;ioctl device function but not a write
          cmp      bx,1            ;is file handle stdout
          je       eq2
          jmp      ne2             ;ioctl device write, but not on stdout
not44:
          cmp      ah,40h          ;dos function 40, write file or device?
          jne      ne2
          cmp      bx,1            ;is this going to stdout
```

Figure 9-4 (Continued)

```
        jne      ne2
        jmp      eq2
ne2:    jmp      notwrite
eq2:
;       switch to temp stack at end of process's region
        switchsk es,si,ax,di

        push     bp              ;save access to argments
        push     cx              ;save number of bytes to be written

        mov      si,dx
prntstr:
        mov      dl,byte ptr [si];get character
        mov      ah,2            ;set up display output function
        int      21              ;display character
        add      si,1
        loopne   prntstr
donestr:

        pop      bp              ;restore access to capt21 frame
        pop      ax              ;restore no bytes written as return value

;       reaccess scheduler's global variables and decrease
;       software protection flags by one level
        gaccess cx
        restorsk es,si,di,dx
        unprotec es,si

;       Set carry bit to indicate no error result for DOS call
        and      word ptr retflg[bp],0fffeh      ;reset carry bit in return frame
        mov      axreg[bp],ax                    ;puts results in ax on stack
        resreg
        iret

notwrite:
;       test for print string terminated by $
        cmp      ah,9h           ;print string terminated by $
        jne      nprnt$
;       switch to temp stack at end of process's region
        switchsk es,si,ax,di

        mov      si,dx
prnt$:
        mov      dl,byte ptr [si];get character
        cmp      dl,24h          ;compare to $
        je       done$
        mov      ah,2            ;set up display output function
        int      21              ;display character
```

Figure 9-4 (Continued)

```
        add     si,1
        jmp     prnt$
done$:
;       reaccess scheduler's global variables and decrease
;       software protection flags by one level
        gaccess cx
        restorsk es,si,di,dx
        unprotec es,si
;       Set carry bit to indicate no error result for DOS call
        and     word ptr retflg[bp],0fffeh      ;reset carry bit in return frame
        resreg
        iret
nprnt$:
;test for keyboard input function
        cmp     ah,01h
        je      chrin
        cmp     ah,06h
        je      eq06
        jmp     neq06
eq06:
        cmp     dl,0ffh            ;if dl=0ffh, then this is a read, else a write
        je      chrin
        jmp     closers
neq06:
        cmp     ah,07h
        je      chrin
        cmp     ah,08h
        je      chrin
        cmp     ah,0ah
        je      chrin
        cmp     ah,0bh
        je      chrin
        cmp     ah,0ch
        je      chrin
        cmp     ah,3fh             ;read from a file or device
        je      read3f             ;arguments much the same as function 44h
        jmp     closers            ;last test fails, try next function
read3f:
        cmp     bx,0               ;is file handle stdin
        je      chrin
        jmp     closers

;       this is some flavor of keyboard input or test
chrin:
        mov     cx,ss              ;temp save of old stack segment
        mov     bx,bp              ;offset of registers in old stack

        switchsk es,si,ax,di
```

Figure 9-4 (Continued)

```
;         push arguments of keyin onto new stack (in reverse order)

          push      cx              ;push old stack segment pointer
          mov       dx,bx
          add       dx,retflg       ;compute offset of flags reg in old stack
          push      dx              ;push offset of flags reg in return frame

          push      cx              ;push old stack segment pointer
          mov       dx,bx
          add       dx,cxreg        ;compute offset of cx reg in old stack
          push      dx              ;push offset of cx reg in return frame

          push      cx              ;push old stack segment pointer
          mov       dx,bx
          add       dx,bxreg        ;compute offset of bx in old stack
          push      dx              ;push offset of bx in old stack

          push      cx              ;push old stack segment pointer
          mov       dx,bx
          add       dx,dsreg        ;compute offset of ds in old stack
          push      dx              ;push offset of ds in old stack

          push      cx              ;push old stack segment
          mov       dx,bx
          add       dx,dxreg        ;compute offset of dx in old stack
          push      dx              ;push offset of dx in old stack

          push      cx              ;push old stack segment
          mov       dx,bx
          add       dx,axreg        ;compute offset of ax in old stack
          push      dx              ;push offset of ax in old stack

;         restore ds to SCHEDULER'S data group
          mov       ax,dgroup
          mov       ds,ax

;         restore es to SCHEDULER'S psp
          mov       ax,word ptr dgroup:_PSPSEG+2
          mov       es,ax

          call keyin
          add       sp,24           ;throw away ptrs to saved ax, dx, ds, bx,
                                    ;cx and flags registers

;         reaccess scheduler's global variables and decrease
;         software protection flags by one level
          gaccess di
          restorsk es,si,di,cx
```

Figure 9-4 (Continued)

```
        unprotec es,si
        resreg
        iret
closers:


;;;;;;;;;;;;;;;;;;;;;;;;;;;;;;;;;;;;;;;;;;;;;;;;;;;;;;;;;;;;;;;;;;;;;;;;;;;;;;;;;;;;;
;       FOR BREVITY, SOME CASES ELIMINATED FROM FIGURE                            ;
;;;;;;;;;;;;;;;;;;;;;;;;;;;;;;;;;;;;;;;;;;;;;;;;;;;;;;;;;;;;;;;;;;;;;;;;;;;;;;;;;;;;;

noterm:                                           ;not a termination interrupt

;       restore registers to state before interrupt for DOS
        resreg
;       now let DOS have control
        int     61H                     ;DOS int 21 relocated to user int 61
;       save registers again
        savreg
;       set zero flag
        setzero
;       set carry flag to indicate error result
        setcarry
;       Re-access scheduler's global data via (es:si) and
;       reduce software protection by one level
        gaccess di
        unprotec es,si
;       restore registers
        resreg

        iret
capt21  endp
        include epilogue.h
        end
```

Figure 9-4 (Continued)

Only a small portion of **capt21** is involved in displaying characters. At the top of the function, the three macros **savreg**, **gaccess**, and **protect** perform important preparatory functions. **savreg** pushes the 8086/88 registers on the stack so that the exact register state can be restored later, should we pass control through to a DOS function that requires no intercept, or when control is returned to the calling function. The macro **gaccess** sets up the registers **es** and **si** to point to the multi-tasker's global variables so that the macro **protect** can turn on the no preempt flag, **noprmpt**, and increment **lvlcalls**. This keeps the function **preempt** from switching tasks in the middle of a DOS function. We can never guarantee that DOS functions are reentrant, and therefore we must allow them to run to completion before allowing a task switch. The macro **unprotec** (invoked after the call to **charout**) decrements **lvlcalls** and if **lvlcalls** becomes zero, turns off the **noprmpt** flag, once again allowing preemptions to occur. Once we have protected ourselves against preemption, we turn the interrupts back on so that we do not freeze out the keyboard interrupt. Following that, **capt21** analyzes **ah** to see if the intercepted function is a function requesting to write the display, and if it is, **capt21** calls **charout** (Figure 9-5) whose jobs are to reset the **es** and **ds** registers so that the C code will properly access global C data, to set up the arguments to the **displayc** function (Figure 9-6), and to perform a call to **displayc**.

The macros **switchsk** and **restorsk** used before and after the call to **charout** are provided so that the C code can operate on the temporary stack provided by **loadprog** for each program. This ensures against overflowing the target program's stack while processing the interrupt. We cannot expect all target programs to allocate enough stack space to handle the stack space requirements of the multi-tasker, which are often rather large. We have made no effort to restrict the stack space used by those programs that simulate DOS and BIOS functions, and even if we had, we still could not guarantee that all target programs would run without stack overflow. Using this temporary stack still is not an absolute guarantee that programs that run without stack overflow under DOS will run without stack ov-erflow under the multitasker, but it ensures that most will.

Finally, just before **capt21 iret**'s to the calling program, it sets the carry bit in the **flags** register within the return frame on the stack, based on the current value of the carry bit in the **flags** register. This tells the calling program whether or not there was an error in the DOS function.

displayc is the workhorse function for character display. It performs integrity checks, writes characters to the display buffer, positions the cursor for the next character, and handles special characters such as carriage return. To increase the speed of the display function and to compensate for the large amount of integrity-checking computation done by **displayc** and the additional computation introduced by the BIOS intercept code for cursor movement, **displayc** writes data characters and their attribute bytes directly to the video display buffer. A pointer to the location of the display buffer is kept in the global C variable **display**, and **displayc** treats the buffer like a C array.

The actual display operation is quite straightforward, but much of **displayc** is code aimed at ensuring the integrity and robustness of the multitasker. On a machine such as the PC, which has no memory protection, an ill-behaved program running under the multitasker can corrupt both its own code and data as well as that of the multitasker. Integrity-checking code is intended to stop a runaway program before it does too much damage. There are no guarantees, of course. If the integrity-checking code is corrupted, the results are unpredictable. Neverthe-less, this code provides some measure of protection.

The integrity code checks for:

1. Potentially infinite recursive calls to **displayc**, as would occur, for example, if there were a **printf** statement in one of the routines called by **displayc** (In this case, **termsched** is called to terminate the multitasking system.)

```
        include model.h
        include prologue.h
a1      equ     @ab

        include process.h

        public charout

charout proc    far
        extrn   displayc:far        ;pointer to C routine that does actual charout
        extrn   _PSPSEG:dword       ;pointer to multitasker's psp

        push    bp
        mov     bp,sp

;       save flags and turn off interrupts

        pushf
        cli

;       restore ds to SCHEDULER'S data group
        mov     ax,dgroup
        mov     ds,ax

;       restore es to SCHEDULER'S psp
        mov     ax,word ptr dgroup:_PSPSEG+2
        mov     es,ax

        mov     ax,7                ;push normal attribute arg onto stack
        push    ax
        mov     ax,a1[bp]           ;push character argument onto stack
        push    ax
        call displayc
        pop     ax                  ;pop argument off stack
        add     sp,2                ;remove attribute arg from stack

;       restore interrupts
        popf

        pop     bp
        ret
charout endp
        include epilogue.h
        end
```

Figure 9-5 charout

```
#include <stdio.h>
#include "proc.h"
#include "window.h"
#include "globdefs.h"
displayc(chr,attr)
        unsigned char chr;        /*Character to be displayed*/
        unsigned char attr;       /*Attribute of character to be displayed*/
        {

        extern unsigned char (*display) [25] [80] [2];
        unsigned int win;         /*Number of window in which to put character*/
        unsigned int pn;          /*Current proc number*/
        unsigned int r,c,lh,lw,ro,co;
        unsigned int vr,vc;
        unsigned int rcur,ccur,mcur;    /*Real cursor position and mode, per bios*/
        int nc,nr,delta;
        unsigned int *psp;
        unsigned int pseg;
        extern int maxcol,maxrow;

        pn = (g->procno);
        win = (g->proctbl)[pn].windno;

        /*Put current cursor position into (r,c)*/
        r = wintbl[win].crow;
        c = wintbl[win].ccol;

        /*Put virtual cursor position into (vr,vc)*/
        vr = wintbl[win].vrow;
        vc = wintbl[win].vcol;

        /*Put origin of window into (ro,co)*/
        ro = wintbl[win].rorg;
        co = wintbl[win].corg;

        /*Put usable height and width of window into (lh,lw)*/
        lh = wintbl[win].h;
        lw = wintbl[win].w;


        ++disp_level;
        if(disp_level > 2)
                {
                strcpy(s,"displayc: disp_level (     ) for procno (     ) in window (     )");

                converti2s(disp_level,&(s[22]));
                converti2s(pn,&(s[41]));
                converti2s(win,&(s[58]));
                errormsg(SCHEDULER,s);
                termsched(disp_level);
                }

        if(tracef)
                {
                /*Integrity check*/
                if(wintbl[win].pnumb != pn)
                        {
                        strcpy(s,"displayc: curr process no (     ) !=pn in wintbl (     )");
```

Figure 9-6 displayc

```
                    converti2s(pn,&(s[27]));
                    converti2s(wintbl[win].pnumb,&(s[49]));
                    errormsg(SCHEDULER,s);
                    /*Suspend, but only once*/
                    if((g->proctbl)[pn].procstate==RUNNING) suspend(pn);
                    --disp_level;
                    return;
                    }

        pseg=(g->proctbl)[pn].pspseg;
        pfusion(&psp,pseg,0);

        if(*psp != 0x20CD)
                {
                /*Temporarily repair psp signature so that trace messages
                  emitted during process switching do not cause an
                  infinite loop*/
                *psp = 0x20CD;
                strcpy(s,"displayc( ): illegal signature at psp        , suspending     ");
                s[9] = chr;
                converti2s(pseg,&(s[39]));
                converti2s(pn,&(s[58]));
                errormsg(SCHEDULER,s);
                /*Suspend, but only once*/
                if((g->proctbl)[pn].procstate==RUNNING) suspend(pn);
                --disp_level;
                return;
                }
        }
if(r < 0 || r > maxrow || c < 0 || c > maxcol ||
   r <= ro || r > ro + lh || c <= co || c > co + lw)
        {
        strcpy(s,"displayc: attempt to display ' ' at illegal pos (    ,    )");
        s[30] = chr;
        converti2s(r,&(s[49]));
        converti2s(c,&(s[55]));
        errormsg(SCHEDULER,s);
        --disp_level;
        return;
        }

if( disp_level <= 2 && (printer_on || (g->proctbl)[pn].prntr)) printchar(chr);

if(chr == '\n') /*Line feed*/
        {
        if(r + 1 > ro + lh) /*Already on last line of window*/
                {
                scroll_window(ro+1,co+1,ro+lh,co+lw,1,NORM_ATTR,SCROLL_UP);

                /*Move cursor to start of last line of window*/
                move_wcursor((ro + lh),(co + 1),win);
                --disp_level;
                return;
                }
        else    /*The cursor is somewhere in middle of window (vertically)*/
                {
```

Figure 9-6 (Continued)

```
                        /*Move cursor to start of next line*/
                        move_wcursor(r + 1,co + 1,win);
                        --disp_level;
                        return;
                        }
                }

if(chr == '\r') /*Carriage Return*/
        {
        move_wcursor(r,co+1,win);
        --disp_level;
        return;
        }

if(chr == BACKSPACE)
        {
        nc = ((c - co - 2 + lw) % lw) + co + 1;
        delta = (c >= nc) ? 0 : 1;
        nr = ((r - ro - 1 - delta + lh) % lh) + ro + 1;
        (*display) [nr] [nc] [0] = ' ';

        move_wcursor(nr,nc,win);
        --disp_level;
        return;
        }

/*Data character (+ its attribute) to be displayed*/

(*display) [r] [c] [0] = chr;
(*display) [r] [c] [1] = attr;

if((lw+co) > c) /*There is room for one more data character on this line*/
        {
        move_wcursor(r,c + 1,win);
        --disp_level;
        return;
        }
else            /*This character is the last character on the line*/
        {
                /*Cause proper cursor movement, with scrolling if necessary*/
        displayc('\n', NORM_ATTR);
        displayc('\r', NORM_ATTR); /*Redundant for display but necessary for printer*/
        --disp_level;
        return;
        }
}
```

Figure 9-6 (Continued)

2. Agreement between the current process number and the process number stored in the window table entry associated with the current process

3. The validity of the program segment prefix (the first two bytes must contain an **int 20** instruction)

4. Coordinate positions that are outside of the display buffer

If one of the integrity constraints is violated, an error message is created and written to the message area of the scheduler's window using the function **errormsg**. These messages are created using conversion routines (e.g., **converti2s**) that are separate from the C run-time I/O routines that would be invoked by **sprintf**. Recall that **displayc** may well be invoked from inside a **printf**, and we have no way to guarantee that there is not some undesirable interaction between the run-time structures of **sprintf** and **printf**.

The main line processing of **displayc** starts just after the integrity checks. It first checks for characters that require special handling. Line feeds will require that the window be scrolled up by one line, if the cursor is currently on the last line of the window. Otherwise, the cursor is moved to the first position of the next line using **mov_wcursor**, which will update the cursor position in the window table. A carriage return moves the cursor to the start of the current line and updates the window table appropriately. A backspace moves the cursor back one character and writes a blank in that position. The backspace logic shown wraps the cursor backwards from line to line and from top of window to bottom. An alternative no-wrap convention could be implemented that would ignore backspaces after the first character of the current line is reached. Which convention is used, is a matter of the user requirements.

Data characters that require no special processing are written directly to the display buffer, after which the cursor is moved to the next character position. If the current character is the last character on the line, **displayc** causes line wrap by recursively calling itself to process a line feed and carriage return.

Emulating BIOS Display Functions

The BIOS interrupt for managing the display, interrupt 0x10, represents the lowest level of control that most programs exert over the display. Indeed, most programs only indirectly invoke BIOS display functions through their invocation of DOS display functions. Nevertheless, some programs do write the display or move the cursor from place to place using BIOS. For example, at one point when the compiler determines that it cannot continue because its memory has apparently been corrupted, it uses BIOS to write messages and dump the stack before it aborts. It probably does this for two reasons: First, it is relatively simple to write a constant string with the BIOS call, and second, the compiler cannot be entirely sure that that part of the DOS code that writes to the display has not also been corrupted. It certainly can be sure that the BIOS has not been corrupted, because it is in ROM.

Accommodating programs that use BIOS to write the display is only one reason that we intercept BIOS display functions. Another and more compelling reason is to manage the cursor position in the window table. This ensures that the proper relationship between the virtual coordinate space and the real coordinate space is maintained, and it ensures that both the application program and the multitasker are using the same virtual coordinate position.

Mapping Screen Coordinates

Understanding the relationship between the virtual coordinate space and real co-ordinate space is fundamental to understanding the routines that emulate the BIOS display functions, as well as understanding the cursor movement utility functions used by the DM. Therefore, we will develop the equations that underlie this relationship.

Let each capital letter followed by a small integer—for example, A0—represent a point in some two-dimensional, infinite plane. That is, A0 represents the 2-tuple (r0,c0) where r0 and c0 are integers representing row and column positions respectively in the plane. Thus, A0 is a vector in the plane from the origin to the point (r0,c0). By convention, we will choose uppercase A to represent absolute positions (i.e., positions in an absolute plane) and uppercase V to represent virtual positions (i.e., positions in a virtual plane). Let the current cursor position stored in the window table be point 0 and some separate, new cursor position be point 1. By this definition, we have defined the following four vectors:

```
A0 - Current point in wintbl[win], in absolute form
V0 - Current point in wintbl[win], in virtual form
A1 - New point in absolute form
V1 - New point in virtual form
```

Now we can use vector arithmetic to compute the vector difference between points 0 and 1 in both the absolute plane and in the virtual plane. Of course, the two resultant vectors must be equal, which gives us the vector equation:

```
A1 - A0 = V1 - V0
```

Another way to think about this equation is to think about the **x** and **y** dimensions separately. Looked at in this way, the equation says that the difference in the two **y** values in the absolute plane must be equal to the difference in the two **y** values in the virtual plane, and likewise for the **x** values. That is, the relative **y** distance between the points is a constant regardless of where the two points are placed with respect to the origin of the plane. The same is true for the relative **x** distance.

Variants of this equation provide the methods for computing absolute co-ordinates of a new point from the absolute and virtual coordinates of the current point, plus the desired virtual coordinates of the new point. Similarly, we can compute the virtual coordinates of a new point in the analogous way. The forms of the equation on which these computations are based are:

```
A1 = V1 - V0 + A0,       and
V1 = A1 - A0 + V0
```

Displaying Characters

The function **writeac** emulates interrupt 0x10, functions 9 and 10. These functions write a character plus its attribute byte, or just write a character. The input parameters to **writeac** are all pointers to register values stored on the stack. These register values will be restored to the registers just before control is returned from the interrupt, and this provides a mechanism for returning results to the calling program. The input parameters for **writeac** as well as the other BIOS emulation functions are set up by an assembly routine **capt10**, which is similar to **capt21**.

Figure 9-7 exhibits the code for **writeac**.

```
#include <stdio.h>
#include "proc.h"
#include "window.h"
#include "globdefs.h"
unsigned writeac(inax,inbx,incx,retflags)
        unsigned *inax; /*Ptr to value of ax register - bios function in ah*/
        unsigned *inbx; /*Ptr to value of bx register - display page*/
        unsigned *incx; /*Ptr to value of cx register - count of characters to write*/
        unsigned *retflags;/*Ptr to value of flags register in return frame*/
        {
        extern unsigned char (*display) [25] [80] [2];
        unsigned int win;      /*Number of window in which to put character*/
        unsigned int pn;       /*Current proc number*/
        unsigned int r,c;
        unsigned tmpax, tmpdx, tmpbx, tmpflags;
        unsigned bioscode;     /*Original contents of ax*/
        int i;
        unsigned char chr, attr;
        unsigned setpos();

        bioscode = (*inax & 0xff00) >> 8;

        /*Capture write character to display function.
          All others handled by BIOS code*/


        pn = (g->procno);
        win = (g->proctbl)[pn].windno;

        chr =(unsigned char) (*inax & 0x00ff);
        if(bioscode == 9) attr = (unsigned char) (*inbx & 0x00ff);
        else attr = NORM_ATTR;

        for(i=0; i < *incx ;i++)
                {
                tmpbx = *inbx & 0xff00;
                /*If more than one character to write,
```

Figure 9-7 writeac

```
          move cursor on copies 2 through n*/
    if(i > 0)
            {
            tmpdx = (wintbl[win].vrow << 8) | (wintbl[win].vcol+ 1);
            tmpax = 0x0200;         /*Set cursor position function*/
            setpos(&tmpax,&tmpdx,&tmpbx,&tmpflags);
            }

    /*Put current absolute cursor position into (r,c)*/
    r = wintbl[win].crow;
    c = wintbl[win].ccol;

    /*Data character (+ its attribute) to be displayed*/
    (*display) [r] [c] [0] = chr;
    if(bioscode == 9)
            (*display) [r] [c] [1] = attr;
    }
return;
}
```

Figure 9-7 (Continued)

Setting and Reading the Cursor Position

setpos, shown in Figure 9-8, emulates the function of interrupt 0x10, function 2. It performs several separate functions:

1. It maps from the virtual input coordinates to absolute coordinates
2. Updates the window table with the new cursor position
3. Folds positions that are past the right boundary of the window onto the following line
4. Scrolls the window up or down when positions are below or above the window
5. Calls the real BIOS interrupt 0x10 code to perform the physical cursor movement

```
#include <stdio.h>
#include "proc.h"
#include "window.h"
#include "globdefs.h"
unsigned setpos(inax,indx,inbx,retflags)
        unsigned *inax; /*Ptr to value of ax register - bios function code in ah*/
        unsigned *indx; /*Ptr to value of dx register - row, column target*/
        unsigned *inbx; /*Ptr to value of bx register - page number in bh*/
        unsigned *retflags;/*Ptr to value of flags register in return frame*/
```

Figure 9-8 setpos

```
{
unsigned int win;           /*Number of window in which to put character*/
unsigned int pn;            /*Current proc number*/

int rabs,cabs,ro,co;        /*Absolute (real screen) coords & dimensions*/
int newrabs, newcabs;       /*Absolute coordinates of new point*/

int rwrel,cwrel;            /*Window relative coordinates for current cursor position*/
int newrwrel,newcwrel;      /*Window relative coordinates for new cursor position*/
int lh,lw;                  /*Usable length and width of window (w/o borders)*/

int vr,vc;                  /*Virtual screen coordinate of current position*/
int rscreen, cscreen;       /*Virtual screen coordinate of new position*/
int rov, cov;               /*Virtual screen coordinates of upper,
                               left window border*/
int botwinv, ritwinv;       /*Virtual coordinates of bottom, right window corner*/

int scrollno;               /*Amount to scroll (if necessary)*/
unsigned scrolldir;         /*Scroll direction*/

process *curproc;
unsigned curpno, sysint();
struct regval srv;


pn = (g->procno);
win = (g->proctbl)[pn].windno;

/*Put current position into abs. coordinates (rabs,cabs)*/
rabs = wintbl[win].crow;
cabs = wintbl[win].ccol;

/*Put origin of window border into abs. coordinates (ro,co)*/
ro = wintbl[win].rorg;
co = wintbl[win].corg;

/*Put usable height and width of window into (lh,lw)*/
lh = wintbl[win].h;
lw = wintbl[win].w;

/*Get virtual coordinates of new position in (rscreen,cscreen)*/
rscreen = (*indx & 0xff00) >> 8;
cscreen = (*indx & 0x00ff);

/*Get virtual coordinates of current position in (vr,vc)*/
vr = wintbl[win].vrow;
vc = wintbl[win].vcol;

/*Compute positions relative to window*/
rwrel = rabs - ro - 1;
cwrel = cabs - co - 1;

/*Compute virtual screen position of upper, left corner of window border*/
rov = vr - rwrel - 1;
cov = vc - cwrel - 1;
```

Figure 9-8 (Continued)

```
/*Compute virtual screen position of bottom right corner of window*/
botwinv = rov + lh + 1;
ritwinv = cov + lw + 1;

scrollno = -1;

/*If cursor falls past the right boundary, fold the position onto
  the next line*/
if(cscreen >= ritwinv) {cscreen = cscreen % ritwinv; ++rscreen;}

/*New relative coordinates = distance between points + old relative*/
newrwrel = (rscreen - vr) + rwrel;
newcwrel = (cscreen - vc) + cwrel;

/*If rscreen falls outside of window, scroll window appropriate amount*/
if(newrwrel < 0) /*Point is above and outside window*/
        {
        scrollno = ABS(newrwrel);
        scrolldir = SCROLL_DOWN;
        newrwrel = 0;
        }
else if (newrwrel >= lh) /*Point is below and outside window*/
        {
        scrollno = newrwrel - lh + 1;
        scrolldir = SCROLL_UP;
        newrwrel = lh - 1;
        }
else scrollno = -1;                           /*No scroll*/
if(scrollno >= lh) scrollno = 0;              /*Scroll whole window*/
if(scrollno >= 0)
        scroll_window(ro+1,co+1,ro+lh,co+lw,scrollno,NORM_ATTR,scrolldir);

/*Compute absolute coordinates of new point*/
newrabs = newrwrel + ro + 1;
newcabs = newcwrel + co + 1;

/*Now move cursor to new position*/

if (win==cwin)
        {
        srv.ax = *inax;
        srv.bx = *inbx;
        srv.dx = (newrabs << 8) | (newcabs & 0x00ff);
        *retflags = sysint(BIOS10,&srv,&srv);
        }
else *retflags &= ~CARRY_BIT ;

/*Record new position in window table*/
wintbl[win].crow = newrabs;
wintbl[win].ccol = newcabs;

wintbl[win].vrow = rscreen;
wintbl[win].vcol = cscreen;

}
```

Figure 9-8 (Continued)

readpos, shown in Figure 9-9, emulates interrupt 0x10, function 3. It reads the current virtual position of the cursor from the window table and returns it in the format defined for function 3.

We make use of another function called **scroll**, which emulates interrupt 0x10, functions 6 and 7. Its interface is analogous to the other C functions that emulate portions of interrupt 0x10. We will leave this routine as an exercise for the reader. See Exercise 9.1.

```c
#include <stdio.h>
#include "proc.h"
#include "window.h"
#include "globdefs.h"
unsigned readpos(inax,inbx,indx,incx,retflags)  /*ah = 3*/
        unsigned *inax; /*Ptr to value of ax register - bios function code in ah*/
        unsigned *inbx; /*Ptr to value of bx register - page number in bh*/
        unsigned *indx; /*Ptr to value of dx register - current row, column*/
        unsigned *incx; /*Ptr to value of cx register - current cursor mode*/
        unsigned *retflags;/*Ptr to value of flags register in return frame*/
        {
        unsigned int win;       /*Number of window in which to put character*/
        unsigned int pn;        /*Current proc number*/
        int cscreen, rscreen;   /*Virtual coordinate of current position*/

        process *curproc;
        unsigned curpno, sysint();
        struct regval srv;


        pn = (g->procno);
        win = (g->proctbl)[pn].windno;

        /*Get current cursor mode*/
        srv.ax = *inax;
        srv.bx = *inbx;
        *retflags = sysint(BIOS10,&srv,&srv);

        *incx = srv.cx;

        /*Return virtual screen coordinates*/
        rscreen = wintbl[win].vrow;
        cscreen = wintbl[win].vcol;
        *indx = (rscreen << 8) | cscreen;

        }
```

Figure 9-9 readpos

Cursor Movement Utility Functions

This represents a good place to present the definitions of the cursor movement utility functions, such as **mov_wcursor**, that up to now we have taken on faith. Table 9-1 summarizes the requirements for these functions.

These functions are designed for use by the scheduler and provide a variety of ways to move the cursor. Those functions that have the prefix "virt" take virtual coordinates as input and those functions without the prefix take absolute coordinates. If the function name has a "wcursor" syllable, it takes an additional argument that specifies the window to which the move is relative. If the syllable is just "cursor," the move is relative to the current window if in virtual coordinates, or the whole screen if absolute. The window table is updated for all routines except **move_cursor**, which is reserved for multitasking functions such as moving the real cursor from one window to another when the window specified as current is changed. The physical cursor is moved for the other functions only if the specified window is the current window since the visible cursor—that is, the cursor that the user actually sees on the video display—is always associated with the current window.

These functions are presented in Figure 9-10. The support functions **virt2abs** and **abs2virt** are a direct implementation of the vector equations developed earlier.

Window Management Functions

The window management functions are few and simple. They provide the ability to create windows, allocate them to and deallocate them from processes, and change the current window.

initwindow, shown in Figure 9-11, is called once per window to initialize that window. The window may be allocated to and deallocated from many processes thereafter, but **initwindow** is never called again. This function does the physical

TABLE 9-1   CURSOR MOVEMENT UTILITY FUNCTION REQUIREMENTS

Routine	Virtual/absolute coordinates	Physical move of cursor	Update wintbl	BIOS intercept code called	Relative to
move_wcursor	Absolute	Physical if current window	Yes	Yes, if physical move	Specified window
virt_move_wcursor	Virtual	Physical if current window	Yes	Yes, if physical move	Specified window
move_cursor	Absolute	Physical	No	No	Screen
virt_move_cursor	Virtual	Physical if current window	Yes	Yes, if physical move	Current window

```
#include <stdio.h>
#include "proc.h"
#include "window.h"
#include "globdefs.h"
virt_move_cursor(row,col)
/*      This function moves the cursor to position (row,col)
        in the virtual screen space of the current window.
        It uses bios 0x10 interrupt with function 2.
*/
        unsigned int row,col;
        {
        unsigned int xtrows;
        extern int maxcol,maxrow,maxcolp1,maxrowp1;


/*      Declare structures which contain the register
        values before and after a system interrupt
        executed by the C function sysint.
*/
        struct regval {int ax,bx,cx,dx,si,di,ds,es; };
        struct regval sreg ;
        struct regval rreg;

/*      Screen wrap logic --
        This logic wraps to top of virtual screen if necessary.
*/
        if((row > maxrow) || (col > maxcol))
                {
                xtrows = col / maxcolp1;
                col %= maxcolp1;
                row += xtrows;
                row %= maxrowp1;
                }

/*      col to dl and row to dh          */
/*      screen number to bh              */
        sreg.dx = col;
        sreg.dx = sreg.dx | ((row << 8) & 0xff00);
        sreg.bx = 0;

        sreg.ax = 0x200;                 /*bios function 2*/

        return(sysint(INTERCEPT10,&sreg,&rreg));

        }
```

Figure 9-10 Cursor Movement Utility Functions

```
move_cursor(row,col)
/*      This function moves the cursor to absolute position (row,col)
        of the screen. This function knows nothing of windows.
        It uses bios 0x10 interrupt with function 2.
*/
        unsigned int row,col;
        {
        unsigned int xtrows;
        extern int maxcol,maxrow,maxcolp1,maxrowp1;


/*      Declare structures which contain the register
        values before and after a system interrupt
        executed by the C function sysint.
*/
        struct regval { int ax,bx,cx,dx,si,di,ds,es; };
        struct regval sreg ;
        struct regval rreg;

/*      Screen wrap logic --
        This logic wraps to top of real screen if necessary.
*/
        if((row > maxrow) || (col > maxcol))
                {
                xtrows = col / maxcolp1;
                col %= maxcolp1;
                row += xtrows;
                row %= maxrowp1;
                }
/*      col to dl and row to dh          */
/*      screen number to bh             */
        sreg.dx = col;
        sreg.dx = sreg.dx | ((row << 8) & 0xff00);
        sreg.bx = 0;


        sreg.ax = 0x200;            /*bios function 2*/

        /*Call bios interrupt 10, bypassing interrupt code*/
        return(sysint(BIOS10,&sreg,&rreg));

        }

move_wcursor(r,c,w)
```

Figure 9-10 (Continued)

```
      unsigned int c;  /*Column to which to move cursor*/
      unsigned int w;  /*Window in which to move cursor*/
      {
      int vr,vc; /*Virtual coordinates*/
      int pn,win; /*Current process number and its window number*/

      pn = (g->procno);
      win = (g->proctbl)[pn].windno;

      /*Transform coordinates to virtual coordinates with respect to the
        window*/

      abs2virt(r,c,&vr,&vc,w);

      /*Do physical movement of cursor, only if movement is in
        the current window*/
      if(w==cwin) virt_move_cursor(vr,vc);

      else
              {
              wintbl[w].vrow = vr;
              wintbl[w].vcol = vc;
              wintbl[w].crow = r;
              wintbl[w].ccol = c;
              }
      }

virt_move_wcursor(vr,vc,w)
        unsigned int vr;/*Row in virtual screen to which to move cursor*/
        unsigned int vc;/*Column in virtual screen to which to move cursor*/
        unsigned int w; /*Window in which to move cursor*/
        {

        int r,c;        /*Absolute coordinates*/
        int pn,win;     /*Current process number and its window number*/

        pn = (g->procno);
        win = (g->proctbl)[pn].windno;

        /*Transform virtual coordinates to absolute coordinates */
        virt2abs(vr,vc,&r,&c,w);

        /*Do physical movement of cursor, only if movement is in
          current window*/
        if(w==cwin) virt_move_cursor(vr,vc);
```

Figure 9-10 (Continued)

```
            else
                    {
                    wintbl[w].vrow = vr;
                    wintbl[w].vcol = vc;
                    wintbl[w].crow = r;
                    wintbl[w].ccol = c;
                    }
            }

virt2abs(vr,vc,ar,ac,win)
        int vr,vc;          /*Virtual coordinates input*/
        int *ar,*ac;        /*Absolute coordinates output*/
        int win;
        {
        *ar = vr - wintbl[win].vrow + wintbl[win].crow;
        *ac = vc - wintbl[win].vcol + wintbl[win].ccol;
        }
abs2virt(ar,ac,vr,vc,win)
        int ar,ac;          /*Absolute coordinates input*/
        int *vr,*vc;        /*Virtual coordinates output*/
        int win;
        {
        *vr = ar - wintbl[win].crow + wintbl[win].vrow;
        *vc = ac - wintbl[win].ccol + wintbl[win].vcol;
        }
```

Figure 9-10 (Continued)

```
#include <stdio.h>
#include "proc.h"
#include "window.h"
#include "globdefs.h"
initwindow(wno,r,c,lh,lw)
        unsigned int wno;       /* window number*/
        unsigned int r;         /* row of upper left corner of window*/
        unsigned int c;         /* column of upper left corner of window*/
        unsigned int lh;        /* usable height of window being created*/
        unsigned int lw;        /* usable width of window being created*/
        {

        char s;
        unsigned seg,off;
        unsigned *ptr;
        unsigned *alloc(), *calloc();
```

Figure 9-11   initwindow

```
/*Initialize window area with blanks*/
scroll_window(r,c,(r+lh+1),(c+lw+1),0,NORM_ATTR,SCROLL_UP);

draw_border(r,c,lh,lw);

wintbl[wno].rorg = r;
wintbl[wno].corg = c;

wintbl[wno].h = lh;
wintbl[wno].w = lw;

/*Initialize window's cursor*/

wintbl[wno].crow = wintbl[wno].rorg + 1;
wintbl[wno].ccol = wintbl[wno].corg + 1;

wintbl[wno].vrow = 0;
wintbl[wno].vcol = 0;


ptr = (unsigned int *) alloc(BUFFER_SIZE * sizeof(unsigned int));
pfission(ptr,&seg,&off);

/*Set up keyboard buffer for this window*/
wintbl[wno].keybuf = ptr;

clearkeybuf(wno);
++numwindow;
}
```

Figure 9-11 (Continued)

setup of the window on the display using the utility function **draw_border**; initializes its entry in the window table, which includes setting up and initializing the keyboard buffer for this window; and increments the number of windows available.

findwindow, shown in Figure 9-12, looks through the window table in search of a window that is not currently assigned to a process—that is, an idle window— and if it finds one, it allocates it, clears its keyboard buffer, and returns its window table index.

clear_window, shown in Figure 9-13, just blanks an entire window.

change_window and **next_window**, shown in Figure 9-14, allow the current window to be changed. **change_window** does the real work. It unhighlights the border of the old current window and highlights the border of the new current

```
#include <stdio.h>
#include "proc.h"
#include "window.h"
#include "globdefs.h"
findwindow()                /*Find a free window & allocate it*/
        {
        unsigned int i;

        /*Find the next available window and show it as in use*/

        for(i=1; i<=numwindow; ++i )
                if(!wintbl[i].inuse)
                        {
                        wintbl[i].inuse = TRUE;
                        /*Initialize window's cursor*/

                        wintbl[i].crow = wintbl[i].rorg + 1;
                        wintbl[i].ccol = wintbl[i].corg + 1;

                        wintbl[i].vrow = 0;
                        wintbl[i].vcol = 0;

                        clearkeybuf(i);

                        return(i);
                        }
        return(0);
        }
```

Figure 9-12   findwindow

window, using the utility function **border_attribute**. Highlighting the border of the current window is the chosen convention to aid the user in remembering which window is current, and hence with which window the keyboard is currently associated. **change_window** also moves the physical cursor to the current cursor position of the new current window, and if the program associated with that window has been suspended, as would happen if it had tried to read the keyboard while its window was not current, the program is resumed.

next_window is a variation that just picks the next window in the window pool as the current window. This allows the user to cycle through the windows.

delete_window, shown in Figure 9-15, de-allocates a window from use and

```
#include <stdio.h>
#include "proc.h"
#include "window.h"
#include "globdefs.h"
clear_window(nw)                        /*Blank current window*/
        unsigned int nw;                /*Number of target window*/
        {

        unsigned int ro,co,lh,lw;

        ro = wintbl[nw].rorg;
        co = wintbl[nw].corg;
        lh = wintbl[nw].h;
        lw = wintbl[nw].w;
        scroll_window(ro+1,co+1,ro+lh,co+lw,0,NORM_ATTR,SCROLL_UP);
        move_wcursor(ro+1,co+1,nw);
        }
```

Figure 9-13 clear_window

```
#include <stdio.h>
#include "proc.h"
#include "window.h"
#include "globdefs.h"
change_window(nw)                       /*Change current window to window nw*/
        unsigned int nw;                /*Number of target window*/
        {

        unsigned int i;
        unsigned int pn;

        /*Restore border of current window to un-highlighted*/
        border_attribute(cwin,NORM_ATTR,INV_ATTR);

        /*Highlight border of new current window*/
        border_attribute(nw,NORMHLIT_ATTR,INV_ATTR);

        move_cursor(wintbl[nw].crow,wintbl[nw].ccol);
        cwin = nw;

        pn = wintbl[nw].pnumb;
```

Figure 9-14 change_window and next_window

```
        if(!outrange(pn) && (g->proctbl)[pn].procstate == SUSPENDED) resume(pn);
        }

next_window()            /*Change current window to next successive window*/
        {
        unsigned int i,j;

        /*Find the next window and shift attention to that window*/

        for(i=0; i<numwindow;++i)
                {
                j = (i + cwin + 1) % numwindow;
                if(wintbl[j].inuse)
                        {
                        change_window(j);
                        break;
                        }
                }
        }
```

Figure 9-14 (Continued)

```
#include <stdio.h>
#include "proc.h"
#include "window.h"
#include "globdefs.h"
delete_window(nw)                    /*Delete window nw*/
        unsigned int nw;
        {
        unsigned int i;
        char msg[128];
        unsigned pno;

        if(wintbl[nw].pnumb == SCHEDULER || wintbl[nw].inuse == FALSE ||
           numwindow <= 1) return;
        pno = wintbl[nw].pnumb;

        sprintf(msg,"Process %.15s (# %d) terminating use of window number %d",
                (g->proctbl)[pno].procname,pno,nw);
        errormsg(wintbl[nw].pnumb,msg);
        errormsg(SCHEDULER,msg);
        wintbl[nw].inuse = FALSE;
        clearkeybuf(nw);
        if(nw==cwin) next_window();
        }
```

Figure 9-15 delete_window

disassociates it from any process. The window must be in use and it cannot be the scheduler's window. If it is the current window, the next window becomes the current window.

errormsg and **windowmsg**, shown in Figure 9-16, are two ways to write messages to windows. **errormsg** is somewhat of a misnomer, since is it used to write most messages to windows, error, trace, and information. **errormsg** requires the specification of the process number as an indirect specification of the window to which the message is to be directed. **windowmsg** allows the window number to be specified directly.

Other functions that we have used, such as **draw_border** and **border_attribute** are sufficiently intuitive that we will leave them as an exercise for the reader.

```
#include <stdio.h>
#include "proc.h"
#include "window.h"
#include "globdefs.h"
errormsg(pno,msg)       /*Write message in message area of window*/
        int pno;        /*Process number*/
        char *msg;      /*Message to write*/
        {
        int wno;        /*Window number*/

        if(outrange(pno)) pno = SCHEDULER;

        wno = (g->proctbl)[pno].windno;
        windowmsg(wno,msg);
        }


windowmsg(win,msg)      /*Write message in message area of window*/
        int win;        /*Window number in which to write message*/
        char *msg;      /*Message to write*/
        {
        int r,c,m;      /*Row, column position and mode of current cursor*/
        int mr,mc;      /*Row, column position of start of window message area*/

        mr = wintbl[win].rorg + wintbl[win].h + 1;
        mc = wintbl[win].corg +1;

        /*Blank window message area*/
        disp_str(blanks,wintbl[win].w,mr,mc,INV_ATTR);

        /*Write message in window message area*/
        disp_str(msg,MIN(MSG_LEN,strlen(msg)),mr,mc,INV_ATTR);

        }
```

Figure 9-16 errormsg, windowmsg and disp_str

```
disp_str(str,len,r,c,attr)
        char *str;
        int len,r,c;
        unsigned attr;
        /*display len characters of string str at (r,c) position of display*/
        {
        extern unsigned char (*display) [25] [80] [2];

        for(;len>0;--len,++c,++str)
                {
                (*display) [r] [c] [0] = *str;
                (*display) [r] [c] [1] = attr;
                }
        }
```

Figure 9-16 (Continued)

9.2 KEYBOARD MANAGEMENT

Requirements

There is only one keyboard for many programs. As with other shared resources in the system, we have to establish a philosophy of sharing the keyboard. The "current window" notion establishes this philosophy—that is, the current window owns the keyboard, and the program running in that window can perform keyboard reads. Programs running in other windows do not, at the moment, have access to the keyboard. What should happen if a program in a noncurrent window performs a keyboard read? It should be suspended and should not be resumed until its window becomes the current window. If we did not suspend the program trying to read the keyboard, we would have the following deadlock condition: The process in the current window holds the keyboard and is waiting for the CPU. A process in some other window holds the CPU and is waiting for the keyboard. Deadlock! In an earlier chapter, we discussed methods for breaking deadlocks and one was to eliminate the "hold-and-wait" condition for one of the participants of the deadlock condition—that is, take his or her resources away until he or she can have all the resources needed to proceed, and this is just what we do. We take the CPU away from the program in a noncurrent window when it requests the keyboard resource.

What should happen if the program in the current window is reading the keyboard but no character is forthcoming? Maybe the user is thinking about what to type. This is a wasteful situation because the program that is reading the keyboard is "busy waiting"—that is, it is just looping and checking the keyboard. Just to complicate matters a bit, this program cannot be preempted when it runs out of time because it is within a DOS or BIOS call. Therefore, no other program can get a slice of the CPU until the program in the current window gets past the read. This condition is very similar to the deadlock described earlier, and we cannot allow the system to stop while the user is thinking. Therefore, we would like the program that is reading to give up the CPU if no character has been typed for "a long time." The way that we cause this to happen is to create a BIOS intercept routine that looks for this condition and, if it finds the condition, **resume**s the current process, causing a context switch to the scheduler. In the simple DM example, we will take the phrase "a long time" to mean just over one second.

On the other hand, we do not want a sluggish response to typing. A character should appear almost immediately after it is typed, not seconds later. This requirement establishes a higher priority for the program in the current window than programs in other windows. It is similar to a scheduling philosophy called "foreground/background," which in simple terms says that one program designated by the user as foreground should get all the resources that it needs, whenever it needs them, and all other programs are considered background. They get the leftovers. This requirement means that when the program in the current window is running and a character is typed, that program should get another time slice. We do not want three other programs to take up at least a third of a second each before control returns to process the next character. This requirement must be implemented within the keyboard management code.

If, on the other hand, the program in the current window is not running and we type a character, we want it to be the very next program scheduled for the CPU. This requirement is handled in the main loop of the multitasker, discussed in the previous chapter.

Architecture

Figure 9-17 shows the structures involved in keyboard management and how the data flows between them. The BIOS service routine associated with the keyboard hardware interrupt is unaltered. As usual, every time a key is pressed, an interrupt is generated and if the key generates a data character, that character is stored in the buffer associated with the service routine. Those characters are transferred to the keyboard buffer of the current window whenever any program performs a software interrupt 0x16 to request some keyboard service—for example, test for character available. This function is performed by the **bios16** routine, which replaces the system bios for the most part. **bios16** does, however, use the system BIOS interrupt 0x16 code to fetch characters from the real BIOS buffer.

We also have replaced the DOS keyboard functions with an emulator called **keyin**. This replacement is forced on us by the requirement to switch contexts while in the **bios16** routine. **bios16** is called from the DOS routines, and therefore those DOS routines must be reentrant. After all, it is high likely that one program in

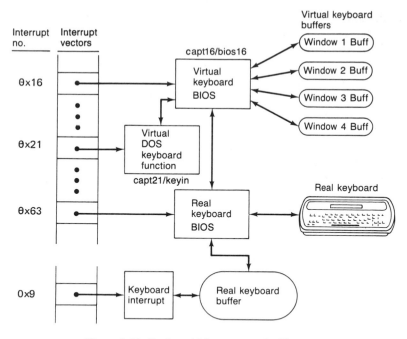

Figure 9-17 Keyboard Management Architecture

the current window will read the keyboard while another program is suspended because it tried to read the keyboard but could not. It appears that DOS switches to a temporary stack while executing the keyboard input functions. Since DOS is operating on the assumption of a single task, it certainly switches to the same stack every time, under the assumption that that stack is free. Should that stack contain any residue from an incomplete keyboard read issued by a now-suspended program, that residue would be overwritten by any intervening keyboard reads. Indeed, this seems to be exactly what happens if we do not replace the DOS keyboard functions. The multitasking system gets extremely confused. Therefore, the multitasker must perform the stack switching on a one-stack-per-program basis and must allow suspension and reentrance of the keyboard read process. **keyin** accomplishes this requirement.

Control gets passed to **bios16** and **keyin** by interrupt intercept routines just like the video display routines. **capt16** intercepts control for **bios16** and **capt21** intercepts control for **keyin**.

Data Structures and Their Management

The keyboard buffers associated with the windows are the central data structure of keyboard management. Each window table entry contains a pointer to its associated keyboard buffer and the storage for the buffer is allocated in the routine

initwindow. (See the definition of **wintbl**.) These buffers are circular buffers similar to the circular buffers that we used in the terminal emulator. Their code appears slightly more complex because the buffer control variables are fields within the window table, but they behave nearly the same as the circular buffers in the terminal emulator. There are a few differences, of course. One difference is that each buffer management function takes an additional parameter that specifies the window number, and therefore the buffer on which the function is to be performed. Another difference is that we have added a new function, **pushkeybuf** that allows us to push a character onto the front of the buffer rather than always queuing characters at the end of the buffer. This function is required because some keys, such as the function keys, must generate two characters, a zero indicating a special key, followed by an ASCII character indicating which specific special key it is. Since some keyboard input functions want only one character returned per interrupt, we need to store the second character of a two-character sequence so that it will be the very next character they read.

The keyboard buffer management functions are shown in Figures 9-18, 9-19, 9-20, 9-21, and 9-22. **beep** is a utility function that generates a tone on the system unit speaker.

Emulating DOS Keyboard Functions

keyin and the functions that it calls attempt to emulate the DOS keyboard input functions faithfully. They do, however, differ in some ways. Since we have changed the meaning of Control-Break, one will, of course, get different behavior in that case. The philosophy of our Control-Break processing is still, in some sense, the same—interrupt and give control to a higher system level. However, the mechanism differs. Due to this difference in the handling of Control-Break, some of the keyboard functions that differed only in whether or not they tested for Control-

```
#include <stdio.h>
#include "proc.h"
#include "window.h"
#include "globdefs.h"
clearkeybuf(w)  /*Set up empty buffer*/
        unsigned w;       /*window number*/
        {
        int flags;
        disable(&flags);             /*Disable interrupts while changing globals*/
        wintbl[w].kbcount = wintbl[w].kbrear = wintbl[w].kbfront = 0;
        restore(flags);
        }
```

Figure 9-18 clearkeybuf

```
#include <stdio.h>
#include "proc.h"
#include "window.h"
#include "globdefs.h"
emptykeybuf(w)
        unsigned w;        /*window number*/
        {
        if(wintbl[w].kbcount > 0) return(FALSE);
        else return(TRUE);
        }
```

Figure 9-19   emptykeybuf

```
#include <stdio.h>
#include "proc.h"
#include "window.h"
#include "globdefs.h"
unsigned nextkeybuf(w)
      unsigned w;       /*window number*/

      {       /*get next character & update circular input buffer*/
      int flags;
      unsigned int current;
      disable(&flags);        /*Disable interrupts while changing globals*/
      if(wintbl[w].kbcount>0)
            {
            current = (*(wintbl[w].keybuf))[wintbl[w].kbfront];
            --wintbl[w].kbcount;
            wintbl[w].kbfront = (wintbl[w].kbfront + 1) % BUFFER_SIZE;
            }
      else current = 0;
      restore(flags);
      return(current);
      }
```

Figure 9-20   nextkeybuf

Break reduce to the same function—DOS functions 7 and 8, for example. Another difference is that we have made no attempt to implement DOS-like function key editing of input lines. This facility is available from DOS to programs that use function 0x0A, buffered keyboard input, to read the keyboard. (See Exercise 9.3.) Other differences, currently unknown, are likely as well.

```
#include <stdio.h>
#include "proc.h"
#include "window.h"
#include "globdefs.h"
putkeybuf(c,w)            /*put one character into the circular buffer*/
        unsigned int c;
        unsigned w;      /*window number*/
        {
        int flags;
        if(wintbl[w].kbcount>=BUFFER_SIZE)
                {
                beep();              /*character lost, buffer overflow*/
                return;
                }

        disable(&flags);            /*Disable interrupts while changing globals*/
        (*(wintbl[w].keybuf))[wintbl[w].kbrear] = c;
        wintbl[w].kbrear = (wintbl[w].kbrear + 1) % BUFFER_SIZE;
        ++wintbl[w].kbcount;
        restore(flags);
        }
```

Figure 9-21   putkeybuf

```
#include <stdio.h>
#include "proc.h"
#include "window.h"
#include "globdefs.h"
pushkeybuf(c,w)            /*push one character onto the front of the buffer*/
        unsigned int c;
        unsigned w;      /*window number*/
        {
        int flags;
        if(wintbl[w].kbcount>=BUFFER_SIZE)
                {
                beep();              /*character lost, buffer overflow*/
                return;
                }

        disable(&flags);            /*Disable interrupts while changing globals*/
        wintbl[w].kbfront = (wintbl[w].kbfront - 1 + BUFFER_SIZE) % BUFFER_SIZE;
        (*(wintbl[w].keybuf))[wintbl[w].kbfront] = c;
        ++wintbl[w].kbcount;
        restore(flags);
        }
```

Figure 9-22   pushkeybuf

Figure 9-23 exhibits the definition of **keyin** and the functions that it calls. Similar to the case with **bios10** the interrupt intercept routine sets up pointers to various register values that are saved on the stack waiting to be restored to the appropriate registers upon return. This provides access to the register values for use by emulation routines, as well as a mechanism for **keyin** to return values as specified by the DOS function definitions. That is, any register value that gets altered on the stack during emulation, will be reflected in the value of the corresponding register upon return from emulation. For example, clearing the carry flag in the flags register on the stack, assures that the carry flag will be clear upon return from the emulation.

This return value mechanism is used in several ways. For example, **keyin** and the functions that it calls make sure that the carry flag is clear in the flags register of the interrupt return stack frame. The carry flag is the mechanism by which newer DOS functions indicate whether or not an error condition has been detected by the DOS function. Clear indicates no error, and set indicates an error condition

```
#include <stdio.h>
#include "proc.h"
#include "window.h"
#include "globdefs.h"
unsigned keyin(inax,indx,inds,inbx,incx,resflags)
        unsigned *inax; /*Ptr to value of ax register passed to dos int 21 function*/
        unsigned *indx; /*Ptr to dx register passed to dos int 21 function*/
        unsigned *inds; /*Ptr to ds register passed to dos int 21 function*/
        unsigned *inbx; /*Ptr to bx, used only for IOCTL device reads*/
        unsigned *incx; /*Ptr to cx, used only for IOCTL device reads*/
        unsigned *resflags;     /*Ptr to value of flags register*/
        {
        unsigned flags;
        unsigned curpno, win, sysint();
        process *curproc;
        unsigned char c;
        unsigned cl;
        unsigned keyboard_char(),ischar;
        struct regval srv;
        unsigned char (*buf)[];
        int i, maxc;
        unsigned seg,off;
        int j;
        unsigned op;

        enable();               /*Assure that interrupts are on so keyboard
                                  can respond*/
        curpno = g->procno;
        curproc = &((g->proctbl)[curpno]);
        /*Only processes in current window may take input from keyboard*/
        win = curproc->windno;
```

Figure 9-23a   keyin

```
op = (*inax & 0xff00) >> 8;


if (op == 0x3f)
        /*Read from keyboard*/
        dos3f(inax,indx,inds,inbx,incx,resflags);
else if(op == 1 || op == 8 || op == 7)
        /*1 = (echo, wait, ctrlbreak check, result in al)*/
        /*7 = (no echo, wait, no ctrlbreak check, result in al)*/
        /*8 = (no echo, wait, ctrlbreak check, result in al)*/
        dos01(inax,resflags);

else if (op == 6)
        /*(no echo, no wait, no ctrlbreak, result char is
          in al if ZF is clear, or no char if ZF is set)*/

        dos06(inax,indx,resflags);

else if (op == 0xa)
        /*0a = (echo, wait, ctrlbreak check, result in [ds:dx])*/
        dos0a(inax,indx,inds,inbx,incx,resflags);

else if (op == 0xb)
        {
        /*(no echo, no wait, ctrlbreak, result status in al)*/
        /*if al==0ff, char is available, else char not avail*/

        srv.ax = BIOSCHECKCODE;
        *resflags = (sysint(INTERCEPT16,&srv,&srv) & ~CARRY_BIT);
        if(*resflags & ZERO_BIT) /*No char avail*/
                *inax = 0;
        else *inax = 0x00ff;
        }
else if (op == 0xc)
        {
        /*(echo =f(al), wait, ctrlbreak=f(al), result is clear buffer)*/
        clearkeybuf(win);
        *inax = (*inax & 0xff) << 8;
        *resflags = keyin(inax,indx,inds,inbx,incx,resflags);
        }
else
        {
        strcpy(s,"keyin: bad op code = 0x    ");
        convertx2s(op,&(s[23]));
        errormsg(SCHEDULER,s);
        }

return(*resflags);
}
```

Figure 9-23a (Continued)

```
dos3f(inax,indx,inds,inbx,incx,resflags)
        unsigned *inax; /*Ptr to value of ax register passed to dos int 21 function*/
        unsigned *indx; /*Ptr to dx register passed to dos int 21 function*/
        unsigned *inds; /*Ptr to ds register passed to dos int 21 function*/
        unsigned *inbx; /*Ptr to bx, used only for IOCTL device reads*/
        unsigned *incx; /*Ptr to cx, used only for IOCTL device reads*/
        unsigned *resflags;     /*Ptr to values of flags register*/
        {
        unsigned curpno, win, sysint();
        process *curproc;
        unsigned char c;
        struct regval srv;
        unsigned char (*buf)[];
        int i, maxc;
        unsigned seg,off;
        int j;

        curpno = g->procno;
        curproc = &((g->proctbl)[curpno]);
        win = curproc->windno;

        c = '\0';
        pfusion(&buf,*inds,*indx);
        (*buf)[0] = '\0';         /*Assure no CTRL_Z left from previous call*/
        for(i=0; i < *incx ; i++)
                {
                enable();         /*Assure that interrupts are on
                                     so keyboard can respond*/

                srv.ax = BIOSREADCODE;
                *resflags = (sysint(INTERCEPT16,&srv,&srv) & ~CARRY_BIT);
                c = (srv.ax & 0x00ff);
                if (c == BACKSPACE)
                        {
                        if(i > 0) i -= 2;       /* -2 + loop incr = -1*/
                        else      --i;          /* -1 + loop incr = 0*/
                        displayc(c,NORM_ATTR);
                        }
                else if (c == 0) --i;   /*Special key, ignore*/

                else if ((*buf)[0] != CTRL_Z)
                        {
                        (*buf)[i] = c;
                        displayc(c,NORM_ATTR);
                        }
                /* CTRL_Z was the first character, just echo character.
                  But do not store character.
                  CRETURN is an exception whose processing is defined below.*/

                else if (c != CRETURN) displayc(c,NORM_ATTR);
```

Figure 9-23b   dos3f

```
        if(c == CRETURN)            /*CRETURN causes loop termination*/
            {
            if (i < (*incx - 1))
                {
                if ((*buf)[0] != CTRL_Z)
                        (*buf)[++i] = NEWLINE;
                displayc(NEWLINE,NORM_ATTR);
                }
            else
                {
                if ((*buf)[0] != CTRL_Z)
                        pushkeybuf(NEWLINE,win);
                }
            if ((*buf)[0] != CTRL_Z)
                    *inax = ++i;        /*Number of characters read*/
            else *inax = 0;             /*Return 0 if CTRL_Z*/
            return(*resflags);
            }
        }
if ((*buf)[0] != CTRL_Z)
        *inax = i;          /*Number of characters read*/
else *inax = 0;             /*Return 0 if CTRL_Z*/
}
```

Figure 9-23b (Continued)

was found and further indicates that the specific error condition will be defined by
the value in the ax register. (See "DOS Interrupts and Function Calls" in the DOS
manual.)

TABLE 9-2   SPECIAL CHARACTER HANDLING

DOS operation	CTRL-Z (EOF)	Carriage return	Backspace	Function keys
0x01	Returns 0x11a	Returns 0x10d	Returns 0x108	Returns 0x100 followed by 0x1<sc>
0x06	Returns 0x61a	Returns 0x60d	Returns 0x608	Returns 0x600 followed by 0x6<sc>
0x07	Returns 0x71a	Returns 0x70d	Returns 0x708	Returns 0x700 followed by 0x7<sc>
0x0a	Returns buffer [N,1,0x1a,0x0d]	Returns buffer [N,0,0x0d]	Processes in buffer	(See discussion)
0x3f	Returns 0 chars with 0x1a in buffer	Returns 0x0d followed by 0x0a	Processes in buffer	Sporadic behavior

```
dos01(inax,resflags)
      unsigned *inax; /*Ptr to value of ax register passed to dos int 21 function*/
      unsigned *resflags;      /*Ptr to values of flags register*/
      {
      unsigned curpno, win, sysint();
      process *curproc;
      unsigned char c;
      struct regval srv;
      unsigned char (*buf)[];
      int i, maxc;
      unsigned seg,off;
      int j;
      unsigned op;

      curpno = g->procno;
      curproc = &((g->proctbl)[curpno]);
      win = curproc->windno;

      op = (*inax & 0xff00) >> 8;

      srv.ax = BIOSREADCODE;
      *resflags = (sysint(INTERCEPT16,&srv,&srv) & ~CARRY_BIT);
      if((srv.ax & 0x00ff) == 0)
              {
              /*Two character sequence, push scan code back onto
                front of key buffer. Will be retrieved on next call*/
              pushkeybuf(((srv.ax & 0xff00) >> 8),win);
              if(op == 1) displayc(' ',NORM_ATTR);
              *inax = (op << 8) | 0;
              }
      else
              {        /*Normal character*/
              *inax = (op << 8) | (srv.ax & 0x00ff);
              /*if op 1, echo character*/
              if(op == 1) displayc((unsigned char) (*inax & 0x00ff),NORM_ATTR);
              }
      }
```

Figure 9-23c   dos01

In general, the **keyin** function just analyzes the DOS function code in **ax** (pointed to by **inax**), and dispatches control to the proper processing routine. Each of the DOS functions implemented by **keyin** and its subfunctions differ in the way that they handle special characters. Table 9-2 defines the empirically determined handling of special characters by the various DOS keyboard input functions. This table is our specification for **keyin** and its subfunctions.

The End Of File character receives special processing only for function 0x3f and only if it is the first character on the line. If it is in the middle of a buffer, it is handled just like any other character. When it is the first character in the buffer,

```
dos06(inax,indx,resflags)
        unsigned *inax; /*Ptr to value of ax register passed to dos int 21 function*/
        unsigned *indx; /*Ptr to dx register passed to dos int 21 function*/
        unsigned *resflags;        /*Ptr to values of flags register*/
        {
        unsigned curpno, win, sysint();
        process *curproc;
        struct regval srv;
        unsigned op;

        curpno = g->procno;
        curproc = &((g->proctbl)[curpno]);
        win = curproc->windno;

        op = (*inax & 0xff00) >> 8;


        /*Not a keyboard input function, should not be possible (see capt21)*/
        if((*indx & 0x00ff) != 0x00ff) return(*resflags);

        srv.ax = BIOSCHECKCODE;
        *resflags = (sysint(INTERCEPT16,&srv,&srv) & ~CARRY_BIT);
        if(!(*resflags & ZERO_BIT))       /*Character is available*/
                {
                /*Now actually get character and update window buffer*/
                srv.ax = BIOSREADCODE;
                sysint(INTERCEPT16,&srv,&srv);
                if((srv.ax & 0x00ff) == 0)
                        {
                        /*Two character sequence, push scan code back onto
                          front of key buffer. Will be retrieved on next call*/
                        pushkeybuf(((srv.ax & 0xff00) >> 8),win);
                        *inax = (op << 8) | 0;
                        }
                else
                        {        /*Normal character*/
                        *inax = (op << 8) | (srv.ax & 0x00ff);
                        }
                }

        }
```

Figure 9-23d   dos06

```
dos0a(inax,indx,inds,inbx,incx,resflags)
        unsigned *inax; /*Ptr to value of ax register passed to dos int 21 function*/
        unsigned *indx; /*Ptr to dx register passed to dos int 21 function*/
        unsigned *inds; /*Ptr to ds register passed to dos int 21 function*/
        unsigned *inbx; /*Ptr to bx, used only for IOCTL device reads*/
```

Figure 9-23e   dos0a

```
unsigned *incx; /*Ptr to cx, used only for IOCTL device reads*/
unsigned *resflags;     /*Ptr to values of flags register*/
{
unsigned curpno, win, sysint();
process *curproc;
unsigned char c;
struct regval srv;
unsigned char (*buf)[];
int i, maxc;
unsigned seg,off;
int j;

curpno = g->procno;
curproc = &((g->proctbl)[curpno]);
win = curproc->windno;


pfusion(&buf,*inds,*indx);
maxc = (int) (*buf)[0];
for(i=-1; i < maxc ;)
        {
        enable();       /*Assure that interrupts are on
                            so keyboard can respond*/
        srv.ax = BIOSREADCODE;
        *resflags = (sysint(INTERCEPT16,&srv,&srv) & ~CARRY_BIT);
        c = (srv.ax & 0x00ff);

        /* (*buf)[i] == the last character put into the buffer*/
        if(c == BACKSPACE)
                {
                if(i > -1)
                        {
                        --i;
                        displayc(c,NORM_ATTR);
                        }
                }
        else if (c == 0);       /*Special key, ignore*/
        else if(i < (maxc - 2) || (i == (maxc - 2) && c == CRETURN))
                {
                (*buf)[(++i + 2)] = c;
                displayc(c,NORM_ATTR);
                }
        else beep();

        if(c == CRETURN)        /*last char is always creturn*/
                {
                (*buf)[1] = (unsigned char) i + 1;
                break;
                }
        }
}
```

Figure 9-23e (Continued)

all characters following it up to and including the carriage return are not entered into the buffer, and 0x3f returns the number of characters read as zero. The other functions give it no special treatment.

As for the backspace character, those functions that buffer characters (0x0a and 0x3f) process the backspace in the buffer eliminating characters and adjusting the character count appropriately. They also reflect the proper contents of the buffer on the screen.

The function 0x3f returns two characters when it reads a carriage return, 0x0d and 0x0a, a carriage return followed by a line feed. Both functions 0x3f and 0x0a require a carriage return to terminate the input operation as long as the buffer is not full. Function 0x3f will allow completion of the read operation without a carriage return if and when the number of characters specified in the **cx** register on input has been read. Function 0x0a, on the other hand, will not return from the operation until it has read a carriage return, even if the buffer is full. It saves the last space in the buffer for the carriage return and if the user tries to overflow the buffer, it simply throws the extra characters away until it receives the carriage return. The carriage return is always the last character in every string that is returned, but the 0x0a function does not include the carriage return in the character count that it returns as the second character of the buffer. The first character position of the buffer, shown as N in Table 9-2, contains the buffer size.

Function keys and keys on the key pad behave somewhat differently. For these keys, the BIOS keyboard code returns two values in the **ax** register. The lower byte, **al**, contains zero, indicating that a special key was struck. The upper byte, **ah**, contains what is called the "scan code," the hardware's designation of the key. In Table 9-2, the symbol string "<sc>" represents the scan code. As a general rule, the DOS routines break out these two fields and return them as two distinct characters, the zero first, followed by the scan code. An appendix of the BASIC manual claims that there are some exceptions to the general rule that the second character is the scan code. It is left as an exercise for the reader to verify if this is true and if so make the proper modifications to the subfunctions of **keyin**.

Intercepting BIOS Keyboard Functions

It would appear desirable not to have to intercept the BIOS keyboard functions if possible, but we must for several reasons. The most compelling reason is that we cannot depend on every program that we would like to run under the multitasker to use only DOS functions to interact with the keyboard. It is easy to find programs that for reasons bad or good will perform direct calls to the BIOS routine. If we depended on only the DOS level emulation to perform the context switches on an illegal keyboard operation, we could have a situation in which an errant program could sneak around the DM and illegally read the keyboard with a BIOS operation. Therefore, we need to intercept the BIOS 0x16 interrupt and since we have to create this BIOS intercept code anyway, it is a convenient, centrally located place in which to place other multitasking services—for example, transferring waiting characters to the correct keyboard buffer. Specifically, the BIOS emulator routine, **bios16**, which is shown in Figure 9-24, performs the following functions:

1. Call the real BIOS to get waiting characters typed from the keyboard
2. Transfer those waiting characters to virtual keyboard buffers
3. Emulate the BIOS interrupt 0x16 read and status check functions
4. Suspend a process that is trying to read the keyboard, if it is not in the current window, is not the scheduler, and the virtual keyboard buffer for that process is empty

```
#include <stdio.h>
#include "proc.h"
#include "window.h"
#include "globdefs.h"
unsigned bios16(inax,retflags)
        unsigned *inax;    /*Ptr to value of ax register passed to dos int 21 function*/
        unsigned *retflags;/*Ptr to value of flags register in return frame*/
        {
        unsigned curpno, win, sysint();
        process *curproc;
        unsigned bioscode;        /*Original contents of ax*/
        unsigned localax;
        unsigned result;
        unsigned peek();
        unsigned nextkeybuf();
        int i;
        struct {int scs, sss,sds,ses;} rv;
        int errflag, resume();
        unsigned flags;


        enable();          /*Assure that interrupts are on so keyboard
                            can respond*/
        curpno = g->procno;
        curproc = &((g->proctbl)[curpno]);
        win = curproc->windno;
        bioscode = (*inax & 0xff00);

        /* Turn off carry bit to indicate no error on return*/
        *retflags &= ~CARRY_BIT;
/* Poll keyboard and buffer any characters waiting for the process in the
   current window.
*/
        localax = BIOSCHECKCODE;
        callb63(&localax,&result);
        while(!(result & ZERO_BIT))
                {
                /*Give this process another time slice*/
                disable(&flags);
```

Figure 9-24   bios16

```
                  (g->clock) = 0;
                  restore(flags);

                  /*Get the waiting character and put in keyborard buffer*/
                  localax = BIOSREADCODE;
                  callb63(&localax,&result);
                  putkeybuf(localax,cwin);

                  localax = BIOSCHECKCODE;
                  callb63(&localax,&result);
                  enable();                     /*Assure that interrupts are on so keyboard
                                                   can respond*/
                  }

/*Now, service the incoming request*/

        if(bioscode == BIOSCHECKCODE)
             {

             if(emptykeybuf(win))
                     {
                     /*If the routine is just looping and waiting for a character,
                       we need to provide the opportunity to get back to
                       the SCHEDULER in case this requires a change of window*/
                     if((g->clock) > 75 && curpno != SCHEDULER)
                             {
                             errflag = resume(curpno);
                             if (errflag == ERROR)
                                     {
                                     strcpy(s,"bios16: resume error\n");
                                     windowmsg(0,s);
                                     }
                             }
                     *retflags |= ~ZERO_BIT;  /*Zero bit on for no char avail*/
                     return;
                     }
             else    /*Put waiting character into al*/
                     {
                     *retflags &=~ZERO_BIT;   /*Zero bit off for char avail*/
                     *inax |= (*(wintbl[win].keybuf))[wintbl[win].kbfront];
                     return;
                     }
             }
        else if(bioscode == BIOSREADCODE)
             {
             while(TRUE)
                     {
                     enable();                         /*Assure that interrupts are on so keyboard
                                                         can respond*/
                     if(!emptykeybuf(win))
                             {
                             *inax =nextkeybuf(win);
                             return;
                             }
                     else
                             {       /*Poll keyboard for a character*/

                             localax = BIOSCHECKCODE;
```

Figure 9-24 (Continued)

```
                                    callb63(&localax,&result);
                                    if(!(result & ZERO_BIT))
                                        {
                                        if(win == cwin)
                                            {
                                            /*Give this process another time slice*/
                                            disable(&flags);
                                            (g->clock) = 0;
                                            restore(flags);
                                            }
                                        localax = BIOSREADCODE;
                                        callb63(&localax,&result);
                                        putkeybuf(localax,cwin);
                                        continue;
                                        }
                                    else if(curpno != SCHEDULER)
                                            {    /*Relinquish control*/
                                            if(win == cwin)
                                                {
                                                /*If no character has arrived for
                                                  1 1/3 seconds, relinquish control.*/
                                                if((g->clock) >25)
                                                        errflag = resume(curpno);
                                                if (errflag == ERROR)
                                                        {
                                                        strcpy(s,"bios16: resume error\n");
                                                        errormsg(SCHEDULER,s);
                                                        errormsg(curpno,s);
                                                        }
                                                }
                                            else
                                                {
                                                strcat(s,"");
                                                strcat(s,"bios16: process no (      ) suspended");
                                                strcat(s," awaiting input, window not current");
                                                converti2s(curpno,&(s[20]));
                                                errormsg(curpno,s);
                                                errormsg(SCHEDULER,s);
                                                suspend(curpno);
                                                strcpy(s,"bios16: process no (      ) resumed");
                                                converti2s(curpno,&(s[20]));
                                                errormsg(curpno,s);
                                                errormsg(SCHEDULER,s);
                                                }
                                            }
                                        /*Else curpno is the scheduler, in which case,
                                          we just keep going around until we get a
                                          character
                                        */
                                        }
                                    }
                            }
            else    /*shift status check, just pass it through*/
                    {
                    callb63(inax,retflags);
                    return;
                    }
            }
```

Figure 9-24 (Continued)

5. Give up the CPU if the current process is reading the keyboard but no character seems forthcoming

6. Pass BIOS calls to check keyboard shift status through to the real BIOS routine

The first thing that **bios16** does on every call is to check the BIOS keyboard buffer to see if there are characters waiting, and if there are, to transfer all that are available into the virtual keyboard buffer of the current window. **bios16** uses the utility function **callb63** to invoke the real BIOS interrupt 0x16 code, which is pointed to by interrupt vector 0x63, one of the interrupt vectors that DOS reserves as "user interrupts." **callb63** serves the same function as **sysint**, but is specialized to interrupt vector 0x63 (the real BIOS interrupt 0x16 code), and it is therefore faster than **sysint**.

Next, **bios16** decodes the subfunction code in **ah** (high-order byte of **ax**) and simulates a keyboard check or read, but passes a shift status check function directly to the real BIOS code. The logic which emulates checking of the keyboard does so by examining the virtual keyboard buffer associated with the process running in the current window, and if it is empty, it may **resume** the current process, thereby giving up the CPU for a time, or it may return the results of the check by setting the zero flag in the flags register. It decides whether or not to give up the CPU by examining the clock. If the clock is greater than seventy-five units, meaning that this process has run for about four seconds without relinquishing the CPU, it calls **resume** and allows the scheduler to choose another candidate. Of course, if there is a character waiting in the buffer, it just emulates a BIOS interrupt 0x16 keyboard check.

The code for emulating the BIOS read is a loop that cycles around waiting for some character to appear in the appropriate virtual keyboard buffer. For each loop in which the virtual keyboard buffer is empty, it polls the real keyboard buffer by invoking the check status function using the real BIOS code. If a character is waiting in the real keyboard buffer, it will issue a read to get it, but first it restarts the clock if the window associated with the executing program is the current window. This effectively gives a program running in the current window another opportunity to issue a keyboard read. The rational for doing this is that programs tend to read the keyboard in bursts, and by restarting the clock we give the typist at least one-third of a second (six clock ticks) to hit the next key. If the program issues a read that waits, the typist gets about one and one-third seconds (see explanation in next paragraph). If the program is just polling the keyboard to test for a character available, the typist may get up to four seconds, under the very special condition that the hardware clock just happens to synchronize with the program logic so that the program is within a DOS or BIOS call every time the clock interrupt fires. This condition is unlikely to hold for very long, but it is possible. These intervals can be adjusted to strike the correct balance between responsiveness and performance degradation.

When the character is read, it is put into the virtual keyboard buffer to be extracted and returned by the next cycle of the loop. However, if no character is available in the real keyboard buffer and the program running is not the scheduler, the current program may give up the CPU by **resume** or **suspend** depending on whether or not it is running in the current window. An additional precondition of giving up the CPU by **resume** is that the clock is greater that 25. In other words, this program has been waiting for the user to type a character for about one and one-third seconds without avail. When a process is **suspend**ed, it leaves a message in the message area of both the scheduler and the window of the suspended process. When the process is later resumed, that message is replaced by one that reports its resumption.

9.3 THE COMMAND INTERFACE

Requirements

Up to this point, we have explained how to switch contexts from one process to another, to write information on the display, read information from the keyboard, terminate programs and even how to initiate programs given a command line, but we have not yet explained how to get a command line from the user to the system, nor have we explained the interaction between the user and the system. This section will explain how this interaction between the user and the system (and more specifically, the scheduler) is accomplished.

We will impose the following requirements on this interaction. We will define the Control-Break key combination as the mechanism whereby we get the scheduler's attention. Control-Break is the key pair established by DOS to interrupt the current application program and get the attention of the program that initiated that application program, usually DOS. Therefore, this key pair is almost never used as data by any application program and therefore, presents little likelihood of conflict between the multitasker and any application program. Almost any other choice of attention getting characters runs some risk of usurping characters that some application program uses as data.

Once we have the scheduler's attention, we will want the interaction to take place in the scheduler's window and operate as part of the scheduler even if we have to wait a short time before the Control-Break gets the scheduler's attention.

Finally, we would like to be able to perform the following functions via this interaction:

1. Initiate new processes (programs)
2. Abort, suspend or resume existing processes
3. Change the current window or redraw the window boundaries

4. Dump various tables (process and window)
5. Turn traces on or off
6. Ask for help
7. Terminate the multitasking system

Architecture

All of these functions are performed by a function called **command**, which is called from the main scheduler loop whenever the **break_cmd** global variable is nonzero. Striking the Control-Break key combination will cause **break_cmd** to be set non-zero. How do we effect the setting of **break_cmd** on a Control-Break key strike? Basically, we replace the keyboard break interrupt (0x1b) with a pointer to an assembly routine called **kbbreak**, which calls the C routine **kbint**. **kbint** sets the **break_cmd**. Now, all of this works because the keyboard break function is invoked from the keyboard hardware interrupt service routine whenever the Control-Break key is struck.

The definitions of these functions are shown in Figure 9-25. **command** is quite intuitive and requires no discussion. Combining the comments with your knowledge of previously described functions should provide sufficient understanding. (The **displaychar** function is left as an exercise for the reader.)

```
#include <stdio.h>
#include "proc.h"
#include "window.h"
#include "globdefs.h"
command()
        {
        unsigned char c,n[3];
        process *pt;
        unsigned pno,wno,tno;
        unsigned i;
        unsigned flags;
        unsigned char bios_getchar();
        unsigned sysint();
        unsigned oldwin;
        unsigned p1,createproc();
        unsigned str[128];
        struct regval srv;

        /*This routine is called from the scheduler.
          This routine is not preemptable.*/

        disable(&flags);
        if(break_cmd == 0) return;
```

Figure 9-25a command

```
if(tracef) printf("command: break_cmd = 0x%x\n",break_cmd);
break_cmd = 0;
enable(flags);


oldwin = cwin;

/*Temporarily change to scheduler's window*/
if(cwin!=0) change_window(0);

printf("Type one character meta cmd>");

/*Get scheduler command and eat creturn*/
c = bios_getchar(); bios_getchar();

if(tracef) printf("command: I just read a 0x%x char\n",(unsigned) c);

displaychar('\n');                 /*Newline*/
pno = wintbl[cwin].pnumb;

/*Decode command*/

switch(c)
        {
        case ABORT:     /*Abort program(s) in current window*/
                if(pno==SCHEDULER) getno(&pno,"process number","ABORT");
                /*First, kill non-active programs (e.g., suspended)
                that are associated with this window*/
                for(i = 1; i < MAXPROCS; i++)
                        {
                        pt = &((g->proctbl)[i]);
                        if(pt->pspseg && (i!=pno) && (pt->windno==oldwin))
                                kill(i);
                        }
                kill(pno);      /*Kill active program*/

                return;

        case NEXT:      /*Move to next window*/
                change_window(oldwin);
                next_window();
                return;

        case COMMAND:   /*Issue a command to start new process*/

                zeroarray(str,127);
                printf("Command>");
                bios_readline(str);

                /*Legal program names are non-null*/
                if(*str!='\0')
```

Figure 9-25a (Continued)

```
                                        {
                                        p1=createproc(str,findwindow());
                                        if(!outrange(p1) && p1>0) resume(p1);
                                        }

                break;

        case PRINTER:   /*Toggle printer flag associated with this program*/
                if(pno==SCHEDULER) getno(&pno,"process number","PRINTER");
                (g->proctbl)[pno].prntr = ((g->proctbl)[pno].prntr + 1)
                                % 2;
                break;

        case SUSPEND:   /*Suspend program(s) associated with curr window*/
                if(pno==SCHEDULER) getno(&pno,"process number","SUSPEND");
                suspend(pno);   /*Suspend active program*/

                /*if we just suspended the process associated
                  with the old window, return without changing
                  back to the old window*/

                if(wintbl[oldwin].pnumb == pno) return;
                break;

        case RESUME:    /*Resume a process*/
                if(pno==SCHEDULER) getno(&pno,"process number","RESUME");
                if(pno!=SCHEDULER) resume(pno);
                break;

        case HELP:
        case HELP2:
                printf("Scheduler meta (or CTRL-BRK) commands are:\n");
                printf( "a-ABORT         n-NEXT WINDOW   c-COMMAND       ");
                printf( "p-PRINTER       q-QUIT\n");
                printf( "s-SUSPEND       r-RESUME        h-HELP          ");
                printf( "?-HELP          b-BOUNDARY\n");
                printf( "w-WINDOW        l-LOOK WINTBL   d-DUMP PROCTBL ");
                printf( "t-TRACE TOGGLE  x-REAL CTLBRK\n");
                printf("Type any character to continue>");
                bios_getchar();
                displaychar('\n');      /*Newline*/
                break;

        case BOUNDARY:  /*Refresh window boundaries*/
                for(i = 0; i < numwindow; i++)
                        draw_border(wintbl[i].rorg,wintbl[i].corg,
                            wintbl[i].h,wintbl[i].w);
                break;

        case WINDOW:
                getno(&wno,"window number","WINDOW");
```

Figure 9-25a (Continued)

```
                        change_window(wno);
                        return;

            case LOOK:
                        dump_wins("CTRLBRK");
                        break;

            case DUMP:
                        dump_queues("CTRLBRK");
                        dump_ptbl("CTRLBRK",(g->numbprocs));
                        break;

            case REALCTLBRK:
                        printf("This may cause the scheduler to abort\n");
                        printf("Are you sure you want to do this(y or n)\n");
                        bios_getchar();
                        if(c=='y') sysint(ORIGCTLBRK,&srv,&srv);
                        break;

            case TRACE:
                        getno(&tno,"trace number","TRACE");
                        toggle_trace(tno);
                        break;


            case QUIT:
                        i = (g->numbprocs) - 1;
                        if(i > 0) printf("There are %d active processes\n",i);
                        printf("Do you really want to quit SCHEDULER (y or n)>");
                        c = bios_getchar();
                        if(c=='y') termsched(0);
                        break;
            }

/*Restore previous window as current*/
if(oldwin!=cwin) change_window(oldwin);
}
```

Figure 9-25a (Continued)

```
toggle_trace(tno)
        unsigned tno;
        {
        switch(tno)
                {
                case 1:
                        tracea = (tracea + 1) % 2;
                        break;

                case 2:
                        traceb = (traceb + 1) % 2;
                        break;

                case 3:
                        tracec = (tracec + 1) % 2;
                        break;

                case 4:
                        traced = (traced + 1) % 2;
                        break;

                case 5:
                        tracee = (tracee + 1) % 2;
                        break;

                case 6:
                        tracef = (tracef + 1) % 2;
                        break;

                case 7:
                        traceg = (traceg + 1) % 2;
                        break;

                case 8:
                        traceh = (traceh + 1) % 2;
                        break;

                case 9:
                        tracei = (tracei + 1) % 2;
                        break;

                case 10:
                        traceq = (traceq + 1) % 2;
                        break;
                }
        }
```

Figure 9-25b command Support Routines

```
/*get number required for a break command*/

getno(no,numbtype,cmd)
        unsigned *no;
        char *numbtype;
        char *cmd;
        {
        char n[20];
        int i;

        printf("Type target %s (hex) for %s command>",numbtype,cmd);
        bios_readline(n);
        displaychar('\n');         /*Newline*/
        sscanf(n,"%x",no);
        }

/*kbint is called from kbbreak assembly routine, by BIOS keyboard interrupt
  service routine. kbint's job is to set the break_cmd flag so that if none
  of the application routines are doing keyboard input (and hence, allowing
  outstanding control breaks to fire), the scheduler will assure that the
  control break is honored as soon as the currently running application
  program is preempted*/

kbint ()
        {
        unsigned flags;
        unsigned peek(),pokeb();
        unsigned bios_break;

        disable(&flags);

        bios_break = peek(BIOSBREAK_OFF,BIOSBREAK_SEG);
        strcpy(s,"kbint: bios_break =        \n");
        convertx2s((unsigned) bios_break,&(s[19]));
        errormsg(SCHEDULER,s);

        /*Turn off flag that signals that break key was struck*/

        pokeb(BIOSBREAK_OFF,BIOSBREAK_SEG,0);

        break_cmd = 1;
        restore(flags);
        }
```

Figure 9-25b (Continued)

```
unsigned char bios_getchar()
        {
        struct regval srv;
        unsigned flags,sysint();
        unsigned char c;

        srv.ax = BIOSREADCODE;   /*function code to read a character*/
        /*Use real bios interrupt service routine, bypassing capture and
          suspend logic in capt16*/

        flags = sysint(BIOS16,&srv,&srv);
        c = (unsigned char) (srv.ax & 0x00ff);
        displaychar(c);              /*echo character*/
        return(c);
        }

int bios_readline(array)         /*read a line up to newline from stdin
                 and store in array, return value is number of chars*/
        unsigned char *array;
        {
        unsigned char c;
        unsigned char bios_getchar();
        int i;

        for(i=0;((c=bios_getchar())!=EOF) && c!='\n' && c!='\r';++i)
                {
                if(c == BACKSPACE)
                        {
                        i = (i > 0) ? (i - 2) : (i - 1);
                        }
                else array[i] = c;
                }
        array[i] = '\0';           /*Terminate string*/
        return(i);
        }
```

Figure 9-25b (Continued)

9.4 SUMMARY

The Framework

The foregoing two chapters have presented the barest framework of a multitasking system with an integrated display manager. The extended example illustrates:

1. *Task Management*. The example contained the rudiments of a multitasking system including task creation, loading, initiation, termination, and sched-

uling. These concepts were described concretely in terms of their effects on the system's data structures including the global variables, the queues, the process table, and the window table.

2. *DOS Interface and Low-Level Services.* The example addressed the general problems introduced by interfacing one operating system to another operating system, and more specifically, the problems introduced by interfacing a multitasking system to a single-tasking system. In addition, developing such an interface provided the opportunity to understand the kind of low-level services provided by personal computer operating systems.

3. *Display (or Window) Management.* The example developed a simple display manager as a strategy for managing two key shared resources—the display and the keyboard. The display is shared by splitting it into multiple windows allowing one process to run in each window. The keyboard is shared by associating it with one of the windows that is identified as the current window. The keyboard may be switched from window to window by the user.

4. *Command Interface.* The example developed a simple command interface by which the user could initiate, manage the execution of, and terminate the tasks running in the various windows.

Possible Extensions

Since this multitasking/window system is a barebones system designed to illustrate only the basic features of this class of systems, there are a variety of extensions, both large and small, that could be made to address its omissions. Many of these are extensions to the display manager. A first big step would be the introduction of transcription buffers, which would allow a variety of interesting and useful features to be added. While this would significantly increase the complexity of managing the screen, it would allow:

1. More than four windows
2. Overlaid windows so that only the immediately important windows would be totally visible
3. Windows with variable size so that they could be scaled to the needs of the task running in them
4. Popup or pulldown menus
5. Temporary borrowing of the full screen for those occasional programs that could justify it

There are a variety of other extensions and facilities that are required to make the system safe and robust enough to be used in day-to-day operation by casual users. These extensions include:

1. File locking and protection so that two concurrently executing programs could not write the same file at the same time

2. A function to initiate a subtask from a task, thereby allowing one program to call another as a subprogram

3. A function to initiate a concurrent task—that is, *fork* a task—from a task, thereby allowing the parallel execution of two tasks

4. A UNIX-style pipe operator and I/O redirection so that the user can easily assemble small, simple programs into larger, more complex functions without having to develop the larger functions from scratch

5. Interprocess communication mechanisms that allow the assembling of programs into richer communication structures than the pipe operator allows

6. Enhanced command processing allowing a superset of the DOS command language

7. A facility to execute a command stream from a batch file

Finally, integration of additional utility programs would extend the functionality and therefore the usefulness of the system. Perhaps the most obvious of these is the integration of the communications software from Chapter 5. This would provide an immediately useful combination, allowing the user to use one window for interaction with a remote computer while using another window for executing local utilities, browsing directories, and so on. Of course, to make such a combination really useful, one would need to add an upload/download file transfer capability to the communications package.

The Final Word

In the preface to this book we stated that two of the the aims of this book are:

1. To present a rich set of examples, coupled with associated principles, in order to help the reader learn about systems concepts

2. To provide a framework for "doing," since doing is the best way to learn concepts

These aims will have succeeded to the extent that the reader is spurred to extend, create, develop and experiment. That's the final word. Experiment!

EXERCISES

9.1. Design a function called **scroll** that emulates interrupt 10, functions 6 and 7, and works within the framework of the example. Impose the following additional requirement: any scroll window that extends outside of the program's assigned window, by virtue of its size or position, is to be clipped. Notice that because **setpos** folds positions past the right window boundary onto the following line, scrolling of windows using **scroll** is not guaranteed to work consistently for programs that write information into columns 78, 79 and 80. See also Exercise 9.2.

9.2. Develop a design for the Display Manager that uses a transcription buffer. Think about how this changes the functions **displayc**, **writeac**, **setpos**, **readpos**, **scroll**, and the cursor movement utility functions. What new functions should be added?

9.3. Develop a design to extend the definition of DOS function 0x0A, buffered keyboard input, that allows function key editing of the input lines. See the function **dos0a**. Implement your design and test it with Edlin.

Appendix A

Listing of .h Files for Assembly Programs

These three files are the standard C86 files for use with assembly programs. The **prologue.h** file is put in front of each assembly language program and it defines the set of data segments required by the C86 compiler. The **model.h** file sets the **@bigmodel** flag to indicate whether or not the program assumes a big or a small memory model. Finally, the **epilogue.h** file marks the end of the assembly code.

The prologue.h File

```
;           prologue.h      11/5/83

;           standard prologue for c86 assembly code

;           DEFINE ARGUMENT BASE RELATIVE FROM BP

IF      @BIGMODEL
@AB     EQU     6
ELSE
@AB     EQU     4
ENDIF

@CODE   SEGMENT BYTE PUBLIC 'CODE'
@CODE   ENDS
@DATAB  SEGMENT PARA PUBLIC 'DATAB'
```

```
@DATAB   ENDS
@DATAC   SEGMENT BYTE PUBLIC 'DATAC'
@sb      label    byte
@sw      label    word
@DATAC   ENDS
@DATAI   SEGMENT BYTE PUBLIC 'DATAI'
@ib      label    byte
@iw      label    word
@DATAI   ENDS
@DATAT   SEGMENT BYTE PUBLIC 'DATAT'
@DATAT   ENDS
@DATAU   SEGMENT BYTE PUBLIC 'DATAU'
@ub      label    byte
@uw      label    word
@DATAU   ENDS
@DATAV   SEGMENT BYTE PUBLIC 'DATAV'
@DATAV   ENDS
DGROUP   GROUP    @DATAB,@DATAC,@DATAI,@DATAT,@DATAU,@DATAV
@CODE    SEGMENT BYTE PUBLIC 'CODE'
         ASSUME   CS:@CODE,DS:DGROUP

;        END OF PROLOGUE.h
```

The model.h File

```
;        define big or small model for library assembly code

FALSE   equ     0        ;for small model
TRUE    equ     1        ;for big model

@bigmodel equ TRUE       ;select this for model desired
```

The epilogue.h File

```
;        end of any assembly code

@CODE    ENDS
```

Listing of .h Files
for Multitasking Functions

The following files are the complete versions of the C header files used by the multitasking and window management programs described in Chapters 7 through 9.

The proc.h File

This is the key header file used by virtually all C functions described in these chapters. It contains **#defines** for a variety of constants, bit masks, interrupt vector numbers, operating system function codes, process states, error flags, macros, and scheduler command characters. In addition, it contains definitions of queues, process table entries, the scheduler's global variables, the pointer to the scheduler's global variables, trace flags, temporary buffers, and some scheduler communication flags.

```
#define FALSE          0
#define TRUE           1
#define MAXPNAME       15      /*Maximum length of a processes name*/
#define MAXPROCS       25      /*Maximum number of processes*/
#define MAXQENTS       75      /*Maximum number of queue entries*/
#define STKSIZE        0x1000  /*Size of interim stack (bytes)*/
#define BUFFER_SIZE    128     /*Size of keyboard buffer*/
#define EXEHDRLEN      0x1c    /*Size of fixed portion of exe file header*/
#define EXESIG         0x5a4d  /*Signature word of an exe file*/
```

```
#define LOADPGSIZ          512        /*Page size (in bytes) used by linker-loader*/
#define PARASIZE           16         /*Paragraph size in bytes*/
#define HEAPSIZE           512        /*Minimum heap size allocated to loaded prog*/
#define CMD_AREA_LEN       126        /*Max length of command line (+ '\0') in psp*/
#define START_DTA_OFF      0x80       /*Offset within psp of starting DTA*/
#define ENVOFFSET          0x2c       /*Environment field offset (in bytes) within psp*/
#define PGPSPLEN           0x10       /*Length of the psp in paragraphs*/
#define BPSPLEN            0x100      /*Length of the psp in bytes*/
#define INTR_ON_BIT        0x0200     /*Interrupt bit in flags register*/
#define TRAP_ON_BIT        0x0100     /*Trap bit in flags register*/
#define CARRY_BIT          0x0001     /*Carry bit in flags register*/
#define SIGN_BIT           0x0080     /*Sign bit in flags register*/
#define DIRECTION_BIT      0x0400     /*Direction bit in flags register*/
#define ZERO_BIT           0x0040     /*Zero bit in flags register*/

/*Special Interrupt Vectors*/

#define INTERCEPT16        0x16       /*Bios interrupt 16 vector*/
#define INTERCEPT10        0x10       /*Bios interrupt 10 vector*/
#define KEYBOARDBRK        0x1b       /*Keyboard break function executed on ctrl_brk key*/
#define POSTTIMER          0x1c       /*Post timer interrupt*/

#define DOSTERM            0x20       /*Address of DOS termination handler*/
#define DOSFNC             0x21       /*Address of DOS function handler*/
#define TERMADDR           0x22       /*Termination address for program*/
#define CNTRL_BRK          0x23       /*Control Break address for this program*/
#define ERRORINT           0x24       /*Address of critical error handler for this program*/

#define GLOBALS            0x60       /*Address of Global variables for SCHEDULER*/
#define REALDOSFNC         0x61       /*New location of vector to the
                                        real DOS FUNCTION (int 21) code*/
#define DOSINT20           0x62       /*New location of vector to real DOS int 20 code*/
#define BIOS16             0x63       /*New location of vector to real BIOS int 16 code*/
#define BIOS10             0x64       /*New location of vector to real BIOS int 10 code*/
#define ORIGCTLBRK         0x65       /*New location of vector to original ctl brk code*/
#define USERINT6           0x66       /*Reserved as user interrupt*/
#define USERINT7           0x67       /*Reserved as user interrupt*/

/* DOS and BIOS variable locations*/

#define BIOSBREAK_OFF      0x71       /*Offset of bios_break flag, used by keyboard
                                        bios to signal DOS that the break key has
                                        been depressed*/
#define BIOSBREAK_SEG      0x40       /*Segment of bios_break flag*/

/* DOS and BIOS function codes */

#define BIOSREADCODE       0x0000     /*BIOS int 16 function to read a char from keyboard*/
#define BIOSCHECKCODE      0x0100     /*BIOS int 16 function to check status of keyboard*/
#define BIOSKEYBRDINT      0x16       /*BIOS keyboard interrupt*/
#define DOSPRINTCHAR       0x0500     /*DOS print character function*/

/* Process states */
```

```
#define RUNNING        0       /*Process is running (only one process)*/
#define READY          1       /*Process is ready to run*/
#define SUSPENDED      2       /*Process is suspended*/
#define SLEEPING       3       /*Process is sleeping*/
#define WAITMSG        4       /*Process is waiting for a message*/
#define WAITSIG        5       /*Process is waiting for a signal*/
#define TERMINATING    6       /*Process is being terminated*/


#define SCHEDULER      0       /*Process number of the scheduler task*/
#define MAXDELAY       0x7fff  /*Maximum delay value*/
#define MINDELAY       0x0     /*Minimum delay value*/
#define EMPTY          -1      /*Empty queue signal*/
#define NOERROR        0       /*Non error return value (actually any val > -1)*/
#define ERROR          -1      /*Error return value*/


/*Macros*/

#define ABS(x)          ((x < 0) ? - (x) : (x))

#define MAX(A,B) ((A) > (B) ? (A) : (B))          /*Maximum of two numbers*/
#define MIN(A,B) ((A) < (B) ? (A) : (B))          /*Minimum of two numbers*/

/******* Scheduler Control Characters (follow Ctrl-brk character) ***********/

#define ABORT      'a'    /*Abort program(s) in current window*/
#define BOUNDARY   'b'    /*Redraw window boundaries*/
#define COMMAND    'c'    /*Make scheduler's window current to give command*/
#define DUMP       'd'    /*Dump globals and process table*/
#define HELP       'h'    /*Show help screen*/
#define HELP2      '?'    /*Show help screen*/
#define LOOK       'l'    /*Look at window table*/
#define NEXT       'n'    /*Associate keyboard with next window*/
#define PRINTER    'p'    /*Toggle printer flag for current process*/
#define QUIT       'q'    /*Quit Scheduler*/
#define RESUME     'r'    /*Resume program(s) associated with current window*/
#define SUSPEND    's'    /*Suspend program(s) associated with current window*/
#define TRACE      't'    /*Toggle one of the trace flags*/
#define WINDOW     'w'    /*Go to window n*/
#define REALCTLBRK 'x'    /*Execute the real control break code*/

/***************** Queue Declarations ***************************************/

typedef int qindex;     /*Index of a qentry record in the qentry table*/
typedef int pindex;     /*Index of a process record in the proctbl table*/

typedef struct qnt       /*Queue entry structure*/
        {
        qindex prev;               /*Previous queue entry*/
        qindex next;               /*Next queue entry*/
        int pn;                    /*Process number*/
        int delay;                 /*Delay value (if delay queue)*/
        } qentry;
```

```
typedef struct que        /*Queue head and tail structure*/
        {
        qindex qhead;              /*Index of head entry of queue*/
        qindex qtail;              /*Index of tail entry of queue*/
        } queue;

/**************** Process Declaration *********************************/

typedef struct procentry          /*Process table entry*/
        {
        unsigned int savesp;                /*Saved sp register*/
        unsigned int savess;                /*Saved ss register*/
        unsigned int pspseg;                /*Psp segment address of this process*/
        unsigned int windno;                /*Window number assoc with this proc*/
        unsigned int procstate;             /*State of the process*/
        char procname[MAXPNAME+1];          /*Name of the process*/
        int pnum;                           /*Process number for this entry*/
        unsigned int mynoprmpt;             /*The noprmpt flag for this process*/
        unsigned int mylvlcalls;            /*The lvlcalls flag for this process*/
        unsigned int intstkss;              /*Seg of temp stack for dos 21 interrupt*/
        unsigned int prntr;                 /*Printer flag*/
        unsigned int reservd[2];            /*Reserved*/
        unsigned int calllvl;               /*Reserved*/
        unsigned int retproc;               /*Reserved*/
        unsigned int retvalue;              /*Reserved*/
        unsigned int waitsig;               /*Reserved*/
        unsigned int msgbuf;                /*Reserved*/
        } process;

struct globals  /*Global variables providing status of the processes*/
        {
        unsigned int clock;            /*Scheduler's clock - used for preemption*/
        unsigned int procno;           /*Process number of currently executing process*/
        unsigned int numbprocs;        /*Number of currently active processes*/
        process proctbl[MAXPROCS];     /*Process tbl array*/
        queue    tbk;                  /*List of processes to be killed/*
        queue    ready;                /*Ready list*/
        queue    doze;                 /*Queue of sleeping processes*/
        qentry qe[MAXQENTS]            /*Table of queue entries*/
        unsigned int preempted;        /*Number of process just preempted, else 0*/
        unsigned int noprmpt;          /*Flag indicating system call in progress,
                                         no preemption allowed.*/
        unsigned int lvlcalls;         /*No. of levels of systems calls in progress*/
        };

typedef char *pointer;

extern struct globals *g;

/**************** Trace facilities ***********************************/

extern int traceq;
extern int tracea;
```

```
extern int traceb;
extern int tracec;
extern int traced;
extern int tracee;
extern int tracef;
extern int traceg;
extern int traceh;
extern int tracei;

extern FILE *tracefile,*fopen();

/************* Temporary Buffers ******************************************/

extern char s[128];
extern char nmsg[128];

extern char parmfile1[128];              /*First parameter file*/
extern char parmfile2[128];              /*Second parameter file*/

/************* Constants **************************************************/

extern char blanks[128];

/************* Scheduler communication *********************************/

extern unsigned break_cmd;               /*Indicates desire to issue a break (or meta)
                                           command to scheduler*/

extern unsigned disp_level;              /*Level of recursion of displayc routine,
                                           integrity checking variable*/
```

The load.h File

This file is used by the functions associated with loading programs. It contains definitions of the parameter blocks used by the DOS program load function, the header record of an ".exe" file, the program segment prefix area, the structure returned by DOS function 0x4e, and the DOS file control block structure.

```
/*** Parameter block used to load overlays (without immed. execution) *******/

typedef struct povblk
        {
        unsigned int env_seg;    /*Segment at which to load file*/
        unsigned int reloc;      /*Relocation factor*/
        }
        poverblock;
```

```
/***************** Parameter block used to load and exec progs ************/

typedef struct pblk
        {
        unsigned int env_seg;
        char *cline;
        char *fcb1;
        char *fcb2;
        }
        pblock;


typedef struct fhdr              /*Fixed part of exe file header*/
        {
        unsigned signature;      /*"0x4d5a"-signature of an exe file*/
        unsigned image_len;      /*Load module image size mod 512*/
        unsigned filesize;       /*No. of 512 byte pages in file*/
        unsigned nreloc;         /*No. of relocation table items.*/
        unsigned hdrsize_para;   /*No. of paragraphs (16 bytes) in header*/
        unsigned min_xmem;       /*Minimum number of paragraphs req'd above prog*/
        unsigned max_xmem;       /*Maximum no. of para. req'd above prog*/
        unsigned stackoff;       /*Offset of stack segment in module (para. addr)*/
        unsigned stacksp;        /*Sp register value at start of execution*/
        unsigned checksum;       /*Negative sum of all words in file*/
        unsigned startip;        /*Value of ip register at start of execution*/
        unsigned startcs;        /*Value of cs register at start of execution
                                   (para. addr)*/
        unsigned firstreloc;     /*Offset of first reloc item in file*/
        unsigned overlayno;      /*Overlay number*/
        } header;


typedef struct                   /*Program Segment Prefix structure -- psp*/
        {
        unsigned int20;                 /*Interrupt 20 instruction for termination purposes*/
        unsigned top_mem;               /*First available segment of memory (paragraph form)*/
        unsigned char dummy;            /*Dummy spacing byte*/
        unsigned char longcall[5];      /*Long call to DOS function dispatcher*/
        unsigned *termaddr;             /*Terminate interrupt vector*/
        unsigned *ctrlbreak;            /*Control-Break Interrupt vector*/
        unsigned *criterror;            /*Critical error Interrupt vector*/
        unsigned char resrved[0x46];    /*Reserved for use by DOS*/
        unsigned char pspfcb1[0x10];    /*Fcb area for first paramter*/
        unsigned char pspfcb2[0x14];    /*Fcb area for second parameter*/
        unsigned char parmlen;          /*Length of command line*/
        unsigned char parmarea[0x80];   /*Unformatted parameter area (default DTA)*/
        } *psp;

typedef struct dir       /*Directory entry description returned by DOS fnc 4E*/
        {
        char dosarea[21];               /*Reserved for DOS use*/
        char fattrib;                   /*File attribute*/
        unsigned ftime;                 /*File time stamp*/
        unsigned fdate;                 /*File date stamp*/
        unsigned lowfsize;              /*Low word of file size*/
        unsigned highfsize;             /*High word of file size*/
        char filen[13];                 /*File name and extension*/
        } direntry;
```

```
typedef struct          /*File control block*/
        {
        char drive;                     /*Drive number*/
        char name[8];                   /*File name*/
        char exten[3];                  /*File extension*/
        unsigned block;                 /*Current block number*/
        unsigned record_size;
        unsigned long file_size;
        unsigned date;
        char resrv[10];
        unsigned char record;           /*Current record number in block*/
        unsigned long random;           /*Random record number*/
        } fcb;
```

The window.h File.

This file is used by the window management software described in Chapter 9. This file contains the definition of a window table entry and several global variables related to the window table.

```
/******************** window table entry ********************************/

typedef struct win
        {
        unsigned int inuse;        /*Is this slot being used*/
        unsigned int rorg;         /*Row of upper left corner of window*/
        unsigned int corg;         /*Column of upper left corner of window*/
        unsigned int h;            /*Usable height of window--boundaries extra*/
        unsigned int w;            /*Usable width of window*/
        unsigned int crow;         /*Current row of cursor for this window on real screen*/
        unsigned int ccol;         /*Current column of cursor for this window on real screen*/
        unsigned int vrow;         /*Current row of cursor for this window on virtual screen*/
        unsigned int vcol;         /*Current column of cursor for this window on virtual screen*/
        unsigned int pnumb;        /*Process number associated with this window*/
        unsigned int (*keybuf)[];/*Pointer to keyboard buffer for this window*/
        unsigned int kbcount;      /*Number of characters in keyboard buffer*/
        unsigned int kbrear;       /*Index of rear of buffer, where next char goes*/
        unsigned int kbfront;      /*Index of front of buffer, where next char
                                      to be read comes from*/
        } window;

extern window wintbl[];            /*Window table*/
extern unsigned int cwin;          /*Current window number. I.E. The window the
                                      user is talking to*/
extern unsigned int numwindow;     /*Number of active windows*/

extern unsigned int printer_on;    /*Control PrtSc has toggled the printer on*/
```

The globdefs.h File

This file is used by a variety of functions and in particular the window management functions. It contains **#defines** for a variety of globally useful constants.

```
#define NORM_ATTR            0x07   /*normal or blank attribute*/
#define INV_ATTR             0x70   /*inverse video attribute*/
#define NORMBLNK_ATTR        0x87   /*normal blinking attribute*/
#define INVBLNK_ATTR         0xf0   /*inverse video blinking*/
#define NORMHLIT_ATTR        0x0f   /*normal with highlighting*/
#define INVHLIT_ATTR         0x78   /*inverse video with highlighting*/
#define NORMBLNKHLIT_ATTR    0x8f   /*normal,blinking,highlighting*/
#define INVBLNKHLIT_ATTR     0xf8   /*inverse, blinking,highlighting*/
#define UNDERLINE_ATTR       0x01   /*underline attribute*/

#define SCROLL_UP            0x06   /*function number to scroll window up*/
#define SCROLL_DOWN          0x07   /*function number to scroll window down*/

#define TOP_BORDER           0xcd   /*Top border character for window*/
#define VERT_BORDER          0xba   /*Vertical border character for window*/
#define UP_LEFT_CORNER       0xc9   /*Upper left corner character for window*/
#define UP_RIGHT_CORNER      0xbb   /*Upper right corner character for window*/
#define BOT_LEFT_CORNER      0xc8   /*Lower left corner character for window*/
#define BOT_RIGHT_CORNER     0xbc   /*Lower right corner character for window*/
#define BOT_BORDER           0xb1   /*Bottom border character for window*/

#define MSG_LEN              77     /*Max message length in window msg area*/

#define ASCII_ZERO           0x30   /*Numeric value of an ASCII zero*/
#define ASCII_A              0x41   /*Numeric value of an ASCII A*/

/*Special characters*/

#define BACKSPACE            0x08   /*Backspace character*/
#define CTRL_A               0x01   /*Control A*/
#define CTRL_B               0x02   /*Control B*/
#define CTRL_C               0x03   /*Control C*/
#define CTRL_D               0x04   /*Control D*/
#define CTRL_E               0x05   /*Control E*/
#define CTRL_F               0x06   /*Control F*/
#define CTRL_G               0x07   /*Control G*/
#define CTRL_H               0x08   /*Control H*/
#define CTRL_I               0x09   /*Control I*/
#define CTRL_J               0x0a   /*Control J*/
```

```
#define CTRL_K       0x0b        /*Control K*/
#define CTRL_L       0x0c        /*Control L*/
#define CTRL_M       0x0d        /*Control M*/
#define CTRL_N       0x0e        /*Control N*/
#define CTRL_O       0x0f        /*Control O*/
#define CTRL_P       0x10        /*Control P*/
#define CTRL_Q       0x11        /*Control Q*/
#define CTRL_R       0x12        /*Control R*/
#define CTRL_S       0x13        /*Control S*/
#define CTRL_T       0x14        /*Control T*/
#define CTRL_U       0x15        /*Control U*/
#define CTRL_V       0x16        /*Control V*/
#define CTRL_W       0x17        /*Control W*/
#define CTRL_X       0x18        /*Control X*/
#define CTRL_Y       0x19        /*Control Y*/
#define CTRL_Z       0x1a        /*Control Z*/
#define ESC          0x1e        /*Escape key*/
#define CRETURN      0x0d        /*Carriage return*/
#define NEWLINE      0x0a        /*Line feed character*/


#define FILENOTFOUND    -1
#define COMFILE          0
#define EXEFILE          1
```

The globinit.h File

This file is used to initialize several variables used by the multitasking software.

```
int maxcol = 79;          /*max col number of screen*/
int maxrow = 24;          /*max row of screen*/
int maxcolp1 = 80;        /*max col of screen + 1*/
int maxrowp1 = 25;        /*maxrow + 1*/

char blanks[] = "                                    ";
```

The prefmain.h File

This file is used to declare and initialize global variable storage used by the multitasking software.

```
FILE *tracefile;
int traceq = 0;                      /*Flag to trace queue operations*/
unsigned ptrtrace = 0;               /*Flag to trace ptr fission & fusion*/
int tracea = 0;
int traceb = 0;
int tracec = 0;
int traced = 0;
int tracee = 0;
int tracef = 0;
int traceg = 0;
int traceh = 0;
int tracei = 0;

/************** Global variables for saving interrupt vectors **************/

int tick_ip;                         /*saved offset of original timer tick contents*/
int tick_cs;                         /*saved ctrl seg of original timer tick contents*/
unsigned *savesched22;               /*Saved termination address of scheduler*/
unsigned *savectlbrk;                /*Saved Control-Break address of scheduler*/
unsigned *saverrhdlr;                /*Saved Error Handler address of scheduler*/
unsigned *saveint20;                 /*Saved address of interrupt 20 service routine*/
unsigned *saveint16;                 /*Saved address of interrupt 16 service routine*/
unsigned *savekeybrk;                /*Saved address of the original keyboard
                                       break function*/
unsigned *saveint10;                 /*Saved address of interrupt 10 routine*/

pointer tvector;                     /*timer interrupt vector pointer*/
pointer dosint21;                    /*DOS interrupt 21 service routine pointer*/

/*************** Global variables for load related functions*********************/

header image_hdr;                    /*Header for load image being created*/

unsigned startseg;                   /*Point to start loading new code*/
psp newpsp;                          /*Pointer to psp of new program*/

poverblock overlay_parm;             /*Parameter block to load a
                                       program as if it was an overlay*/
oblock parmb;                        /*DOS parameter block for loading and executing
                                       a program, used in multproc only as info
                                       storage structure*/

char parmfile1[128];                 /*First parameter file of a cmd*/
char parmfile2[128];                 /*Second paramter file of a cmd*/

/*************** Multi-processing status variable ******************/

struct globals gbl;                  /*Initialize global variable structure*/

struct  globals *g;
```

```
/****************** Window table and status variables *********************/

window wintbl[10];              /*Window table*/
unsigned int cwin;              /*Current window number. I.E. The window the user is
                                  talking to*/
unsigned int numwindow;         /*Number of active windows*/

unsigned int printer_on = 0;    /*Control PrtSc toggle flag*/

/***** Display buffer pointer (for monochrome display set to 80 chars) ******/

unsigned char (*display) [25] [80] [2];

/*************** Structure of a long pointer: Two words (ip,cs).***************/

union
        {
        struct globals *gtmp;
        unsigned int gparts[2];
        } gptr;

/********************* Buffers ***********************************************/

        char s[128];
        char nmsg[128];

/************* Scheduler communication **************************************/

unsigned break_cmd;             /*Indicates desire to issue a break (or meta)
                                  command to scheduler*/

unsigned disp_level;            /*Level of recursion of displayc routine,
                                  integrity checking variable*/
```

The fileio2.h File

This is a C86 header file used for debugging purposes to reference some variables in the C86 run-time library routines for file IO under DOS2. Source for this file available from Computer Innovations, Inc.

The _default.c File

This is a C86 header file used to reduce run-time requirements for multitasker stack + heap space in order to allow more space for application programs to be loaded after the multitasker. Source for this file available from Computer Innovations, Inc.

Index

TO ORDER YOUR DISKETTE

A diskette, containing the programs listed in this book, is available from Prentice-Hall for $50.00.

To order, mail check or money order to

Book Distribution Center
Route 59 at Brook Hill Drive
West Nyack, NY 10995

Systems Software Tools (diskette) 88187-0

Tan Joo Tong